RACISM UNTAUGHT

REVEALING AND UNLEARNING RACIALIZED DESIGN

Lisa E. Mercer and Terresa Moses

Foreword by Cheryl D. Miller

The MIT Press
Cambridge, Massachusetts
London, England

The MIT Press would like to thank the anonymous peer reviewers who provided comments on drafts of this book. The generous work of academic experts is essential for establishing the authority and quality of our publications. We acknowledge with gratitude the contributions of these otherwise uncredited readers.

Printed and bound in the United States of America.

Library of Congress Cataloging-in-Publication Data

Names: Mercer, Lisa E., author. | Moses, Terresa, author, illustrator. | Miller, Cheryl D., 1952- writer of foreword.
Title: Racism untaught : revealing and unlearning racialized design / Lisa E. Mercer and Terresa Moses ; foreword by Cheryl D. Miller.
Description: Cambridge, Massachusetts : The MIT Press, [2023] | Includes bibliographical references and index.
Identifiers: LCCN 2022052711 (print) | LCCN 2022052712 (ebook) | ISBN 9780262048583 (hardcover) | ISBN 9780262376433 (epub) | ISBN 9780262376426 (adobe pdf)
Subjects: LCSH: Design—Social aspects. | Racism.
Classification: LCC NK1520 .M47 2023 (print) | LCC NK1520 (ebook) | DDC 744—dc23/eng/20221116
LC record available at https://lccn.loc.gov/2022052711
LC ebook record available at https://lccn.loc.gov/

10   9   8   7   6   5   4   3   2   1

CONTENTS

FOREWORD

Cheryl D. Miller

A perfect storm of the COVID-19 pandemic's "stay at home" lockdown orders in 2019, the murders of Breonna Taylor and George Floyd, and Black Lives Matter protests gave us all a front-row, global view of an awakening of social consciousness and reckoning across humanity. This featured cinema streamed across my devices, moment by moment. Decades ago, I had seen this exact movie, albeit, at my neighborhood theater. Dr. Martin Luther King Jr. had been assassinated. The world seemed to be in suspended animation. Streets burned.

At full attention, Zoom technology and social media became the designers' protest march. Instagram posts became our picket signs. Zoom became the dais for what was once my generation's boom box and microphone lectern. Design as protest became the new civil rights manifesto. The concept of the "design challenge" flooded social media platforms with activist memes and GIFs as picket banners. I had been there as a teen and found myself returning to the scene of the same crime.

I knew a fresh sense of Black pride and nationalism as well as reparations toward a more diverse community would arise next. When King was murdered, "I'm Black and I'm Proud" mantras were chanted. The Afro bush replaced ideas of white beauty and straightened hair. These were all cultural action points. Benefactors of reparations for business, academic, and organizational benefit and opportunity poured into the Black community. Everyone took an empathetic seat in the Black experience; we all stood by the street curb watching the events march by. Black designers were missing in action, to the greater audience. We were fighting a silent war, winning and losing battles for inclusion. That was then, and this is now.

The pandemic kept us glued to the screen, and the wheel of change was turning once more. The design student's responses and uprisings would define a new deliverable. In my lifetime, I would begin to see the change I had always dreamed of for the graphic design industry. Black designers, Indigenous designers, and designers of color were making demands—and they were being met.

History was repeating itself. I was living to see it unfold, once again. With sequestered time on my hands, I stayed glued to the screen. Like a book I had previously read, I was turning the pages of a new edition. The young design scholars were protesting, demanding, marching, picketing, and student online uprisings were abounding. Young scholars were screaming "Design for social justice!" and took action for their demands to be met. White professors were being charged with racial allegations; many were forced to retire. Votes of no confidence filings against art and design colleges and university administrations were occurring every day.

Social media student protests were hitting to the core of the situation and putting a crack in the ceiling that had once lowered on my generation of design practitioners. "Dismantle!" "Decolonize!" "Decenter Whiteness!" "Anti-racist Pedagogies!" I am best known for my legacy contribution of design justice advocacy, specifically to the graphic design industry. I am a designer, educator, writer, and design social justice activist, and a liberation design theologian, revision historian, and decolonizing historian. These titles to say, I actively come against any- and everything that seeks to oppress and disenfranchise Black designers, Indigenous designers, and designers of color. Scholarship is my weaponry.

My *PRINT* magazine's seminal article, "Black Designers Missing in Action," was based on scholarship. The 1987 article was published and structured from my 1985 Pratt Institute graduate thesis, "Transcending the Problems of the Black Designer to Success in the Marketplace." The article started a design-wide movement both in industry and academia. My research opened the conversation on the role of diversity in design practice. The article was the catalyst for AIGA (then the American Institute of Graphic Arts) to begin its national discourse on diversity, equity, and inclusion in the design industry. I have received lifetime legacy revered accolades that were amassed from creating scholarship and documenting recorded history. I have stood up for design justice since the end of the civil rights era.

The culture shifted, and the design scholar protests online put me squarely in the citadel of the new scholars, scholarship, theories, and pedagogies. Fondly, I am referred to as the "OG [original] BIPOC" graphic designer. Living past the "one drop" rule of being identified as African American, I have now found myself able to freely identify as authentically mixed-race. I have succeeded despite the oppression of the lingering culture of Jim Crow laws and the intrinsic DNA of white supremacy and racism found deep in the catacombs of design history.

In my current scholarship, I have dared to decolonize the Euro-Anglo white male–centered canonical history of graphic design. My core research and discoveries conclude the slave artisan as the first Black designer in North America from the shores of West Africa.[1] A new cadre of astute, dynamic, exhaustive design scholars graciously have invited me to speak and lecture at their conferences. Many have included me in the next iteration of the design justice movement.

Particularly at one conference, I embraced a term I gleaned from designer, scholar, and activist Jacquelyn Ogorchukwu Iyamah: *white default*.[2] We were presenters at the Harvard Graduate School of Design's "Black in Design" Zoom conference. I deeply resonate with her terminology. Working with the theme, I define my process for breaking down barriers whereby "whiteness" is no longer the governing standard as a norm. Like a magnet, white default, if allowed, can monopolize our visual storytelling of persons, places, things, brands, products, or services. White default will gravitate to whiteness as a measurement for everyone, no matter the race, creed, color, or gender orientation.

My best metaphoric reference is the launch of the 1959 fashion doll. Perched on a stand, the long-limbed, thin-torsoed blonde Barbie was for every young girl in America, no matter their race, creed, or color. White default had created a doll for everyone, except for my community of friends. I am grateful that Barbie has grown past her beginning start-up, but that was 1950s America.

I have met a fierce new league of design scholars who are brilliant and valiant in their assignments to eradicate white supremacy and racialized design. They want all signs of oppression erased from the design academy, academia, even the classroom and the design studio practice. Virtual conferences have allowed for collaboration and curation and for the next generation of design thinkers and scholars to gather and convene.

I have met and know well Professors Terresa Moses and Lisa E. Mercer, strategic voices in this new collegiate space. They are contributing scholars in the sharing of new and exciting approaches to eradicating injustices against Black communities, Indigenous communities, and communities of color that have been caused by systemic racism. They contend that if racism can be taught, it can be untaught. Their book reveals their tested strategies for eradicating the construct of race in design.

They have developed what they describe as the Racism Untaught framework and toolkit. Reminiscent of my era's forerunner scholars, Jane Elliot and Elsie Y. Cross, best known for unteaching racism and diversity, equity, and inclusion consulting, Moses and Mercer enlist us all into the assignment of being designers for a new community. They deputize us into the tenets of learning human-centered design and design thinking process tools.

The Racism Untaught framework teaches us to unlearn racialized design. The framework is a research process that identifies the problem or gap in our understanding, and then it works to create innovative, anti-racist solutions. Best understood, the framework identifies the void and finds the solution to fill it. Interacting with the framework, the book's authors have developed the Racism Untaught process. The accompanying toolkit implements the research process: context, define, ideate, prototype, and impact, which will draw us to findings of liberation, transformation, healing, protection, and creative freedom.

The toolkit is a visually welcoming interactive board journal. The graphic system is easy to follow, and thoughts, emotions, feelings, and impressions are categorized on colorful contextualized cards. The toolkit explores how we have been socialized to normalize racism and how we can dismantle forms of oppression. When moderated through a set of organized prompts, participants are gathering conclusive research to help reach informative conclusions. The toolkit is designed to help participants become aware and learn something of the process to unlearn any racial biases one might possess.

The toolkit can be orchestrated through a sixteen-week course; an eight-, five-, or two-hour workshop; and any corporate seminar. The toolkit helps to extract our personal data to move us forward in actualizing any anti-racist protocol. The authors' goal is to show us how to create anti-racist, anti-oppressive design systems. Our visual storytelling must turn toward a sensibility to eradicate these racial inclinations and oppressive biases. The creation and production of communication artifacts must be free from racialized design and stereotypical inferences. The framework and toolkit teach us to see ourselves first before the creative process even begins.

The Racism Untaught framework and toolkit calls us as partners from academia, industry, and community to embrace a new hope found in a reformative process to heal from racial injustices. Moses and Mercer give us the tools to identify racialized design, to use the design research process, and to intervene in the development of new conventions for anti-racist outcomes.

Moses and Mercer call us to visualize, imagine, and revision an anti-racist practice that will help us unlearn systems of oppression. Ratifying a community agreement of responsibility to grow and change, they charge us to make a promise to sustain our learning. These professors have done the work to push us to revisit, reform, retool, and redesign oppressive systems that seek to disenfranchise Black people, Indigenous people, and communities of color.

Teaching this transformative process in the foundational stages of a design curriculum is important. Even as a corrective antidote to past behaviors, embracing *Racism Untaught: Revealing and Unlearning Racialized Design* as a pedagogical tool offers hope in eradicating racialized design. I believe racialized design oppressions and aggressions will end with the enlightenment revealed in this framework and toolkit. *Racism Untaught* must institute our core belief system and structure. *Racism Untaught* offers a new framework and process for nurturing future design practice and vibrant agents.

For those possibly once unaware of the challenges faced by Black people, Indigenous people, and people of color in the practice of design, *Racism Untaught* makes us vividly aware. *Racism Untaught* opens minds and hearts to visualize a new era of storytelling. From production to fulfillment of promise . . . to a new ethos, a new culture that fosters and ushers us; we walk a new path. We can now stand on a new road, where history doesn't repeat itself and doesn't have to be our new story.

Dr. Cheryl D. Miller's legacy includes recognitions focused on her writing, research, scholarship, and advocacy for Black designers. She has been recognized with the following: the AIGA Medal, AIGA Medalist 2021, the Cooper Hewitt National Awardee 2021, the IBM Honorary Design Scholar 2021, and the One Club Creative Hall of Fame Inductee 2022. She has received three honorary doctorates, from Vermont College of Fine Art in 2021, the Maryland Institute College of Art in 2022, and the Rhode Island School of Design in 2022. She is a distinguished senior lecturer at the University of Texas School of Design and Creative Technologies in Austin, Texas; a professor of diversity, equity, and inclusion in communication design at the Art Center in Pasadena, California; and an adjunct professor at Howard University in Washington, DC.

PREFACE

We begin with an acknowledgment of the context in which we are writing this text. The purpose of this acknowledgment is a meaningful practice we include each time we hold space with each other—grounding us in meaning and purpose.

ACKNOWLEDGING SPACE, TIME, AND CULTURE

We first want to acknowledge *space*. The space in which we are writing this text and the spaces in which it will be read. The work we engage with happens in a "settler colonial system that continues to deprive Indigenous people of access to their lands"[1] and brings consistent epidemic-wide violence against missing and murdered Indigenous women. This work happens within the system of white supremacy that holds and supports a culture of anti-Black racism leading to the deaths of countless Black people, both nationally and internationally. With this work, we remain committed to acknowledging the complex history of this land by honoring the truth of violence, murder, genocide, displacement, migration, and settlement that bring us together in this moment.

We also recognize that the words we write here are not enough in our fight against systemic racism and we remain committed to the work of eradicating the injustices against all Black people, Indigenous people, and people of color. We are keenly aware that the meanings of words shift over time and culture. One example of this cultural language shift is through the term BIPOC, an acronym for Black, Indigenous, and people of color, which we have intentionally tried to avoid throughout the text in the effort to not further the idea of an undifferentiated mass. Although this textual change might feel strenuous, we are mindful about the impact of our words on the broader culture. Provided the context we will use terms such as, people of the global majority, communities or individuals who hold racialized identities, racially marginalized identities, Black and brown people, and the like to describe historically racialized and underinvested communities. Throughout this text, we will be intentional in defining what we mean by terms such as *racism*, *race*, and *oppression* to remain consistent with their meanings in the time, culture, and context in which we exist now. We leave ourselves grace because we understand that justice and liberation, among many things, inevitably mean changes in language and in the ways we identify and identify with terms. We welcome these changes and find comfort in the gray areas of this work, recognizing the many layers, intersections, and nuances within our culture.

It is also paramount to recognize the cultural change after the murder of George Floyd that resulted in the largest protests ever seen both in the United States and globally.[2] These protests were a catalyst and rallying cry at local, national, and global levels for the Black Lives Matter movement—a movement inextricably linked to our and many of our peers' work. Although we have been working on this research years prior to this pivotal moment in time, we are elated to see the expansion of toolkits, language, and works situated within the ecosystem of this work that provides opportunities to address racism. We are introducing and exploring our own anti-racist journeys in the development of the Racism Untaught framework, but we want to emphasize that our work is in tandem and conversation with many scholars, organizers, and designers committed to the eradication of racism. Without their work, our design approaches would not be as rich in content and critical thinking, and so we gladly reference the work of others who add to anti-racist approaches within the industry, academy, and community. This work *requires* us to work together toward collective liberation (more in chapter 6). While we have been diligent in adding those who have inspired our work, we will undoubtedly miss some who have influenced the broader conversations on race, racism, and systemic oppression. To those who we have inadvertently missed, we believe their work is important and should be used beside our work and the work of those we have referenced.

Racism Untaught is a written account of the iterative nature of the framework, toolkit, and additional learned concepts that we have had the opportunity to engage with to further the creation of design interventions that can help us and our communities unlearn racism. We are intentional in our language and style of writing to expand what are recognized and valued as new ways of developing knowledge in the academy. We seek to spotlight the lived experiences of people of color, those who have come before us, and those who are yet to be in this space so that their research will also be valued and heard. We are working on challenging the status quo of the type of work that is held in high regard in the academy.

ACKNOWLEDGING OUR IDENTITIES

A person's social identity informs their everyday lived experiences, and we are using this text as a means to normalize how these experiences influence design outcomes. We lead by example in our classes, workshops, and now here by recognizing our own positionality and lens in this work.

I, Lisa Elzey Mercer, identify as a cisgender woman of Mexican descent. When I was growing up, I was always proud of my ethnically mixed-race family. I am a Sagittarius sun, Taurus rising, and Aquarius moon. My older sister Maria and I were raised by my mom, Jeannie, who is a first-generation Mexican immigrant, and my dad, Mark, who contracted polio as a baby and, as a result, has a significant facial disfigurement. I am a mom to three teenagers with my partner of twenty-four years, Bob. Each of these identities have influenced the way I see the world and have carried me through this work.

I, Terresa Moses, identify as a Black queer cisgender woman. I am a Sagittarius sun, Virgo rising, and Aries moon. I am an army brat born in Panama City, Panama. I have lived internationally but was raised primarily in Texas, located in the southern United States. I was raised by my Black mother, Christine, the primary caregiver for me and my two older sisters, Nicole and Jennifer. I acknowledge the struggle, joy, culture, and ancestral influence that guides my lens in this work.

THECLASS
ROOMREM
AINSTHEM
OSTRADIC
ALSPACEO
FPOSSIBIL
ITYINTHE
ACADEMY

INTRODUCTION

As Black women and women of color in academia, we do not have the luxury of ignoring the social construct of race and how this conditioned ideology crafts a narrative about us before we have even opened our mouths. Racialized ideologies and their perpetuated actions are often inescapable and normalized when communities of color experience racialized violence.[2] Despite the normalization of racialized ideologies and the harm it causes people who hold racialized identities in our society, academia (like many overwhelmingly white spaces) is not comfortable addressing racism in and outside of the classroom.[3] Those who hold positions of power in academia (faculty and administration) and in the broader design industry have historically overlooked issues of race in hopes that if it is not talked about, it will eventually just go away. Unfortunately, those with racial power have the privilege to take a "colorblind approach to race result[ing] in a denial of these experiences and meanings, and prevent us from addressing the social, cultural, and historical implications of race."[4]

An apathetic approach to issues of racism, perpetuated in the actions and inactions of those in positions of authority, leave conversations about racism to those who those in power believe hold more knowledge of racialized experiences. These are often the few people of color who experience racialized oppression within a particular institution.[5] In academia, this shows up in ways such as placing full responsibility on the one course that students are required to take for their diversity credits as the means to fully explore race, even though racism touches all aspects of our social structures. There is little responsibility or accountability for individuals with institutional power to think critically about systemic racism and intentionally weave discourse about systemic oppression into their curricula and design practices. This is not only a disservice to our students but a disservice to our broader community at large. The failure to address systemic racism allows students to leave a college or university without being challenged to question their own ideologies, which perpetuates systemic oppression. This failure on our part as educators in the academy allows those who matriculate through higher education to graduate and comfortably enter their designated industry with those same racist and oppressive ideologies never once being questioned about their positionality and agency for justice-centered outcomes.[6] This avoidance is described as a form of white-informed civility that "(re)produces whiteness"[7] in our institutions and beyond. We call this the *cycle of racialized oppression* (visualized in figure I.1, based on the lens of systemic oppression created by the National Equity Project[8]): racialized *cultural* ideologies, racialized policy and practice formations within *institutions*, racialized *actions* supported by said institutions, and racialized *personal* ideologies, which mirror our broader cultural values.

To break this racialized cycle, individuals with racialized power must be willing to be uncomfortable and work with communities to disrupt, dismantle, and destroy systems of oppression and create a collective future free from violence. This liberation-centered work involves conversations, education, and intentional relationship building in spaces that offer room for mistakes and transformative justice. If there is one place where topics of discomfort can be easily woven into the cultural discourse, it is an anti-racist, trauma-informed, and healing-centered project-based learning environment. As bell hooks states, "The classroom remains the most radical space of possibility in the academy."[9] The influence of white supremacy and colonialism has those of us in academia stuck in a way of doing that oppresses and continues perpetuating racialized ideologies. The Eurocentric canon leaves individuals who are situated in the academic space without the support necessary to shift pedagogy and curriculum toward justice-centered outcomes. We were seeking ways of working outside of the Eurocentric canon we ourselves were taught, so we began to conduct research focused on anti-racism and community-centered design approaches. We created Racism Untaught to explore how we might contribute to the cultural shifts necessary for communities who hold racialized identities to thrive. Through this project, we have made it our mission to explore how we might leverage design research and anthropological research methods to create anti-racist design approaches.

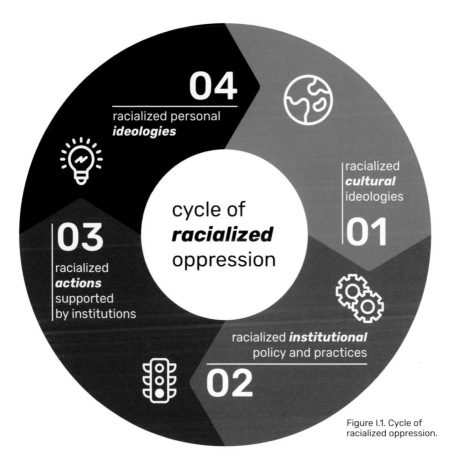

Figure I.1. Cycle of racialized oppression.

This project undertaking was not without its additional costs—a *cultural taxation*[10]—to us as nontenured faculty women of color. How were we, in our vulnerability and powerlessness, to challenge racialized ideologies within the institution, all while continuing to engage students in coursework that explores their positionality in the context of race? We are inherently "battling the exhaustion and burnout that comes from being one of the few faculty members of color and being tapped not only to mentor and sit on every committee that desires a perspective of someone who holds a racialized identity, but also to help students process their own experiences with microaggressions and racial traumas."[11] Leaving issues of race and racism as a problem for the faculty with racialized identities to solve is the calling card of many organizations, including the predominately white institutions (PWIs) that we teach at. Nonwhite faculty are disproportionately charged with teaching these concepts in their courses and are commonly made to feel as though "diversity" is their dilemma. Problematically, students and faculty alike begin to associate research and teaching about racial justice entirely with faculty of color. Topics of racism then become siloed as a part of people of color's culture rather than an issue that affects all of us. The fact remains that issues of race and racism should not be left up to the oppressed because we are not granted the power to shift cultural aspects of our institutions. We are simply used as a means of tokenization and an absolution of guilt for white people. We need strategic and intentional help from those who benefit from systemic racism to address these issues—changing the cultural narrative because this is everyone's responsibility.

The Racism Untaught framework was codeveloped with the mindset that everyone can be a part of anti-racist approaches even if they benefit from racialized systems of oppression. The framework was then crafted into a system of tools (a toolkit) and is used to help participants in co-participatory spaces (workshops, courses, and project processes) create anti-racist approaches in academia, industry, and community. The Racism Untaught toolkit is used in workshops (see figure I.2.) that have been conducted with thousands of participants in a variety of project-based learning environments, college-level courses, and numerous national and international presentations. While the framework was initially developed for educators as a set of tools and interventions for participants to analyze and reimagine racialized artifacts, systems, and experiences, our industry partners use the Racism Untaught toolkit to integrate anti-oppressive collaborative processes into the landscape of their organizations. This is in hopes that they might dismantle their own processes long before they realize they had developed yet another artifact, system, or experience of racialized design. In the introduction, we outline the development of the Racism Untaught framework and toolkit using iterative methodologies to improve upon each of our developed anti-racist design interventions.

Figure I.2. Participants at the pilot workshop, gathered around a workboard.

OUR PURPOSE IN WRITING *RACISM UNTAUGHT*

Racialized experiences and anti-racist approaches are intentionally designed. And because we believe we are *all* designers (further explored in chapter 2), it is imperative that anti-racist approaches be included in design education and design industry processes so that racial justice and liberation can ultimately be realized in our world. The Racism Untaught toolkit is a means to explore ways in which we have all been taught racist ideologies and that we must purposefully use educational design interventions to dismantle how we perpetuate forms of oppression. Our subtitle, *Revealing and Unlearning Racialized Design*, alludes to the ways the Racism Untaught toolkit helps participants understand how elements of racism and oppression show up in designed artifacts, systems, and experiences and how we might use design to co-create anti-racist/oppressive design approaches. Each chapter is followed by a case study of a facilitated Racism Untaught learning experience (college-level course, industry workshop, or community workshop) and its outcomes.

Chapter 1, "The Framework," is focused on the theoretical and applied research used to create the Racism Untaught framework and toolkit that provide participants with the opportunity to identify racialized design challenges and critically assess anti-racist design approaches. It is important to understand what the toolkit is in order to understand how it is applied to explore the iterative, generative, and design-led interventions introduced throughout the framework, which are meant to disrupt the status quo of the design research process; understand why these approaches are foundational to dismantling normative design research and design practice; and understand how the framework has been used to develop the toolkit and its collaborative anti-racist design by way of case study exploration.

Chapter 2, "Defining Design," explores how we are all, in fact, designers of artifacts, systems, and experiences and how the designs we each develop and implement in the spaces around us affect historically oppressed communities. We will provide examples of each of the three areas we have identified and provide context-based evidence that explores the role design plays in perpetuating systems of oppression.

Chapter 3, "Positionality," investigates the different ways participants of the Racism Untaught framework can delve into their predetermined social identities created and upheld by our culture and how these identities affect the way individuals engage in the design process within their communities. This chapter focuses on the onboarding processes necessary to implement the Racism Untaught toolkit, as well as the social identity activities the authors have implemented in specific settings to help prepare participants to engage in open conversations about race, racism, and racialized design. The fundamental question that guides this chapter is, How does the knowledge or unawareness of a person's social identity reflect the understanding of that person's own identity and affect the ways they engage in design decision-making processes?

Chapter 4, "Shared Language," seeks to understand the ethics of knowing and the importance of a shared vocabulary to discuss and identify racialized design. The ability to identify and discuss elements of oppression is imperative for understanding and guiding the social shift in participatory design. In this chapter, we speak to the importance of shared vocabulary to speak to our own social experiences with racialized design and to convey knowledge and validation of these experiences. This enables collaborative partners from multiple disciplines to change patterns—working together to disrupt the continuum of this overgeneralization.

Chapter 5, "Anti-oppressive Interventions," provides users of the framework with the opportunity to further understand how design perpetuates and reinforces the status quo and various levels of oppression: individual beliefs, agentic action, institutional, and cultural. This chapter investigates anti-oppressive interventions integrated in the Racism Untaught framework that help participants gain further context for the oppressive elements. It explores how deeply oppression runs within our society and our ability to create productive and effective tools and design interventions focused on one ism at a time. The Racism Untaught framework is iterative and allows for design-led interventions that are imperative in the design research process to prompt dialogue and critical analysis when working collaboratively toward a solution of responsible, equitable, and liberatory design.

Chapter 6, "A Collective Liberatory Future," explains how to effectively engage in the work of critically assessing, analyzing, and reimagining racialized design. Through collaborative practices, the design research process and design interventions can create design solutions that challenge racism and oppression and increase the capacity to develop forward-thinking and anti-racist design solutions.

CREATION OF THE TOOLKIT

The development of the toolkit was due to a shared interest in providing ways for other educators to guide conversations on race and racism. It became evident in our conversations with each other and colleagues at peer institutions that they were also interested in holding this type of space. The Racism Untaught toolkit is not used to prove that racism exists; rather, the toolkit's framework helps participants acknowledge racist artifacts, systems, and experiences, and then works to deconstruct, dismantle, and reimagine them in a collaborative and participatory group environment. Racism was not invented in isolation; therefore, dismantling it requires that we work together. Barbara J. Fields and Karen Elise Fields discuss racism in their book *Racecraft*: "Race as culture is only biological race in polite language: No one can seriously postulate cultural homogeneity among those whose racial homogeneity scholars nonetheless take for granted."[12] When working to dismantle the social construct of race, it is important to acknowledge the inequality of power, privilege, and prejudice. Our definition of *racism* is the social construct of race as the primary determinant for the racially dominant culture to uphold conscious or subconscious beliefs, actions, and/or benefits that support systemic racial prejudice and oppression through power and privilege—in short: prejudice + power over + privilege = racism. A specific example of racism is white people having power over Black people, Indigenous people, and people of color in the United States.

OUR FIRST ANTI-RACIST RESEARCH PROJECT

We began working together in 2016 to map out anti-racist movements so that we might apply design research methods and processes to create effective solutions for community and police relations (see figure I.3). Our goal was to create a dynamic interactive informational system (see figure I.4) that correlates all the data we gathered to help address and create effective solutions for police reform. This included training and hiring practices of law enforcement, community engagement, how authority is perceived and taken, and the building of empathy in the system of policing. We put together a team that consisted of four designers, a Statistician, a sociologist, and a former public defender. We met regularly to remain informed on our findings and keep us all moving forward as we used the design research process to craft approaches to these issues. In parallel, we aligned an advisory team that provided feedback for ensuring we met our goal and were cognizant of the ways in which our positionality might interfere in our ways of understanding. The advisory team consisted of a professor in communication and media, a professor in philosophy, a community activist, and even a police chief.

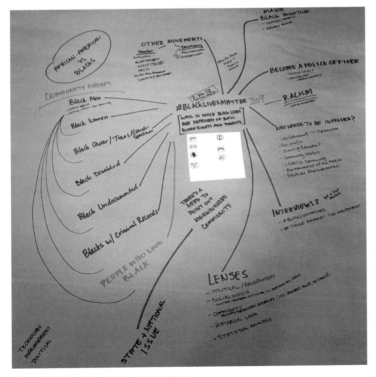

Figure I.3. #BlackLivesMatter concept map.

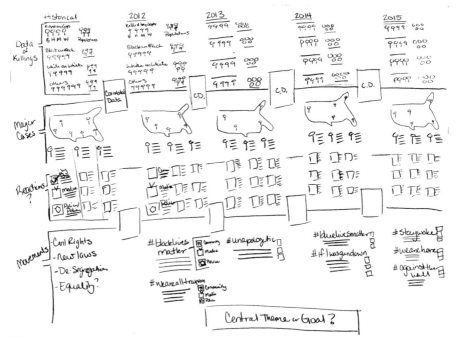

Figure I.4. Informational system low-fidelity sketch.

We worked together on this guiding question: How can activist movements and their portrayal in civic and social media be unified or redefined to overcome the negative and tragic community and police interactions? We worked on gathering data, understanding systems of oppression, and creating community relationships that would guide the forthcoming actions on our research. Then, in November of 2016, the forty-fifth president of the United States was elected. The hope we carried in our work was deflated. We knew we would be shifting our focus to add an abolitionist lens to our work and address the heightened racial division and institutionalized support of racism in the United States. We sent an email to our team and advisors that we would be halting the extensive work we were engaging in for us to determine how we wanted to move forward.

A SHIFT TO RACIALIZED STORYTELLING AND COUNTER-STORYTELLING

We use the term *racialized* in the phrase *racialized storytelling* as an adjective describing racism and elements of racism. As an example, faculty women of color are culturally taxed, creating a racialized experience. The word *racialized* or phrase *to racialize something* can also be used as a verb to explain the process in which systems of oppression use the social construct of race to support the oppression of Black people, Indigenous people, and people of color. For example, due to many years of colonization, Black people in the United States have become racialized. Racialization, both the adjective and verb, are further explained and supported by using the five tenets of critical race theory, as defined by Nicholas Daniel Hartlep.

The tenet most specific to the discourse on racialization that we introduced is a foundational mantra of critical race theory: "the social construction of race."[13] It is our connection to societal implications about racial identity that creates racialized policies and practices meant to discriminate, alienate, and oppress Black people, Indigenous people, and people of color.

Within the five tenets, "the idea of storytelling and counter-storytelling"[14] most specifically describes the shift in our research, scholarship, pedagogical approaches, and curriculum. *Counter-storytelling* is defined by Daniel G. Solórzano and Tara J. Yosso as "a method of telling the stories of those people whose experiences are not often told."[15] The shift in our research toward counter-storytelling as a methodology was a means to center the experiential knowledge of Black people, Indigenous people, and people of color within scholarship. This form of ethnography defined by Wendy Gunn as "the description of cultures"[16] allowed us to validate individual and cultural storytelling, which highlighted the often forgotten narratives of those who sit at the margins of society.

For many communities that have been racialized, storytelling is a way to collect our shared history and to remember the work of our ancestors. We reviewed our data, research, and stories to consider ways to shift our research and work toward an anti-racist agenda. Was there a way to use design to more effectively communicate the stories of Black people harmed not only by police, but by other forms of institutionalized and systemic forms of racism? As designers, our creative abilities give us the means to collectively share stories in ways that invoke change and inspire action and advocacy for communities that have historically been underrepresented, underserved, and underinvested. In our previous work, we identified over twenty accounts of police violence from 2012 to 2016 in conjunction with all the movements that sparked due to community outrage. We reviewed historical movements such as the civil rights movement, Black Power movement, We Are All Trayvon Martin movement, and the Black Lives Matter movement, to craft a full narrative and use historical contexts to positively shift our pedagogy and curriculum. This more than relevant issue—or, we came to find, set of issues—could and should be used in our design courses as a means to explore race in the United States and how we as designers can approach these issues in an anti-racist way. To that end, Terresa created a project called Community Youth Storytelling, which reveals the power of storytelling.

In the fall of 2017, Terresa developed an idea to uplift community voices by creating a community-engaged undergraduate project that would benefit both the student and community members. Before the details of the project were solidified, Terresa developed a relationship with the director of Neighborhood Youth Services (NYS), an after-school program for families with a low economic background and situated in a community with a high population of people of color. She held meetings with the NYS staff to understand the stories of the families they served and what would be most beneficial to the children. They discussed many issues, including representation, having youth input heard and reflected, and what prompts would be most engaging for children to imagine and dream outside of their current circumstances. The NYS staff asked that a conversation focused on power, privilege, and identity happen with the NYS staff members and the university students before they interacted with each other and the NYS youth. Once these details were defined, Terresa moved forward in creating the full project outline for the university students.

The project description read: "Students will develop illustration and typographic layout skills to successfully create a bound book."[17] While the assignment read like any other design project, there were quite a few ways in which Terresa intentionally made room for community engagement and identity exploration. In this project, students not only advanced their technical skills of design principles but also developed their ability to foster client relationships and explore the importance of racially diverse representation in children's books. During the introduction of the project assignment, students were instructed to research book authors and illustrators. This meant having a conversation and intentional discussion of what kinds of authors dominated the children's book industry and who was being visually represented in children's books. They used this information to dig deep into the creation of their mood boards and inspirational pieces, which would come later in the project schedule. Terresa brought in a guest speaker from within the university to talk through concepts like identity, ethics, power, and privilege. These discussions helped students understand the responsibility they now had when working with the community youth at NYS.

Students met with their "client" to debrief, understand their vision, and get their feedback (see figures I.5–I.7). Before their first meeting, staff from the NYS program gave a short presentation on the sensitivity required for successful relationships with the children, many of whom were from racially diverse backgrounds, to help the majority white university students understand that their racial and socioeconomic identities may be quite different.

Figure I.5. Two university students sketching characters for NYS youth during first meeting.

Figure I.6. University students sketching bugs with NYS youth during first meeting.

Figure I.7. University student sketching with NYS youth on couch during first meeting.

The students sat still as a group of high-energy children flooded the workspace and found open chairs, couches, and benches next to the university students. They had in hand their wrinkled stories, which they had worked on earlier based on prompts the staff and Terresa had created. Prompts included questions related to an animal short story, a monster short story, or a superhero short story, such as: What do your characters look like? What are some of your favorite colors? What is your favorite cartoon? Is your story action, romance, funny, or scary?

Students then took time to listen to the children tell their stories. The students took meticulous notes, mimicking the real-life experience of a client debrief meeting. Before the students left that first session, they had asked enough questions to be sure they understood what the children were saying and where the story started and ended.

After the first session, students began working through the design process. As a design scholar, Terresa emphasized the importance of refining their proficiency in illustration, color theory, typographic pairings, typographic grid and layout, and understanding the client debrief. They started by creating mood boards and sketching out their design on a book map to help them break up the story where they saw fit. After creating a few spreads as sketches and one as a fully vectored illustration, students had the opportunity to present their progress to the NYS youth. The second session with NYS was even livelier than the first, with the children asking questions about how they created the drawings and adding their own ideas to the book spreads. Before the third and final session, students revised their work, finished their illustration and type layouts, and had their books perfect bound. After the completion of the books (see figures I.8 and I.9), the students came back to NYS to present the results to the youth, offering not only the book but a short presentation about the process of the design. The youth were absolutely floored at how their narratives and stories came to life.

Figure I.8. University student and youth book concept, example 1.

Figure I.9. University student and youth book concept, example 2.

Introduction

A THREE-MONTH IDEA

During a lunch meeting in April 2018, we took out sticky notes and butcher paper and began brainstorming—a typical process we learned while completing our graduate degrees together. Our goal was to research the art of storytelling using visual elements like photographs, illustrations, or videos. We were particularly interested in racialized experiences and stories of discrimination, oppression, and police brutality. We were hoping to use design to effectively communicate these narratives in order to change perspectives and positively change institutional discrimination. The value that exists at the intersection of design and storytelling lies in contextualizing not only a problem but also an experience and in the opportunity for us to gain an understanding of an experience outside of our own. In *Design Is Storytelling*, Ellen Lupton explains: "Whether creating an interactive product or a data-rich publication, designers invite people to enter a scene and explore what's there—to touch, wander, move, and perform. . . . Storytelling can help products and communications hook the imagination of users and trigger actions and behaviors."[18]

We scheduled weekly meetings with each other to explore this idea further. We were working to gain an understanding of the best ways to start a national awareness campaign on the stories and voices of systemically oppressed communities. We were immersed in examples of similar awareness campaigns and social movements and how these stories can change the perspectives of individuals and impact positive change in our communities. We noted that people in these movements were focused on dispelling stereotypes, changing the narrative, taking a position of offense, and creating a space where voices were heard to streamline missions and affect positive change.

We pulled from our own experiences of incorporating complex social issues in our curriculum. One example was an interactive undergraduate design course facilitated by Lisa and a colleague in industrial design during the spring semester of 2018 at the University of Illinois Urbana-Champaign (UIUC). They conducted a sixteen-week design studio in which students constructed an immersive reality design challenge in two parts: (1) the production of a reality headset and controller that could be used in a detention center and (2) the design and creation of a mobile app to launch a designed and tested virtual reality (VR), augmented reality (AR), mixed reality (MR), or extended reality (XR) experience. Thirteen industrial design students and twenty-four graphic design students were divided into twelve groups. Each group included an industrial design student and two graphic design students.

Students were focused on the development of emerging technology, immersive reality experiences for people who were incarcerated and working toward reentry into society. To better understand the audience students were designing with, they worked with Dr. Rebecca Ginsburg, the director of the Educational Justice Project (EJP), a model college-in-prison program that demonstrates the positive impacts of higher education for people who are incarcerated. The researchers wanted students to understand the importance of creating empathic reality experiences as a vital and necessary part of the creative design process. It was vital for them to understand and empathize with the needs of people who are incarcerated. As a class we watched the movie *13th*, a documentary produced by Ava DuVernay in 2016 that focused on the Thirteenth Amendment, systems of oppression, punishment, and who is seen as a criminal in the United States. Dr. Ginsburg also lectured on this topic two diffᵉrent times over the sixteen-week course. She talked to students about the crimes committed on or near our campus and how Black students were disproportionately incarcerated at a higher rate than white students for the same crimes that white students had committed.

The first eight weeks were focused on the production of a reality headset and controller that could be brought into and used in a detention center. Students considered how comfortable the headset was to use and that it needed to be easy for it to be used by multiple people. Students began by making hand-drawn sketches (see figure I.10). Then students created a second prototype from Styrofoam and cardboard (see figure I.11) that fully realized the headset in a three-dimensional representation. The final deliverable for the headset was a movie of a 2D rendering, with the exploded view of the rendering showing the relationships of the various parts. The second eight weeks of the course were focused on developing immersive reality technologies to help people who were incarcerated with working toward reentry. The intention of these experiences was to help people who were incarcerated become comfortable with common experiences in everyday life outside of a detention center. Ginsburg, plus a team of alumni from the EJP, curated a list of scenarios for students to select from when creating an educational, empathic, immersive experience. A few examples include ordering a McRib at McDonald's, using autopay at Walmart, using automated order boards at fast-food restaurants, paying for gas at the pump, how to text, and how to use emojis. Dr. Ginsburg stressed to the students the ethical implications that some of these scenarios could include. Some of the scenarios required an understanding of culture or parole violations the students might not have, which led us into an important discussion of codesigning and working collaboratively to ensure we understood the impact of our designs. Students had the choice to either select a proposed scenario or develop their own in conversation with Lisa or the second instructor. After conferring with Dr. Ginsburg, students developed two additional scenarios: experiencing coffee shop culture and purchasing tickets for public transportation using different forms of payment. The first prototype was a large-scale sketch in which students began to question the experience and the functionalities needed in an immersive reality experience (see figure I.12). The second prototype was a digital rendering of the mobile app that prompted the experience, as well as the experience that was prompted from the mobile app (see figure I.13).

Figure I.10. Immersive reality sketches.

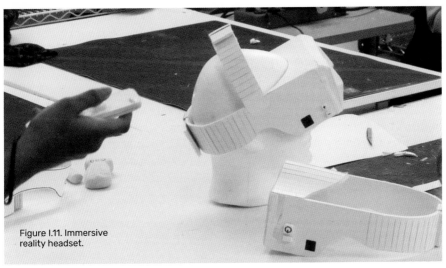

Figure I.11. Immersive reality headset.

Figure I.12. Phase 2, low-fidelity sketch of immersive reality experience.

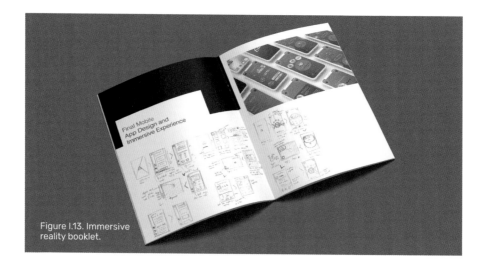

Figure I.13. Immersive reality booklet.

A second example of incorporating complex social issues into our courses was a multilayered, community-engaged undergraduate project facilitated by Terresa entitled *The Movement Imprinted*. This project intentionally focused on the Black experience and created an opportunity for students to consider not only Black narratives, but also Black design inspiration. Students were instructed to create an original poster design (see figure I.14) using imagery and text to evoke the likeness of an assigned Black activist. The student was to understand who this individual was both personally and professionally, what started their interest in activism, what they are best known for as it relates to social justice, and what social norms or systems of oppression this person challenged. After researching the activist based on the supplied guiding questions, students were then required to illustrate this individual in a style inspired by that of an assigned Black designer. This project allowed for conversation about the lack of representation of Black designers in the design industry. The students studied the work of the designer—annotating three major visual works—and were also instructed to research the designer's personal and professional career, their contributions to the design industry, and the change they made in the field of design. It was important to the foundation of the project that students understood not only the lives of the activists but also the lives of the Black designers who contributed to society in major ways.

Students designed a correlating eight-page booklet (see figure I.15) that held the information they had gathered about the activist and designer, along with information about themselves. The design of the pamphlet honed the student's skills in typographic combination and grid, color theory, hierarchy, and data visualization. The pamphlet was branded to coincide with their poster design and included a cover and back cover, a spread about the activist, a spread about the inspirational designer, and a spread about themselves, their work, and their poster design process.

Figure I.14. Project poster examples. Mockup by authors, spring 2017–spring 2020.

Figure I.15. Project poster booklet. Mockup by authors, spring 2019.

The project was purposefully facilitated during Black History Month in February and coincided with the annual Freedom Fund Dinner of the Duluth, Minnesota, branch of the National Association for the Advancement of Colored People (NAACP). Students exhibited their work in a gallery fashion, and their pieces were sold via silent auction. Students donated at least half of their proceeds to the NAACP. All students were required to attend the exhibition, and many invited their family and friends to attend and see their work. Each year, every piece was sold. Terresa continued this project every February for four years, using the *The Movement Imprinted* as the title, with subtitles that correlated with each semester's theme: *Faces of Change* (see figure I.16); *Music of the Revolution* (see figure I.17); *Moments in the Movement*; and *The Life, the Work, the Fight*.

Figure I.16. *The Movement Imprinted* 2017 exhibition, *Faces of Change.*

Figure I.17. *The Movement Imprinted* 2018 exhibition, *Music of the Revolution.*

Students were elated to see their work on display at such an early stage of their careers, in their Graphic Design 1 course—adding a level of consideration and meticulousness to this project. The unintended added pressure heightened class critiques and their own critical analysis of the social constructs that affect Black communities.

When we presented this work at conferences, many of our colleagues at peer institutions asked us how we walked students through the critical analysis of these situations to produce anti-oppressive outcomes. We both explored, within our own research and in the courses we taught, how we use the design research process to critically analyze racism in the classroom. This, in turn, became our focus on helping other design educators use the design research process to assist students with exploring issues of racism. The questions that guided our work were: How might we improve the design curriculum by incorporating multicultural references through critical thinking tools? And how can design positively and effectively integrate anti-racist concepts into project-based learning environments?

We named the framework Racism Untaught because we knew that what we were interested in creating would challenge learned racialized societal norms. It was in this brainstorming phase that we leaned on our own knowledge as designers. First, we knew that we needed a workspace to brainstorm (first referred to as the *card fold-out board* and later called the *workboard*); second, we needed elements to prompt participants to think through each step (later referred to as the *cards*). With all this in mind, and an existing design research framework with which we were quite familiar, we opened Adobe Illustrator and created our first workboard.

The design research process began with empathy building, a period of discovery, then conducting qualitative or quantitative research, ideating based on the learned factors from that research, prototyping those ideas, and in between each prototype revisiting research to ensure the development of an idea would be useful to the community. While we both utilized this framework with success in our own work, we both wanted to question the status quo in the implementation of the design research framework in this work. We wanted to ensure that the critical pauses and interventions we naturally took in our own work were more explicit for other people. The interventions in the Racism Untaught framework are an exploration of the ways we took pause and worked to intentionally understand the impact of our work. We do not relate to the capitalistic notion of "Move fast and break things";[19] unless you are breaking stuff, you are not moving fast enough. Instead, we wanted to provide designers with a more intentional practice so that they can slow down and understand just how their agency is affecting change.

OUR SHIFT IN PEDAGOGY

It is no secret that higher education, along with many institutions across the country, is facing a reckoning with its own perpetuated racism.[20] How many broad-reaching statements, performative emails, social media posts, and statements can an institution send out that claim that "Black lives matter" without the representation of Black students, staff, and faculty—without real anti-racist action and without the programs in place that support the identities of Black students, Indigenous students, and students of color on a predominantly white campus? Within education, the word *decolonize* is an inescapable term to describe the ways in which we engage in and transform pedagogy and research. It centers whiteness instead of centering various epistemic and cultural sources of knowledge and the dissemination of that knowledge.[21] The overuse of *decolonization* has gentrified what it means to be radical and disruptive in the academy. The concept of *decolonization* assumes we all have the same agency to enact these changes. We recognize that the power to make these changes is not binary, but we also recognize that Black people, Indigenous people, and people of color do not hold the same opportunities and power to decolonize. Instead of doing the minimum when it comes to decolonizing our syllabi, design educators need to ask ourselves:

- How do we transform courses into a community of inquiry?
- How do we structure a supportive sequence of courses for students from various backgrounds and lived experiences to succeed?
- Who do we believe holds knowledge in the classroom?
- How does my positionality indicate or affect my perception and understanding of a topic?
- How do we deconstruct settler-imposed systems that oppress Black people, Indigenous people, and people of color?

In panels and invited talks, we are often asked, What is the difference between being *not racist* and *anti-racist*? Angela Davis famously states to this clearly when she states, "In a racist society, it's not enough to be nonracist, we must be anti-racist."[22] Someone who claims they are *not racist* is willfully ignorant of the ways their social identities uphold systems of oppression. They lack concern about oppressive issues because they benefit from the same oppressive system that negatively affects people of color. This might show up as a white person who expresses a "color-blind" approach to life; they have the privilege of ignoring race and claiming they see the world in this way. *Anti-racism*, on the other hand, is the acknowledgment of the ways we uphold systems of oppression and how we engage in intentional actions to dismantle those systems. Being anti-racist is living in a consistent and mindful way, in which we are aware of the privileges and power we hold and then work to actively dismantle oppressive systems that exist around us. In essence, we need to be intentional in moving past decolonization efforts and toward actions that focus on liberation.

One example of being intentional in our own ways of moving toward liberation is working toward eliminating coded language that shows up in academia. For instance, the terms *diversity*, *equity*, and *inclusion* are coded language that allows discourse about racism without tackling the issue of racism. Furthermore, coded language allows racialized actions to be blamed on those that are oppressed rather than calling out the culture of racism that exists within our institutions—for example, "We cannot diversify our faculty because Black people are not interested," rather than what should be said, which is, "Because we as an institution perpetuate actions that support racism, Black people are not interested in working in environments that systemically cause them harm." Notice the difference in accountability, blame, and urgency in each of those statements. Another factor that supports our journey toward liberation is the way we choose to support students and faculty of color, who are often culturally taxed on a predominantly white campus. This support could be reflected in lessening the service/teaching load a faculty member of color has or providing a cocurricular opportunity/credit for a student of color who is leading an affinity space for students of color. The acknowledgment of their efforts should not only affirm their work but also include reparation-based actions that support their racialized experiences. Collective liberation is explored further in chapter 6.

It is our hope that the Racism Untaught framework will be used as a tool of anti-racist support for institutions of higher learning, industry, and community organizations. Examples of outcomes and the use of the toolkit can be found on the following pages (see figures I.18 and 1.19). More information about the toolkit and learning opportunities are available on our website at **racismuntaught.com**.

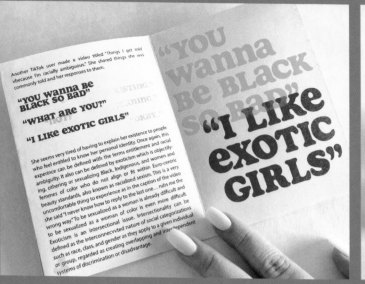

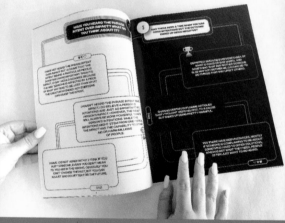

Figure I.18. Collage of Racism Untaught student work.

Queens
SYRUP

up fit for a Queen

VIOLA DAVIS

Triple Threat

DEWANDA WISE

reedom Fighter

LAVERNE COX

Sex Kitten

> "My life changed when I realized I deserve to be seen, to dream, to be fully included, always striving to bring my full humanity."

About Me

Laverne Cox is a fierce trans Black actress and activist born to a single mother in Mobile, Alabama in 1972. Throughout her career she has been a voice and advocate for LGBTQ+ rights.

Achievements

› Winner of a Daytime Emmy Award in Outstanding Special Class Special as Executive Producer for Laverne Cox Presents: The T Word.
› Emmy nomination for "Outstanding Guest Actress in a Comedy Series."
› First Openly Trans Woman to appear on the cover of TIME Magazine
› Courage Award from the Anti-Violence Project

THE UNITED STATES HAS BEEN WHITEWASHED FOR FAR TOO LONG.

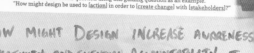

Figure I.19. Collage of Racism Untaught industry and community work.

IDEATE

Use an artifact(s), system(s), and/or experience(s) to create something that will help solve your design _. Incorporating the qualitative and _hnographic research methods from self(ves) how you can affect change _e solution? Lastly, use the quadrant _ below _lot your idea.

NEWS

PROTEST

INFORMATION

PROCESS

THERAPY

CLASS

CONFERENCE

TRAINING

EDUCATION

COMMUNITY

TRAUMA

INTRAPERSONAL

SMALL GROUP RELATIONS

LARGE GROUP RELATIONS

GAMIFICATION

INTERPERSONAL RELATIONSHIP

MOBILE APPLICATION

REPORT

PRISON/ INCARCERATION

GRAPHIC NOVEL

ILLUST

NARRATIVE

POST CARD

AUGMENTED REALITY

EXPERIENCE DESIGN

MIXED REALITY

BOOK

LIKE ALL SYSTEMS, SYSTEMS OF OPPRESSION, INEQUALITY, AND INEQUITY ARE BY DESIGN. THEREFORE, THEY CAN BE REDESIGNED

1

THE FRAMEWORK

In the introduction, we explained how we developed the original idea for the framework over the span of three months. In this chapter, we will share (1) why the design research process fits the need to reimagine forms of racialized design, (2) the steps of the Racism Untaught framework, (3) how we determined where we needed to integrate design interventions, and (4) the iterative improvements we made to the framework and each of its parts (interventions, cards, and naming conventions).

THE DESIGN RESEARCH PROCESS

The design research process is a framework that begins with the identification of a problem or gap in our knowledge and then works toward an outcome to either find an innovative solution for the problem or to fill the gap. The process is often done collaboratively with people from various disciplines and areas of industry, but it is inherent to the way designers work. Some have called the design research process *human-centered design* or *design thinking*. Don Norman explains human-centered design in his 1988 book *The Design of Everyday Things*: "an approach that puts human needs, capabilities, and behavior first, then designs to accommodate those needs, capabilities, and ways of behaving."[2] IDEO, a global design company, is typically credited with coining the term *design thinking* in the 1970s.[3] The company used the term "to describe the elements of the practice we found most learnable and teachable—empathy, optimism, iteration, creative confidence, experimentation, and an embrace of ambiguity and failure."[4] Both human-centered design and design thinking refer to the *design research process*, a research methodology for creating innovative design outcomes. The method is typically an iterative five-step process that begins with building empathy, defining the problem or gap of knowledge, ideating an outcome, prototyping that outcome, and then testing the outcome. The process can also be described as a three-step iterative process of observing a problem or gap of knowledge, ideating an outcome that could fill that gap or problem, and testing that idea. Either process, whether it follows five steps or three, includes multiple iterations while converging on an idea, then diverging to test it, and then eventually converging and narrowing in even more until an outcome is reached.[5]

The path is not always obvious and can feel ambiguous at times; it is not a process that produces one possible outcome, nor is it a process that is repeatable with the same outcome.[6] The interconnectedness of each step can lead participants on different paths of knowing. Horst Rittel and Melvin Webber saw the design of methodologies as "new goal-oriented actions" and ways to solve problems. They explained the value of design methodologies in the 1970s as a way of creating smarter solutions for increasingly complex societies. They explained the necessity of a process "as we seek to improve the effectiveness of actions in pursuit of valued outcomes, as system boundaries get stretched, and as we become more sophisticated about the complex workings of open societal systems."[7] They saw wicked problems as barriers that keep us from planning adequate systems, noting that "it becomes morally objectionable for the planner to treat a wicked problem as though it were a tame one, or to tame a wicked problem prematurely, or to refuse to recognize the inherent wickedness of social problems."[8] Richard Buchanan focused on design thinking and wicked problems in his 1992 article "Wicked Problems in Design Thinking," where he acknowledged the changes in the contemporary practice of design as moving from a "trade activity to a segmented profession to a field for technical research and to what now should be recognized as new liberal art of technological culture."[9] In the Racism Untaught framework, we intentionally made changes to the naming of the steps and included interventions to disrupt the status quo to ensure we were centering an anti-racist form of thinking and doing.

One example of the changes we made (more examples are outlined later in this chapter) is that we changed the name of the first step, typically called *empathy*, to *context*. We believe that if we wait for everyone to empathize with racism, then we will be waiting too long. Building context will happen in parallel with participants as they grow in their empathetic design response.[10] John Gumperz, a founding figure in anthropology and sociolinguistics, questioned, "How does social knowledge—including the indispensable 'context'—enter into the interpretation of utterances from the viewpoints of participants?"[11] He saw context as an important process that would help people create cultural understandings. Gumperz explained *contextualization cues* as a way to conversationally discuss what was being signaled. "Speaking itself creates and re-creates contexts, ties, often in ways that speakers find hard to access in a conscious way."[12]

A second example of the changes we made is the naming of the last step, typically called *test*, which we have titled *impact* (see figure 1.1). We emphasize impact over intent because we have heard many people state, "That was not my intention." But just because the intention or the "desire for discrimination"[13] was not apparent, it does not negate the harm committed. Racism can happen with or without a conscious intention.[14] For this reason, we emphasize understanding the impact of our design outcomes. If we can identify and discuss why an artifact, system, or experience is a form of oppressive design, then we can create a shared understanding of impact over intent.[15] This is a paradigm shift happening in many institutional spaces (explained further in chapter 4). How do we ensure that the iterative approach we are using to reimagine a form of racialized design will be anti-oppressive?

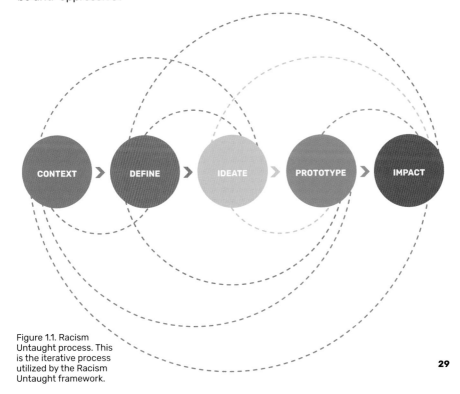

Figure 1.1. Racism Untaught process. This is the iterative process utilized by the Racism Untaught framework.

THE RACISM UNTAUGHT FRAMEWORK

When participants interact with the Racism Untaught framework, they are applying an iterative five-step process (see figure 1.2). Each step has a set of corresponding cards, which we will discuss further ahead. The elements and steps involved in using the Racism Untaught toolkit are described in the following sections.

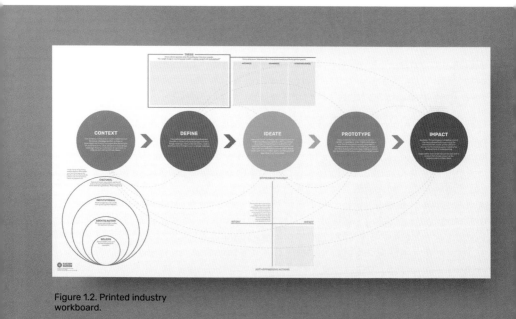

Figure 1.2. Printed industry workboard.

ONBOARDING ACTIVITIES

Before beginning work with the Racism Untaught toolkit, participants are prompted with various onboarding activities (further outlined in chapter 3). This step is intended to help participants understand the positionality of their identities and how those identities shape their everyday experiences and design outcomes. These activities lead to a discussion that helps build a community among the participants through conversations about their social identities. The activities include the Socio-Cultural Identities worksheet and the Social Identity Profile.

PROMPTS

Participants are prompted with a racialized artifact, system, or experience, as outlined in chapter 2. They are then guided through each step of the Racism Untaught framework and the additional design interventions to think critically about the racialized prompt and how to reimagine that form of racialized design. In workshops, the prompts are sometimes collected from one of the pre-workshop activities and are anonymized to use as a prompt in the workshop. You can view examples in each of our case studies in this book.

STEP 1: CONTEXT

In the first step, *context*, we use the following language to describe the instructions: "Use the elements of racism and other forms of oppression in the corresponding card deck to create context around the racialized/oppressive design prompt (artifact, system, or experience) and discuss how racism/oppression is perpetuated with the given prompt." This step's corresponding cards include an element of oppression and its definition. There are approximately seventy-five elements of racism, thirty elements of sexism, and fifteen elements of ableism. Examples of this language are outlined in each of the six case studies and in chapter 4 (see figure 1.3).

Figure 1.3. Context cards. This is how the context cards looked in the first iteration of the printed toolkit.

The following substep is present on the workboard for the next part of context: "Next, use the Levels of Oppression model to further contextualize the racialized/oppressive design prompt. Consider how the prompt is perpetuated in each level." This is a circular model (based on the lens of systemic oppression[16]) to further contextualize your instance of oppression. We encourage participants to consider where in the levels of oppression the problem was created and how each level perpetuated it. The largest concentric circle is titled Cultural, which represents the systems of norms, values, beliefs, and trusted systems of acquiring truth that preserve, protect, and maintain oppression (i.e., white supremacy). The next largest concentric circle within the Cultural circle is titled Institutional, which refers to structural oppression that results from agentic oppressive behavior. The second smallest concentric circle within the levels falls in the Institutional circle and is titled Agentic Action, where oppressive beliefs translate into oppressive behavior. The smallest of all the circles is titled Beliefs, which represents personal beliefs, ideas, and feelings that perpetuate oppression. This design intervention and the visualization are further explored in chapter 5.

STEP 2: DEFINE

We use the following language on the workboard for the *define* step: "Use theories and methods in the corresponding card deck to an approach to the design challenge. A theory is the lens in which one views the racialized/oppressive design prompt, while the methods are the ways in which one might gather supporting data." This step includes theories and methods for participants to contextualize their racialized prompt further. There are approximately twenty theories and forty methods. This step introduces novel ways of developing new knowledge to disrupt the status quo. Participants often use the same methods and ways of thinking to analyze a form of racialized design. Examples of this language are outlined in each of the six case studies and in chapter 4 (see figure 1.4).

Figure 1.4. Define cards. This is how the define cards looked in the first iteration of the printed toolkit.

We frequently ask participants to go through a period of discovery before creating their thesis question and doing additional research. This period of discovery includes an annotated bibliography, a literature review, or a popular media search to help them gain further context into the racialized prompt. In a shorter workshop setting, this often looks like a collage of article titles, screenshots of articles and images, or pull quotes that can help the participants further contextualize their racialized prompts. The development of a collage is a generative tool that can facilitate collaboration and discussion.[17] Often this is the participants' first time working together. The time they spend together creating this collage provides a space for participants to share preconceptions and new insights before they move on to the next step. This information also helps them in the next substep of define. We use the following language to describe the thesis question substep: "Create a thesis question using the following guiding question as an example: How might design be used to [action] in order to [create change] with [stakeholders]?"

Above the sample question, we provide the participants with three areas to help them think through the development of their question in a collaborative space: (1) the action they want to pursue, (2) the change they want to make, and (3) with whom they would like to work. We ask each of the participants to brainstorm separately, starting with change(s), before prompting them to consider what action(s) need to happen for that change to occur and then who they need to work with to ensure the change will be sustainable. After all the participants have added their ideas to each section, the group collaborates to formulate a question.

Once they have created a research question, they focus on answering it. Participants select additional methods or theories to collect secondary and primary research in order to define the racialized prompt further and address their thesis question. Participants could spend the duration of the project going back to this step to gain more quantitative and qualitative data. Once the initial research has begun and the various factors have been gathered, the participants move on to the third step.

STEP 3: IDEATE

We use the following language on the workboard for the *ideate* step: "Use the artifacts, systems, and/or experiences in the corresponding card deck to create an idea that will reimagine the racialized/oppressive design prompt." Examples of this language are outlined in each of the six case studies and in chapter 4 (see figure 1.5).

Figure 1.5. Ideate cards. This is how the ideate cards looked in the first iteration of the printed toolkit.

The ideate step results from the analysis of the primary and secondary research collected in the second step, define. This analysis will result in an artifact, system, and/or experience to create a design solution that will begin to gather more user data from the audience. Each card offers a term and is categorized in the three design areas: artifacts, systems, and experiences. With these cards the participants can ideate ways they might pursue change. This step has the largest number of cards, with over forty-five artifacts, forty systems, and thirty experiences. In the first part of this step, we ask participants to use the cards to help them think of avenues in which they might affect positive change given the racialized design they were assigned. We encourage participants to use all three categories in the group brainstorming process. We also encourage them to think radically in this step. We do not want participants to feel the boundaries from the "real world" and ask them to forget budgets, existing policies, or ways of working.

The following language is for the substep of the ideate step: "Through discussion, you will use this quadrant map to help evaluate the value of each idea. On the x-axis, consider the intent of the idea in comparison to the impact. On the y-axis, consider how far your idea might shift its participants from systemically oppressive thought(s) to anti-oppressive action."

On the quadrant map (see figure 1.6, further outlined in chapter 5), the x-axis reads, "Use this quadrant map to help assess the value of each idea. On the x-axis, consider the intent of the idea in comparison to the impact. On the y-axis, consider how far an idea might shift participants from systemically oppressive thought(s) to anti-oppressive action(s)." On the x-axis, the participants are asked to consider the intent of the idea in comparison to the impact. On the y-axis, participants are asked to consider how far their ideas have shifted systemically

OPPRESSIVE THOUGHT

Through discussion and critical thinking, use this quadrant map to help evaluate the value of each idea. On the x-axis, consider the intent of the idea versus its potential impact. On the y-axis, consider how far your idea shifts systemically oppressive thought(s) to anti-oppressive action.

INTENT

IMPACT

ANTI-OPPRESSIVE ACTIONS

Figure 1.6. Quadrant map. This is how the quadrant map looked in the first iteration of the printed toolkit.

The Framework

oppressive thoughts. We ask each participant to write a fully developed idea on a sticky note. At this stage, all ideas are welcome, and no ideas should be omitted. Once participants have written down one or two ideas, they begin to use the quadrant map to delimit or combine solutions with another to ensure they move forward with one idea that has the most impact. They work together to consider the value and impact of each idea. We encourage participants to consider how the combination of ideas will work toward impact, rather than good intentions. Often participants will go back to the define step to understand whether their expectations are working toward impact or only focused on good intentions. After the participants have decided on the best idea to move forward, they move on to the next step.

STEP 4: PROTOTYPE

The following language denotes the fourth step on the workboard, *prototype*: "Use the low-, mid-, and high-fidelity prototyping methods in the corresponding card deck to determine which processes will be used to reimagine the racialized/oppressive design prompt. Fidelity refers to the function of your artifact, system, or experience. A low-fidelity prototype is nonfunctioning and is initially presented to communicate your idea. A mid-fidelity prototype is limited in functionality and a high-fidelity prototype has minimal modifications needed for the final deliverable." Examples of this language are outlined in each of the six case studies and in chapter 4.

There are approximately ten low-fidelity cards, ten mid-fidelity cards, and five high-fidelity cards (see figure 1.7). The prototype step is meant to refine the design solution through the iteration of moving from prototype to define or other steps of the framework. The participant should use research between each prototype creation to refine and improve upon each design iteration. It is important to (1) remember the iterative process within this framework, (2) ensure participants continue to collect user information, and (3) note how they react to and work with a design approach. A low-fidelity ideation is nonfunctioning and is initially presented to communicate your idea. Once user information is collected on the low-fidelity prototype, then an analysis of that information should result in factors that can then be applied to a mid-fidelity prototype. A mid-fidelity prototype is limited in functionality but functional enough to collect more insights from users through research such as user groups, workshops, or other means of collection. Once these factors have been collected from users, then they are implemented in a high-fidelity prototype (one step before final deliverable), which will potentially need minimal modifications before the outcome is completed. Each prototype (low-, mid-, or high-fidelity) may be conducted more than once to ensure a true understanding of the users' needs.

Figure 1.7. Prototype cards. This is how the prototype cards looked in the first iteration of the printed toolkit.

STEP 5: IMPACT

The following language is present on the workboard for the *impact* step: "Use the impact methods in the corresponding card deck to measure the impact on the design implementation." There are approximately twenty-five cards in this step of the framework, which may be applied in an academic or organizational setting. Examples of this language are outlined in each of the six case studies and in chapter 4 (see figure 1.8). The only difference in this step for the academic framework is the inclusion of a rubric that demonstrates both a high level of comprehension and proficiency of the determined deliverable(s) and the ability to incorporate the methods and processes at an advanced level of understanding. Instructors and students use the academic rubric to evaluate the project together, creating a collective responsibility of learned concepts and their ability to incorporate the methods and processes at an advanced level of understanding. The student should be able to (1) exhibit an understanding of racialized design and anti-racist concepts, (2) apply concepts they have learned in new situations, (3) use critical thinking to draw connections among ideas, (4) justify their design choices, and (5) create an original idea. At the end of the workshop, participants are provided with a certificate of completion and are able to share their work on an online professional platform or social media.

Figure 1.8. Impact cards. This is how the impact cards looked in the first iteration of the printed toolkit.

PILOT WORKSHOP STUDY

In August 2018, we ran our first Racism Untaught workshop. The participants were attendees at the Design + Diversity conference, and they came from different sectors of design, including academia, industry, and community. The workshop took place the day before the conference at the Design for Inclusivity Industry Summit, when roughly eighty to ninety participants came together to experience a series of events. The Racism Untaught workshop was one of the forty-five-minute sessions attended by the participants, who came with different lived experiences specific to race and racism. Most participants present at the conference were already interested in and focused on areas concerning social impact, diversity, equity, inclusion, and access work. They were looking to learn and add language, tools, or ways of thinking to their roles on committees, boards, or organizations.

Figure 1.9. Pilot workshop board. This is an example of how the workboard looked in the pilot workshop.

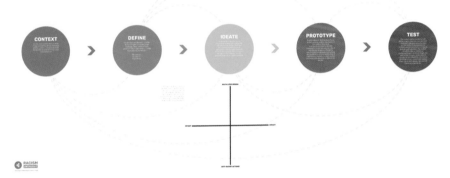

All participants were divided into seven groups. Each group had four to eight participants who sat at their own table supplied with a Racism Untaught toolkit. The toolkit included a workboard (see figure 1.9), on which participants had sticky notes, markers, and cards that corresponded with and matched the color of each step. We gave each group a prompt before they started working on the first step, context. The prompt was provided in two different formats: first a video that illustrated and spoke out loud the racialized lived experience, and second a piece of paper with the experience written out with correlating illustrations (see figure 1.10). The prompt read:

> I called some fellow community members over to my apartment building for a meeting on a Sunday afternoon. There were six of us in total. Five of us were African or of African heritage and one was Asian. We met in a large conference room at the front of my building. The room had a large glass door which automatically locked once you closed it. We had just started our meeting when an older white man came to the door and tried to open it. We all looked up, and puzzled I might add, because we

weren't expecting any more guests. He began talking and raised his voice so that we could hear him and asked "Can someone get my newspaper off the floor? All the newspapers are on the floor, can someone come get these!?" It was very clear that he believed one of us worked at this apartment building, but since the apartment's grand opening almost two years ago, there have been no employees of color.

Figure 1.10. Apartment prompt: experience. This is the prompt that was illustrated and shared as a video with a voice-over of the written prompt.

Once the prompt was shared with the participants, they were guided through the framework with an informal session script that included the time allotted for each step, the actions participants would be prompted with, and a reaction to each step. The participants began with the first step, context, and were given ten minutes to place the cards that included the elements of racism around the context circle that they all agreed were present in the prompt. This exercise provided participants with a way of understanding and a realization of the numerous ways racism showed up in the prompt.

In the second step, define, the participants had ten minutes to select from the cards listing various methods and theories and then place them around the define circle. Then the participants were asked to determine a thesis question or research statement that would help them understand the prompt through the application of these methods and theories.

In the third step, ideate, participants had ten minutes to review the cards that gave examples of artifacts, systems, and experiences, and they were asked to place the cards they could imagine applying to the factors they had learned in their research to reimagine the prompt. The workshop ended after step 3, but the next two steps, *prototype* and *test*, were explained to the participants to make sure they understood the entire framework (see figure 1.11).

Figure 1.11. Workboard in use at pilot workshop. Printed workboard being used by participants at a conference in 2018.

ITERATIVE CHANGES TO THE TOOLKIT

Since 2018, multiple questions have guided our research for Racism Untaught. These questions have helped us understand the iterative changes necessary to develop our research and the framework. Since the pilot workshop in August 2018, we have continuously refined this research while conducting over forty workshops in academia, industry, and the broader community. During the first two years of this research study, one of our questions was, "How can design assist in identifying racialized designs and critically assess anti-racist concepts?" The second question was, "How does the knowledge and awareness of one's own positionality and social constructs influence how they engage in the design research process?"

We were keenly aware that making iterative changes over time would be a crucial factor to the framework's efficacy and successful operation in a course, workshop setting, or community space. With this in mind, we use the workshops (a collaborative participatory space, discussed further in chapter 3) as a methodology to help us continually improve on the toolkit. This way of gathering qualitative data is further emphasized in Rikke Ørngreen and Karin Levinsen's 2017 article "Workshops as a Research Methodology." The authors identified workshops as a research approach that "is an explicit method choice that allows us to iterate, and thus refine and moderate, our research design over time and in different contexts."[18] The workshops have also provided insight through observations and feedback from participants[19] to iteratively develop interventions, shared language, and innovative ways of thinking to integrate within or in addition to the toolkit. The workshops became a space meant for participants and us, as the facilitators, to explore new ways of doing, thinking, and innovation.

We acknowledge and value the insight and experiences that participants bring with them from different disciplines and industries, and we make it a point to state in each workshop, "We are *all* designers of artifacts, systems, and experiences." This is further explored in chapter 2. Using the Racism Untaught toolkit creates a space for participants to think collectively and critically explore oppressive artifacts, systems, and experiences. Participants engage in a sequence of situated actions that begin with working toward a shared context of a racialized design prompt. Context is imperative, as emphasized by anthropologist Lucy Suchman, who stated that "nothing can be understood without first understanding its context."[20] Suchman also introduced the term *situated action* as a way to discuss the development of an intentional space for shared understanding,[21] which is our intention for participants who interact with the framework.

We made a few adjustments to the five steps of the design research process before we first ran the pilot workshop. One of those changes was to change the name of the first step from *empathy* to *context*. We intentionally made this change based on our ethnographic experiences as people of color. If we wait for everyone to gain empathy in the realm of issues of race and racism, we would be waiting forever. While empathy is important in the design process, it is not something that is easily gained in one step; rather, its development runs parallel to the whole process. Changing this step to context allowed participants to break down racism regardless of their racial identity and where they were in their personal anti-racist journeys. Tarana Burke, founder of the #MeToo movement and coauthor with Brené Brown of the book *You Are Your Best Thing*, discusses how our personal experiences shape our understanding and how awareness is key. The authors explain, "If we believe that historical and cultural context matter, then it makes sense that those events don't happen in a vacuum. They happen to people and show up as personal experiences. It's very important, even good, if we are conscious that it is our personal experiences shaping our theology."[22] Since creating the Racism Untaught framework and toolkit, we have learned the importance of designing interventions that prompt pauses and critical thought throughout the process. In the next section, we explore those specific changes.

WORKBOARD LAYOUT

Although the workboard has always included the design research process, we have made changes to work toward ethical and responsible ways of analyzing and reimagining oppressive design. Many participants have asked how they could implement Racism Untaught in the spaces where they worked, including people from each sector of academia, industry, and community. We wanted to ensure that people understood how to work through the toolkit if we were not facilitating it. This desire prompted us to develop two guidebooks, one for academia and one for industry. The academic version included more information specific to the running of a course—for example, a syllabus, a rubric, readings, and group development. Eventually, we combined both versions of the guidebooks because we found that each sector was interested in the onboarding process we implemented.

We wanted the toolkit to have an overall friendly feel since we expected that participants might feel overwhelmed with the idea of analyzing and reimagining a form of racialized design. We intentionally created a colorful space inviting people to interact with the toolkit. The order of the colors per step is as follows: context is teal, define is red, ideate is yellow, prototype is green, and impact is purple. We use the teal color in the first step as a friendly opener, and we chose purple for the last step because purple represents peace and liberation. We flipped the green and red colors while making iterative changes to the framework because, much like a traffic signal, red means stop, yellow is caution, and green means go. On the workboard, from the very first iteration, gray dotted lines have connected the steps. The dotted lines are an important part of the framework and remind participants of the iterative nature of the design research process. We also wanted to keep the gray lines in the process due to the emphasis on continued learning for participants, who might need to move back to the define or context step, even if they are at the prototype step.

In conjunction with the workboard, we have created cards with terms and definitions that are correlated with each step. In the first iteration of the framework, we had approximately ninety cards in total. We now have more than 375 cards (discussed further in chapter 4). The language that has been incorporated into the framework has been a thread of this research that has been more rewarding than we initially anticipated.

The workboard has undergone four major iterations, which have made the exploration of racialized design accessible to a variety of people and industries (design, social work, real estate, etc.) We made our fifth major change in December 2021 to provide more accessibility and to package the toolkit more easily. We have essentially broken down each step and substep into its own 15 × 15" workboard (see figure 1.12). To keep the toolkit available online we revised the digital workboard as well (see figure 1.13).

ACCESSIBILITY

As we facilitated the workshops, we have learned how to offer access to the tools and framework to meet a broad array of needs. We provide the terms that appear on the cards of each step in list form so that the participants can print all the written content from the framework. We provide the file digitally, and participants can either enlarge it or make the text larger before they print the document. We have invited people to provide additional assistance for specific participants on an as-needed basis. This includes American Sign Language (ASL) translators and the use of a closed-caption option in virtual workshops.

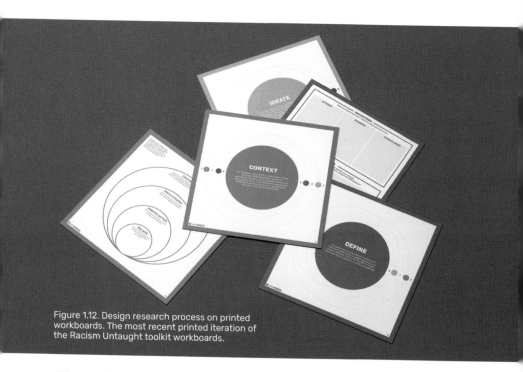

Figure 1.12. Design research process on printed workboards. The most recent printed iteration of the Racism Untaught toolkit workboards.

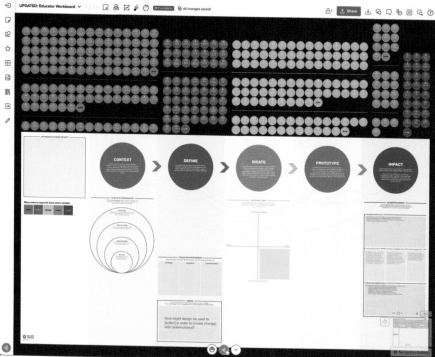

Figure 1.13. Design research process on digital workboard. The most recent digital iteration of the Racism Untaught toolkit workboards.

RACIAL-AFFINITY SPACES

After observing participants engage with one another in workshops, we saw great value in providing racial-affinity spaces for Black people, Indigenous people, and people of color to engage with the toolkit. Creating this optional space prevents additional racial harm from happening in the space while still allowing everyone to participate. This racial harm happens in the form of being asked to explain a racialized experience you have personally been harmed by and teaching white colleagues about race; it can be quite exhausting. Mary Conger, EdD, founder of the American Dialogue Project in New York City, and Ali Michael, PhD, an organizational culture consultant and race educator in suburban Washington, DC, state that "bringing white people and people of color together to discuss race can be like placing pre-algebra students in a calculus class . . . people of color are often so far ahead of the white people that they would have to slow down in order to let us catch up. We [white people] are first graders when it comes to talking about race. Black people are Ph.D. students."[23] In an industry workshop, a participant shared: "I enjoyed being in the Black, Indigenous, and people of color group, where we felt comfortable talking about our experiences. I felt like I was supported and not saying anything new (a good thing), rather than teaching or being tokenized."[24]

Since offering the space, each workshop of sixty participants has had at least one racial-affinity space, and we often have two. The onboarding survey asks participants who hold identities that have been historically racialized if they want to join a racial-affinity space: "Participating in anti-racist workshops or trainings is often culturally taxing for Black people, Indigenous people, and people of color who are often made to teach their white colleagues about the everyday racism they experience. We'd like for this workshop to be a positive experience for all participants. Would you like to be part of a breakout room that is exclusively for people who identify as Black, Indigenous, and people of color?" This is the information we use to create the racial-affinity spaces.

ONBOARDING

We immerse toolkit participants in an onboarding process that can increase their understanding of how their positionality might affect the dynamics of any design outputs, as well as the roles they might play in advocating for anti-racist design decision-making. Understanding their positionality against and within the context of racism and racist ideologies can help designers unlearn how we operationalize systemic practices of oppression that negatively shape the everyday lives of Black people, Indigenous people, and people of color around the world.[25] These activities are shared with participants in an email typically sent out ten days before the workshop's first session begins. These activities, the way they are shared, and the wording with each activity have changed over time.

Survey. We ask participants to complete a survey two to three days before the workshop begins. The survey intends to collect anonymized instances of racism experienced or observed by the participants within their institution. We use these instances as racialized prompts that participants can use to create anti-racist solutions. We also ensure that the survey responses will be seen only by the Racism Untaught workshop facilitators before they are anonymized and that no one from the participants' organizations will have access to the data collected from the survey.

Community agreement.　We ask participants to visit our community agreement on an online collaborative whiteboard and leave additional ideas in at least three categories (further explored in chapter 3). We include Other/Additional categories to ensure that we create space for any ideas we have not thought of ideas that do not fit within the other categories. We added this agreement to the onboarding process because we needed participants to interact with the online collaborative whiteboard. This familiarity helped reduce questions and concerns with the online collaborative space.

Socio-Cultural Identities worksheet.　We ask participants to complete this worksheet before the first session. Once this worksheet is completed, we ask participants to create their Social Identity Profile slide in an online collaborative document. Participants fill in their name and pronunciation, pronouns, and the identities they have chosen to share. We ask that one of the identities be the social construct of race as this workshop is about race and racism. If participants are not able to complete this step before the workshop starts, we ask them to provide the five social identities they would like to share, but we limit the online document to viewing mode only. In that way, participants will not actively be working on the development of their slides while other participants are sharing their social identities.

A SHARED INFORMATIONAL DOCUMENT

We have developed a shared online document for participants to use when we run a virtual or in-person workshop. When participants are online, the document is very helpful because it has all the links in one place. The document also includes the facilitators' names and phone numbers. We provide phone numbers for participants to contact us anonymously in case they have any concerns about a conversation in their room. Participants can also use the Help button in a digital workshop to alert us if they need assistance in their digital room, such as to facilitate the next step or advise on a difficult conversation. Additional links include the following:

- *Workshop Facilitator Presentation Deck:* This is what the facilitators will be presenting from to facilitate the workshop. As we have continued to learn the best way to facilitate, we have added additional visuals to help participants understand what is being asked of them.
- *Socio-Cultural Identities worksheet:* This worksheet is provided in a larger print and is a part of the pre-workshop activity for participants (discussed earlier).

- *Social Identity Profile slide:* This slide deck is in an online shared document and is part of the pre-workshop activity for participants. If the workshop is conducted in person, we print the completed slides for participants who have completed the work and we bring blank slides for participants to fill out. If the workshop is conducted virtually, then we use the online shared document.
- *Racism Untaught worksheet:* Also provided in larger print, this worksheet is available for participants to print and/or use to take notes.
- *Workshop digital report-out:* This online shareable slide deck is available for each group to report their progress in a final presentation.
- *Cards from workboard in list form:* All the written parts of the framework are listed in this document.

LAND ACKNOWLEDGMENT AND STATEMENT OF UNITY

Starting with our first workshop, we have read a land acknowledgment to affirm the ancestral lands we stand on. We share a link to the Native-Land.ca website, developed in 2015 by Victor Temprano, who lives on Okanagan territory.[26] The work is Indigenous-led, with an Indigenous executive director and board of directors who oversee and direct the organization, which details native land in a digital map format.[27] We ask participants to acknowledge the ancestral lands they are on and share that information with us either verbally or, if we are in a virtual workshop, by using the chat feature.

After the 2020 murder of George Floyd and during the COVID-19 pandemic, we changed our land acknowledgment to a statement of unity. We acknowledge the land, then add a second paragraph, which reads:

> We acknowledge the need to end the violence against missing and murdered Indigenous women—a local and national epidemic that can be traced back to the arrival of European colonizers across Turtle Island. We acknowledge and fight against the legacy of white supremacy and culture of anti-Black racism, which has led to the murders of Jamar Clark, Philando castile, George Floyd, Winston Smith, Daunte Wright, Amir Locke, and countless other Black Americans across this nation. Black lives matter. We stand with our Hmong, Asian, Asian American, and Pacific Islander communities against the rise of xenophobic violence since the start of the COVID-19 pandemic. We recognize that words are not enough, and we remain committed to the work of eradicating the injustices against all Black people, Indigenous people, and people of color caused by systemic racism.

PROMPT

Initially we used an artifact, system, or experience that exemplified a form of racialized design as a prompt for participants when beginning to work with the framework. We created an archive of racialized design examples that participants could use and begin to analyze through the process we had created. We even pulled examples of our own racialized experiences and created videos with recorded audio. When we started to work with industry and community partners on a continuous basis, we needed to include a way for them to break down their everyday racialized experiences. We began to use the survey that participants interacted with in the onboarding activity to learn about the racialized design around them. We explained this and asked participants to share their stories if they were comfortable doing so:

> During this workshop, we will be discussing and creating design approaches for real instances of racism at your institution/organization. We define racism as "the social construct of race as the primary determinant for the racially dominant culture to uphold conscious or subconscious beliefs, actions, and or benefits that support systemic racial prejudice and oppression through power and privilege." To that point, are there any instances of racism that you have experienced or observed at your institution/organization that you feel comfortable writing about and that we can analyze to create design approaches? Please tell your story without using specific names; these experiences will be shared without any personal identifiers.

We are thus able to create prompts specific to each partner (academia, industry, or community) and can prompt the participants with a racialized form of design that they experience daily. From the beginning, we decided that anonymizing the prompts and making them slightly ambiguous provided participants with the space to discuss context with each other. In general, we want participants to find the answers themselves rather than providing our own interpretative answers. Liz Sanders and Pieter Jan Stappers explain in their book *Convivial Toolbox* the importance of this type of ambiguity in the design research process: "Leaving holes can be used to trigger people's imaginations. Similarly, an open-ended sentence can be a very inviting way to ask a question. By having people complete the sentence, rather than provide an answer, we are likely to learn much more about the person and get a much wider variety of responses across people."[28]

LANGUAGE

The cards provide participants with the shared language necessary to discuss their own racialized experiences or experiences they have witnessed, further explored in chapter 4. A shared language's value in expressing an idea is generative in that it allows a person to gain even further understanding of their identity. Miranda Fricker explains the value of language in her book *Epistemic Injustice*, in which she notes why it is so essential for a culture to have a way to discuss discrimination using specific terms. Without language, she argues, "the injustice sends the message that they are not fit for participation in the practice that originally generates the very idea of a knower. . . . It is a form of injustice that can cause deep and wide harm to a person's psychology and practical life, and it is too often passed over in silence. My discussion has been driven by the hope that we might become more socially articulate about this somewhat hidden dimension of discrimination, and thereby be in a better position to identify it, protest it when it happens to us and, at least sometimes, avoid doing it to others."[29] Because our work is rooted in equity, we do not want to further perpetuate feelings of exclusion by using inaccessible language; by avoiding doing so, we are actively bridging the academy, industry, and community.

We established an advisory team at the very beginning (in June 2018) to consult with us and provide feedback. The initial advisory team started with four people: a philosopher and race theorist, an intercultural initiatives lead, a community activist and sociologist, and a historian and researcher. From the meetings with our advisors, we learned the value of crafting clear, unambiguous definitions and providing clear examples for our participants. Our advisory team also challenged us to not think of our context cards as *symptoms* of racism but as *elements* of racism. The elements of racism provided participants with a way to organize conversation and create a shared language around the issues of race and racism.

Starting from the first workshop, each group was given five blank cards in addition to each set of cards. The participants were asked to provide any additional terms they did not see represented in this toolkit and wanted to include. We acknowledge that culture and language change over time, and we still provide the blank cards to ensure that participants will feel open to adding their ideas to each step. We have added additional cards to all of our steps and now have the liberty of exploring different intersections of oppression, including sexism and ableism. We have plans for adding more cards specific to different forms of oppression.

DEFINE CARDS
Initially, the define cards did not include an identifier that stated if the term was a method or theory. After running the Racism Untaught framework in a graduate course, the students mentioned that knowing this information would be helpful. We then added that information to each card in the define step.

QUADRANT MAP
The next intervention that we included from the pilot workshop was the quadrant map intervention in the ideate step. We understood quadrant maps to be an excellent way to break down and dissect ideas or concepts, from effective to noneffective, positive to negative. We knew that we wanted participants to work in groups and to continue, throughout the whole process, to question if their ideas were moving their outcomes from a form of racialized design to anti-racist actions and from good intent to positive impact. We stated on the workboard near the quadrant map: "Through discussion, use this quadrant map to help evaluate the

value of each idea. On the x-axis, consider the intent of the idea in comparison to the impact. On the y-axis, consider how far your idea has shifted systemically racist thinking."

TEST AND EVALUATE

Although the last step in the design research process is normally titled *test*, we did not see this as the goal for the outcomes in this framework. We wanted participants to work toward a shared understanding of the impact of their outcomes. We initially titled this step *evaluation* to collaboratively create a rubric with the participants. In a workshop we conducted two months after the pilot workshop, in the fall of 2018, we changed the last step's title to *evaluate*. We eventually changed that title to the current name, *impact*.

Within academia, participants also defined a rubric that demonstrates both their comprehension of the determined deliverable and the ability to incorporate the methods and processes at an advanced level of understanding. Academia, industry, and community participants used this step to measure their design impact on the implementation of their ideas. This step can help guide participants toward a better understanding of the unintended consequences and is not focused only on the final solution. Designers play a key role in ensuring that they are a part of the larger system in developing design solutions. We have an ethical responsibility to maintain open minds when we are designing systems and must make decisions for our audience, rather than being biased by our habits, experiences, and culture.[30]

TRAIN-THE-TRAINER

We began offering the train-the-trainer program to provide partners with the necessary knowledge to facilitate the workshops in their organizations and provide a space for their employees to analyze racialized design. This program gives them access to a guidebook and the framework itself, digitally or printed. We provided them with seven sessions to learn how to facilitate Racism Untaught. The process included onboarding, context, define, ideate, prototype, impact, and off-boarding steps.

Participants step away from the training program with various tools and resources to guide projects focused on anti-racism, including a certificate of completion. Facilitators and participants will gain the experience and knowledge necessary to develop anti-racist themes in the culture of the workplace. We hope that facilitators will find new ways in which participants can use design research to identify how systems perpetuate racism and then, in turn, gain the ability to dismantle those systems.

INVITING ENGAGEMENT WITH THE TOOLKIT AND FRAMEWORK

Partners are typically recommended to us from academia and industry. We have created two flyers, one for each sector, that outline ways people can work with us to cultivate learning environments that further explore issues of race and racism. We outlined our goals as twofold: (1) to guide educators and students to utilize design research methods and processes to solve systemic problems and inspire further work in the public sector or a passion for public service; and (2) to facilitate workshops that help participants learn how to identify artifacts, systems, and experiences that perpetuate elements of racism.

Racism Untaught has iteratively changed not only due to the initial workshop but also because of national and international events. The COVID-19 pandemic played a role in how we have moved the toolkit online and continued to safely facilitate workshops for academia, industry, and community. We are excited for the future of Racism Untaught and will never cease to think iteratively and critically about its design in order to create anti-racist approaches in academia, industry, and community. To learn more about how to partner with us, visit our website **racismuntaught.com**.

ACADEMIC CASE STUDY
UMD Undergraduate Class

FRANK & NANCY: REBRANDING AUNT JEMIMA AND UNCLE BEN'S

COURSE
ART 3933: Graphic Design 3
sixteen-week course, in-person, spring 2019
This course was typically reserved for instruction on package design. To reach those objectives, the facilitator used racialized package designs as prompts during the course.

TEAM
Facilitator: Terresa Moses.
Participants: Eighteen undergraduate students—three groups of six students each. Only one of the three groups will be the focus of this case study, referred to as the lead group. Students were guided through the framework as a group. The racial makeup of the class was two students of color and sixteen white students.

◑ ONBOARDING ACTIVITIES: TWO WEEKS

The course began with activities meant to build community and the classroom culture for the semester. On the first day of the course, rather than overviewing the syllabus, participants were instructed to create short presentations about themselves. This activity was titled What's Going On? The participants were allotted four slides, each with a prompted question they could answer using text or images. Participants were reminded that they could share as much or as little as they wanted within the two minutes allotted for individual share-outs. The four questions were: (1) Who are you? (Introduce yourselves with pronouns, tell us your name story, and/or talk about your identities); (2) What are your top five strengths, or what do you bring to the table?; (3) What is your major, and what do you want to do with design?; and (4) What did you do over the winter break, and/or are you working on any design projects? Participants were given twenty minutes to craft their slideshow to present to the class.

The second activity participants engaged in was facilitated by one of the Racism Untaught advisors and the director of education for inclusive excellence at the university, Dr. Paula Pedersen. She started the course session by creating a classroom alliance that participants could add to before agreeing to take responsibility in the course culture. Among many prompted questions to create the alliance, she asked, "What do you want/need from yourself and others in order to be/learn your best?" This simple exercise instantly changed the classroom culture and provided an opportunity for participants to use their agency in the learning process. Second, Pedersen facilitated a game of bingo with a twist. The directions were: "Find someone to talk with and choose a topic to discuss from one of the squares. Initial each other's sheet, then find a new person with whom to discuss a new topic." We rang a bell every two minutes to signal participants to move to the next person and topic. Adapted from Kathy Obear, *Alliance for Change Consulting*, for the purposes of the class, there were six questions on the bingo sheets that asked participants about concepts centered on their level of comfort and nervousness when discussing issues to do with race, how well they understood racism, their awareness of their own socialization to whiteness, their empathy for the experiences of Black and brown peers at a predominately white institution, and what they were excited to learn about in regard to racism and design. At the end of this activity, Pedersen facilitated a short discussion in which participants voiced similar answers, which Pedersen and Moses sensitively navigated. Finally, Pedersen facilitated a version of the "Where I'm From" poem by George Ella Lyon,[31] entitled "Where I'm REALLY From."[32] In this adaptation of Lyon's community-based I Am From project,[33] Pedersen referenced racial bias and other forms of oppression from her past. She referenced cultural appropriation, exoticism, racial slurs, homophobia, internalized sexism, religious and racial prejudice, and white privilege. In her poem, she stated, "I am from National Geographic magazine. I couldn't wait to visit grandma and grandpa so I could look at the exotic pictures of tribal peoples from far away. They were so colorful." With the majority of white participants engaged in her words, there was a sense of awe at Pedersen's vulnerability. It is not the cultural norm in the academy to meet students with this sort of honesty due to the fear that comes with vulnerability and the toxic culture of expertise—a colonial concept. After Pedersen recited her rendition of the poem, participants were instructed to craft their own poems in a similar fashion, critically analyzing their positionality and learned biases. In addition to the poems, participants were asked to craft visual collages about themselves that they would present to the class as projected images while they read their poems.

In addition to crafting their own poems, participants were instructed to find examples of racialized design that they could discuss during the next session. These examples of racialized design prompted conversation around racism in everyday life, which set up the next guest speaker to dive further into how racism shows up in the systems around us. Dr. Jeanine Weekes Schroer, one of the Racism Untaught advisory team members and an associate professor of philosophy at the university, visited the class session to speak about levels of oppression. As participants shared their examples of racialized design, Schroer explained which of the elements of racism were present in the design and how those elements perpetuated throughout the different levels of oppression.

Participants ended their onboarding with discussions on their new realizations about racism present in their society. They were provided the opportunity to begin journaling about their learning experiences in a document that they would eventually turn into a visual journey map.

◀ CONTEXT: ONE TO TWO WEEKS

THE PROMPT: TWO RACIALIZED ARTIFACTS

Aunt Jemima's Pancake Mix and Uncle Ben's Rice are two ready-made food brands that perpetuate Black archetypes meant to signal good-tasting food to the consumer.[34] This signaling dates back to the era before the emancipation of enslaved Africans in the United States, when Black people were responsible for and expected to cook meals for their slave master and their slave master's family. The Aunt Jemima persona, introduced in 1890, and the Uncle Ben persona, introduced in 1942, were both racial stereotypes created to represent the roles previously expected for enslaved Black people while signaling slavery nostalgia to white consumers. Both brands perpetuated negative perceptions and economic limitations placed upon Black people.

THE CARDS

During the first part of step one, participants began by identifying elements of racism that they believed applied to the racialized prompts. When the participants selected an element of racism, they discussed as a group whether they agreed on the use of that element to describe their prompt. Participants were required to briefly explain why the term applied and why it may not have applied. This group of six selected fifteen elements of racism (see figure 1.14). The ones the group identified include the following:

- *Explicit bias:* Attitudes and beliefs about a person or group of people on a conscious level, usually expressed as a direct result of a perceived and or socialized threat. *Rationale:* The brands both clearly represented awareness of the expected role of Black citizens, which was exploited for capital gain.
- *Exoticism:* Objectifying, othering, sexualizing, and or dehumanizing woman and femmes who hold a identities that have been racialized who do not align with or fit within Eurocentric beauty standards, also known as racialized sexism. *Rationale:* The Aunt Jemima brand emulates the "mammy" archetype often depicted in old Southern-set films depicting a domestic slave that was entrusted with duties such as preparing meals and the rearing of children. She should be always joyful to emphasize her thankfulness and her subservient behavior as a means of gratitude for a life that was above other enslaved Africans within the same plantation.
- *Prejudice:* The perceptions and assumptions directed toward a Black person, Indigenous person, or person of color solely based on their racial identity.
- *Rationale:* A Black woman such as Aunt Jemima is assumed to be a laborer for white consumers.
- *Stereotyping:* A widely held trope based on an individual's racial identity. *Rationale:* A Black man who is loyal to his master above all others is known as an Uncle Tom, signaling brand trust to white consumers.

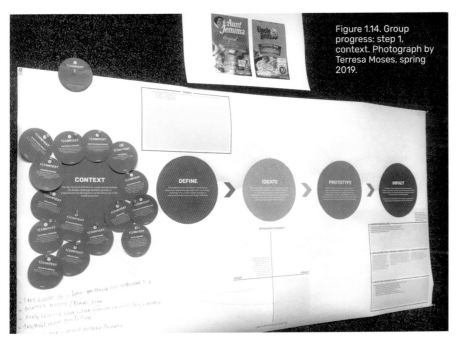

Figure 1.14. Group progress: step 1, context. Photograph by Terresa Moses, spring 2019.

THE LEVELS OF OPPRESSION

In the newest version of the Racism Untaught framework, participants would work together with the *levels of oppression model* to further contextualize the instances of oppression that showed up within and supported the Aunt Jemima and Uncle Ben's brands. They would have considered how and where oppression is introduced, reinforced, and perpetuated within the model. This case study, however, took place before the levels of oppression model was integrated as an additional design intervention. The following are examples of how the participants broke down the levels of oppression specific to their racialized prompt:

- *Beliefs:* Personal beliefs, ideas, and feelings that perpetuate oppression. *Rationale:* Black people are natural-born cooks.[35]
- *Agentic action:* When oppressive beliefs translate into oppressive behavior. *Rationale:* White people trust and purchase brands with Black faces in their branding.
- *Institutional:* Structural oppression that results from agentic oppressive behavior. *Rationale:* Corporations place the faces of Black people on food packaging to signal "good food" to sell to white consumers.
- *Cultural:* Systems of norms, values, beliefs, and trusted systems of acquiring truth that preserve, protect, and maintain oppression. *Rationale:* Black people are mostly shown as blue-collar workers, such as cooks, in movies and television.

◖ DEFINE: FOUR TO FIVE WEEKS

During the second step, participants in the group were instructed to write a collective eighteen-source annotated bibliography and a collective three-thousand-word literature review. Each participant in the group was required to annotate at least three individual sources with three to five sentences each describing the source. In addition, each participant was required to write at least five hundred words within the collective literature review, which they broke up into separate topic sections. The literature review helped provide the participants with additional cultural context specific to the history of both the Aunt Jemima and Uncle Ben's brands, how the brands related, how Black archetypes showed up in food packaging, and what racial implications these brands had on current-day society. Here is an excerpt from the group's literature review: "Aunt Jemima was also being depicted as illiterate in all of the ads [the brand] would put out. The words would be spelled wrong or in a form that [the brand] would portray as a black person's way of saying something. This just proves that the companies know what they are doing when they put out these ads."[36]

The annotated bibliography included a list of citations to books, articles, and documents, both peer-reviewed and not, followed by a brief descriptive and evaluative paragraph. This gave the participants opportunities to understand how their racialized prompt and similar prompts, like Cream of Wheat, were being talked about, analyzed, and theorized. Here is another excerpt from the group's literature review, referencing a similar brand:

> One product that has very similar packaging to these two products is the Cream of Wheat product. They are another brand that offers quick ready-made products. On the package there is a black man in the outfit of a chef. This man's name is Rastus, which is the first problem with this brand. The word rastus has two meanings, the first being, a stereotype of the jolly, former slave, and a character of the coon type often featured in minstrel shows. The second is a pejorative name used by white folks for African American males in the 20th century. When Kraft Foods acquired Cream of Wheat, the marketers viewed the Rastus figure in purely positive terms but that is not the case for much of society.

The thesis question they developed from what they learned from secondary sources was: "How might design challenge racialized imagery and language in ready-made package design to promote cultural and experiential inclusivity?"

In addition to the collective annotated bibliography and literature review, each participant added to their group's collective research proposal. The research proposal outlined the theories the group decided to use as well as their individual research methods to further contextualize the racialized prompt. The define step included cards of methods and theories that might be used to help participants explore further. The participants chose some of the following methods:

- *Competitive analysis:* Understanding what already exists that might compare with or be similar to your work (i.e., competitors)
- *Era map:* A visual that provides historical context to the subject being studied, mapping distinct eras in the context and describing them across topics of interest (see figure 1.15)
- *Guided interviews:* One-on-one conversations where you guide the user through a set of predefined questions, in addition to follow-up questions to clarify any points
- *Graffiti wall:* A shared writing space where individuals are prompted with a question and anonymously respond with their opinion
- *Popular media search:* Searching popular forms of media to gain further context (see figure 1.16)

ERA MAP

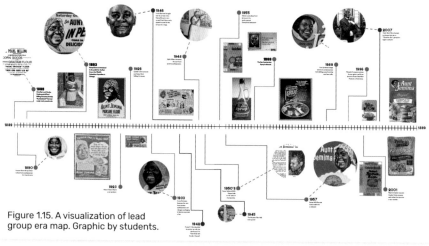

Figure 1.15. A visualization of lead group era map. Graphic by students.

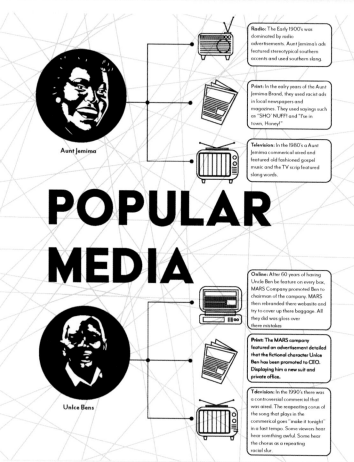

Aunt Jemima

Radio: The Early 1900's was dominated by radio advertisements. Aunt Jemima's ads featured stereotypical southern accents and used southern slang.

Print: In the ealry years of the Aunt Jemima Brand, they used racist ads in local newspapers and magazines. They used sayings such as "SHO' NUFF! and "I'se in town, Honey!"

Television: In the 1980's a Aunt Jemima commerical aired and featured old fashioned gospel music and the TV scrip featured slang words.

POPULAR MEDIA

Unlce Bens

Online: After 60 years of having Uncle Ben be feature on every box, MARS Company promoted Ben to chairman of the campany. MARS then rebranded there websaite and try to cover up there baggage. All they did was gloss over there mistakes

Print: The MARS company featured an advertisement detailed that the fictional character Unice Ben has been promoted to CEO. Displaying him a new suit and private office.

Television: In the 1990's there was a controversial commercial that was aired. The reapeating corus of the song that plays in the commerical goes "make it tonight" in a fast tempo. Some viewers hear hear somthing awful. Some hear the chorus as a repeating racial slur.

Figure 1.16. A visualization of lead group popular media search. Graphic by students.

At the end of the define step, participants gave a twenty-minute group research presentation on the secondary and primary data they collected and what they learned from each other in the process. The presentation reinforced the idea that while participants conducted their research methods individually, discussing the research they conducted helped to provide insight into the factors they each learned. During the presentation, the course facilitator invited guests to provide feedback to the groups on their progress and provide other considerations. These discussions provided them with additional information from which they could draw in the next step, ideate.

◀ IDEATE: ONE TO TWO WEEKS

THE CARDS

During the first part of the third step, participants shuffled through the ideate cards to help them think of avenues through which they might affect positive change given the racialized package design they were assigned. Each card fell within one of the three categories of design explained earlier in this chapter. The participants were encouraged to use all three categories of design in the ideation process. Some of the cards the lead participant chose were the following:

- *Identity marks/brands:* Marks that are used to identify and represent a company or organization. This term fell within the *artifact* section of design.
- *Economy:* The system of relating to, or based on the production, distribution, and consumption of, goods and services. This term fell within the *system* section of design.
- *Experience design:* The connectedness of everything in a process. This term fell within the *experience* section of design.

QUADRANT MAP

The second part of the third step created opportunities for more specific ideas and for measuring the implementation of those ideas using the quadrant map. Each participant created a list of ideas based on the areas of design they pulled from the deck of cards. Participants were encouraged to write down all their ideas, omitting none, which they placed on individual sticky notes. Participants then placed their sticky notes on the quadrant map to gain a better understanding of how far their idea would take their stakeholders from oppressive thought to anti-oppressive action, and then how far the idea moved culture norms from good intentions to positive impact. Participants were encouraged to critically analyze the interaction of their product in grocery stores by considering packaging and utilitarianism, the consumer experience, and the process of approval. In addition to their crafted thesis question, participants also considered how they might be proactive about anti-racism in their new design.

The lead group decided on a social awareness campaign that included a name change, rebrand, and intentional and invested apology. They chose to approach their design challenge by analyzing the existing packaging to create a new package design that would recognize their past racial harm, educate the consumer, and create an opportunity to signal to the consumer that the whole family should be involved in the cooking process. The participants wanted the package design to be familiar while actively contributing to an anti-racist food culture. It was hoped that the new package design would move stakeholders to anti-oppressive action.

PROTOTYPE: FOUR TO FIVE WEEKS

During the fourth step of the toolkit, the participants began to outline and prototype the idea(s) that were the most promising from the ideate step. They started this process by assigning roles in their group and crafting a design team and design agenda. Two participants worked on the new package designs for Aunt Jemima, two participants worked on the new package designs for Uncle Ben's, and two participants worked on crafting their final group report. While they each had their own roles, participants provided critique and constructive feedback at each step of their prototypes. Prototypes occurred in three steps, each one growing in functionality and applying the factors garnered from user testing completed between each prototype.

Low-fidelity prototype. This is the initial, raw presentation of an idea. As the participants sketched and brainstormed about their new brands, they knew the first step was removing the names and faces of the Black archetypes from the packaging. The participants used this week of low-fidelity prototyping to craft intentional names that still spoke to the product while calling out the company's racially systemic stereotyping. Although there was talk of hesitation around purchasing the product for analysis due to the unavoidable investment in the current racist brand, the group decided it was best to purchase one of each product. The participants analyzed the current packaging in depth, measuring dimensions and thoroughly reading through the verbiage on the boxes.

Mid-fidelity prototype. This prototype has limited functionality but presents enough interactions and possibilities for participants to understand the idea. As the participants moved into vectorizing the newly decided-upon brand names and package designs, feedback from guest critics encouraged the participants to dig deeper into the impact they hoped to have. There was an overall feeling of inadequacy in just removing the names and faces from the original boxes. The participants wanted the new brands to be more than just *not racist*—rather, actively *anti-racist*. With that, they began researching corporate apologies for racialized incidents and how they might go further than a simple tweet or press release. They wanted to create an intentional financial investment in their recognition of the racism the brand perpetuated over the past 120 years.

Through their brainstorming process, they decided on crafting another package design that would act as an interim package design with the opportunity to educate and point to the brand's racist history. Participants wrote in their final report in reference to Uncle Ben's: "In our transition packaging, we wanted to make a statement, we wanted to make people look twice at the product. We named the product 'Uncle Who?' because we took Ben's image off the packaging (see figure 1.17). We wanted it to be obvious that the packaging was changing. On the back of the box, we chose to include a statement about how the original packaging of Uncle Ben's is racist." And in reference to the Aunt Jemima brand, participants wrote: "The [transition] box will also have a new label stating 'Racist since 1889' which will let the people know just how long it took for a rebrand (see figure 1.18). This product has been sitting on the counter for more than 100 years and a new box will shock people but get them to think." For the transition boxes, 100 percent of profits from the box was intended to go to the original families of the people the brands were based off of, Frank Brown and Nancy Green, with a large percentage of sales from the final new package design continuing to be invested with the families.

High-fidelity prototype. This prototype needs minimal changes, if any; it is one step away from the final deliverable. Participants digitized and used cardboard to mock up the new designs. In reference to Uncle Ben's rebrand, the participants

Figure 1.17. Uncle Who? rebrand transition box mockup.
Graphics and package design by students, spring 2019.

Figure 1.18. Yours Truly rebrand transition box mockup. Graphics and package design by students, spring 2019.

Figure 1.19. Quite Frankly rebrand high-fidelity mockup. Graphics and package design by students, spring 2019.

Figure 1.20. Yours Truly rebrand high-fidelity mockup. Graphics and package design by students, spring 2019.

set the new brand name as Quite Frankly, saying that it "derives its name from the original face of Uncle Ben's Rice, Frank Brown (see figure 1.19). The term 'To be frank' means to be honest. So, while rebranding this product we wanted to send a new message. We wanted a product that didn't have hidden lies or ill-intentions." And in reference to Aunt Jemima's rebrand (see figure 1.20), the participants set the new brand name as Yours Truly, "to imply to whoever is buying it that these pancakes are in fact made by them, and them alone. Not some black woman working for you in your home, not a common household wife, just simply YOU."

◀ IMPACT: ONE WEEK

The lead group included quite a bit of language about the history of the brands on the transition packaging, but to continue educating consumers, the participants suggested a more permanent placement for the language on the companies' websites. This is just one way the participants decided to create further impact with their new designs. The website idea was inspired and could be measured using the selected impact cards:

- *Vision statement:* Showing and telling a comprehensive outline of what the organization will bring to the wider community
- *Mission statement:* A short formal summary of the values of a company, organization, or individual

- *Implementation plan:* Addressing and creating the execution plan to realize solutions

RUBRIC

The grading for this case study included work from each step of the iterative process the student utilized. The rubric (see figure 1.21) breaks down the whole project into the following categories:

- *Understanding—30 percent of grade:* The research methods the participant group conducted were strong in their connections to one another and helped the group understand how to best effect positive change in the food packaging industry.
- *Application, critical thinking, justification—45 percent of grade:* The prototyping of the package designs was thoughtful in each step. The research conducted between the low-, mid-, and high-fidelity prototypes led the group to new ways of visualizing and crafting apologies that did not simply ease consumers, but also educated and created lasting reparational change. They used critique times to craft specific improvements necessary to produce package designs that would inform and right wrongs.
- *Create deliverable—25 percent of grade:* The final deliverables for this case study included new package designs for the Aunt Jemima and Uncle Ben's brands, a final designed book showing the participants' work throughout the semester, and a final presentation that was given in front of guest critics and faculty members.

❿CHALLENGES

The participants were afraid to talk about racism and their positionality in the context of a racialized system. Initially, many of the participants were afraid to say the wrong thing, but crafting a culture of learning, constant questioning, and the mirrored vulnerability of the facilitator greatly contributed to openness among the participants. Having guest speakers and critics also helped reaffirm the new knowledge they were gaining from a variety of people in academia and community with varying identities.

Participants needed reassurance that they had agency to make decisions about the brand that would positively impact the food packaging industry. Questions like "Can we change the name?" and "Are we allowed to use a different kind of packaging?" are examples of issues on which participants needed assurance.

❿FINAL REPORT: ONE WEEK

During the final week of the course, the participants presented their final outcomes in a designed presentation and a process book. The process book included all the work they completed during the sixteen-week course (see figure 1.22). It included a journey map for each participant, a visualization of their prompted journal entries, which outlined their learning process through the course. The

ACADEMIC RUBRIC

Use this **academic rubric** to evaluate the project. Move the
workboard cards to the associated areas or write the content of the
workboard cards to note how the project will be graded.

UNDERSTANDING (30%)

Incorporating research methods that provide empathy for the user and a
reframing or definition of the challenge. Including but not limited to:
brainstorming, thesis question, annotated bibliography, benchmark analysis,
heuristic analysis, and/or literature review.

APPLICATION (15%)

The ability to develop a low fidelity
prototype(s), articulate learned
concepts in a non-functioning
design solution(s), and test the
initial idea(s) with users. Develop a
list of key factors asking the
questions: what worked, what needs
to be improved, are there new ideas,
and do you have new questions?

CRITICAL THINKING (15%)

Apply key factors gleaned from
low-fidelity prototype(s) to your
mid fidelity prototype(s),
developing a second set of key
factors based off of user testing.
Ask the same or similar questions
to: what worked, what needs to be
improved, are there new ideas, and
do you have new questions?

JUSTIFICATION (15%)

The development of a high
fidelity prototype(s) providing a
proof of concept that addresses
real user needs based off of
research acquired through low
and mid fidelity prototype(s).

CREATE DELIVERABLE (25%)

Final artifact(s) as well as a compelling story of the design process. Evidence of:
*   Aesthetics: demonstrate effective visual communication
*   Critique: the ability to give and receive effective feedback
*   Justification: ability to effectively articulate design choices
*   Organization: research, prototypes, and process
*   Usability: the overall functioning of the design solution
*   Skills: execution of final deliverable based on initial goals for project

Figure 1.21.
Racism
Untaught
rubric.

Figure 1.22. Final Racism Untaught toolkit workspace. Graphics and sketches by facilitator and students, spring 2019.

participants also created a final presentation that reviewed a summary of their work throughout the course in front of invited academic and community guests.

Participants often step away from this class appreciating the opportunity to discuss racism in relation to design—many for the first time ever. Participants relay their understanding and see great value in moving past *not racist* and into *intentionally anti-racist* design decisions. They recognize the agency they have as designers and the impact their designs have once their creations are placed into the public domain. The following are quotes from the students in this group about their experiences during the project:

> This was a fun project that not only helped our skills, but gave us a better insight into racism. We learned from research, design development, and other influences to create an entire new image for two products. This project is one that would hopefully help others to think about certain products that are not so carefully thought out, and think about how they could fix them in a way that we did. Ignored racism in design is something that needs to end because it is still very much alive today. As designers, our goal is to help end that in our futures.[37]

> Seeing this project come together has been such a cool process and I feel as if I can be a better designer because of this. The knowledge I gained from this project is so important and I am grateful to have such impactful professors. At the end of this project I feel as if I am more aware of racism. I keep my eyes open and am careful in how I design certain things. I [will] make sure the reasoning behind my designs is correct.[38]

Seeing this project come together makes me proud because as a team we created a rebrand that speaks about the ignored racism within each brand and has new meaning. As we come to an end of this project I can say that I learned more than just how to rebrand a certain product—I learned to make it correct and inclusive.[39]

Through the rebranding process, I was able to incorporate all my research and interviews into a feasible solution that was anti-racist. Looking back at the entire project, I truly believe I was untaught racism.[40]

At the end of the journey map but not at the end of my journey. This project has opened my eyes to the open and subtle racism I see in my everyday life. I will continue to call out and speak up about the discrimination I encounter throughout my life.[41]

DESIGNPRAC
TICECANBEU
NDERSTOODA
STHEMEDIUM
BETWEENVAL
UESANDIDEAL
SOFACULTUR
EANDTHETAN
GIBLEREALITY.

—Lesley-Ann Noel and Renata Leitão[1]

DEFINING DESIGN

When we share the Racism Untaught framework, it is important to us that each participant knows, no matter their discipline or area of industry and community, that everyone is a designer. This broad perspective of who is a designer is meant to provide each of the participants with the agency to redefine, reimagine, and redesign the systems of oppression they interact with—working collaboratively toward a pluriverse where each of us supports dismantling systems of inequity.[2] Through our development of the framework, we determined three conclusive areas in which racialized design—artifacts, systems, and experiences—can be identified (see figure 2.1).

RACIALIZED DESIGN

We define *racialized design* as design that perpetuates elements of racism. As we mentioned in the introduction, *racialized* is both an adjective (a descriptor) and a verb (action, to racialize). Racialization would not exist without one of the five tenets of critical race theory defined by Nicholas Daniel Hartlep: "the social construction of race."[3] Social constructs are simply ideas that have been accepted and normalized by our society and culture. The idea that race predetermines outcomes and opportunities for Black people, Indigenous people, and people of color upholds the construct and legitimizes the act of racialization. We came to understand the concept of racialization as a mixture of the perspectives of multiple researchers.

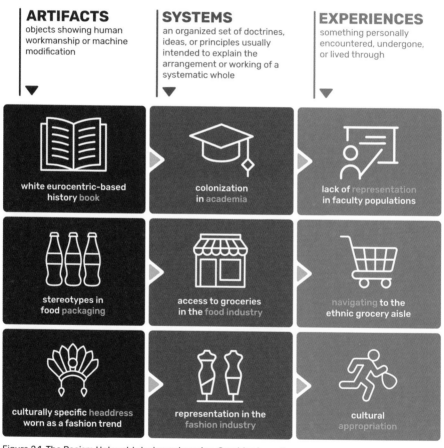

ARTIFACTS
objects showing human workmanship or machine modification

SYSTEMS
an organized set of doctrines, ideas, or principles usually intended to explain the arrangement or working of a systematic whole

EXPERIENCES
something personally encountered, undergone, or lived through

white eurocentric-based history book

colonization in academia

lack of representation in faculty populations

stereotypes in food packaging

access to groceries in the food industry

navigating to the ethnic grocery aisle

culturally specific headdress worn as a fashion trend

representation in the fashion industry

cultural appropriation

Figure 2.1. The Racism Untaught design categories. Graphics by author.

RACIALIZATION AS SOCIAL GRAMMAR

Eduardo Bonilla-Silva, a professor of sociology at Duke University, proposed the use of the term *racialized*, which represents "the more general concept of racialized social systems as the starting point for an alternative framework. This term refers to societies in which economic, political, social and ideological levels are partially structured by the placement of actors in racial categories or races."[4] In his article "The Invisible Weight of Whiteness: the Racial Grammar of Everyday Life in America," Bonilla-Silva compares the normalized racial domination to grammar: "a racial grammar if you will—that structures cognition, vision, and even feelings on all sort of racial matters."[5] This grammar "normalizes the standard of white supremacy as the standard for all sorts of social events and transactions."[6] It creates a racialized field where racial domination is normalized, and it shapes how we see, or do not see, racialized matters. Furthermore, he uses grammar as a "conceptual metaphor"[7] to understand the logic and rules we have in our culture that perpetuate racism. It is a form of social grammar, where we as a society allow domination or power to be normalized.

The power of whiteness controls what is and is not considered racialized. Bonilla-Silva concludes that the real focus of racism is the invisible whiteness in our culture—the Eurocentric culture of dominance in the United States. To elaborate on this point, he uses the example of both white and racialized news segments in which he found a pattern of describing white women who had been shot or kidnapped as *beautiful*.[8] In scenarios of the same context where the victim was Black or brown, the attribute of *beautiful* was rarely if ever included in the description of the victim. Again, whiteness is controlling the narratives of Black and brown communities and benefiting from their oppression and negative perceptions by way of more media exposure for more "innocent" (i.e., white) victims. Racism like this exists because of the perceived higher value of white life.

Scenarios like these play out repeatedly in popular media through words and imagery. For example, in Iowa, three white men were arrested on charges of burglary, and on the same day, four Black men were arrested on charges of the exact same crime. The images used in the local media to represent the white men were pictures of each of them dressed up in clean suits, while mug shots were used as the images in the local media for the Black men.[9] There is a toxic and life-threatening societal preservation around the concept of whiteness that perpetuates an assumed innocence. These white stories have become a culturally universal norm, not only in our popular media, but in popular culture more broadly: entertainment, books, and movies. Another way this is demonstrated is by walking on the campus of predominantly white colleges or universities: "The demography and symbols in HWCUs [historically white colleges and universities] create an oppressive racial ecology. Where just walking on campus is unhealthy; where students who are from marginalized communities feel, as one observer commented, as 'guests [who] have no history in the house they occupy. There are no photographs on the wall that reflect their image. Their paraphernalia, paintings, scents, and sounds do not appear in the house.'"[10] Far too many campuses look just like this one, preserving the lives and histories of whiteness while completely erasing and building negative perceptions of people of color.

To combat this overwhelmingly white representation by increasing the narratives of underrepresented stories, the School of Social Work at UIUC organized a committee that focused on working with artists who self-identified as members of a marginalized community to display their work on campus and in the halls of the school. They received an impressive number of artists, but there was one artist—a graduate student from the School of Art and Design—that stood out. This student self-identified as a Black man, and the work he submitted proposed a large-scale piece that would depict the Black community. Although there was a desire to represent untold narratives, hesitation arose when discussions around the idea of an all-Black mural commenced. The committee spoke with the artist about their concerns, and the artist responded by stating, "During times of immense adversity, it is our responsibility as human beings to be empathetically responsive to voices that cry out in pain as they are representative of parts of our own self. It is our responsibility to be resilient against forces that would maintain the status quo, and it is our responsibility to dismantle every system, every institution, born and rooted in the oppression of disenfranchised and marginalized peoples."[11] His work is the first thing you see when you walk into the School of Social Work. It is a twenty-three-foot wide, nine-foot tall large-scale mural titled *Year 401*. The piece has a golden yellow background with red narrow flowing shapes that swirl around the depictions of four Black individuals, each facing a different direction. The support of this artwork was a pivotal moment in the committee's realization of the need to highlight cultural representations as a step toward inclusion within their school, truly "elevating and empowering the voices of underrepresented populations and groups."[12] The visual series has since added seven additional installments, including various experiences, cultures, and identities.

RACIALIZATION AS GAZE

Sue Hum, an associate professor of English at the University of Texas in San Antonio, uses the term *racialized* to elucidate design as a form of racial gaze and identify racialized forms of design. She further defines the word *design* in the form of a verb and noun to explain areas of visual rhetoric.[13] In considering the term *racialized* in parallel with the three design identifiers, we are able to critically analyze and identify artifacts of racialized design (more obvious, visible, and/or tangible); shared experiences of microaggressions and implicit bias (less obvious, visible, and/or tangible), and systemic forms of racism perpetuated by our culture (pervasive and essentially invisible). Sue Hum points out the value in identifying the "visual-rhetorical intersection and the design decisions influencing that intersection."[14] In her article "Between the Eyes: The Racialized Gaze as Design," she argues that "the racialized gaze as Design provides a valuable theoretical framework for visual rhetoric, exegesis, and cultural analysis by directing our attention to how designers may unwittingly sustain practices of racialization and perpetuate racially based on socio-cultural exclusions. . . . Design has the means to imagine future human dispositions and to enact dynamic social action through visual meaning-making."[15] Identifying forms of racialized design and ensuring the acknowledgment of habitual cultural norms that ultimately perpetuate forms of racism is crucial. As designers, we must consider our positionality as this will affect how clearly one sees racism in our broader society. Understanding this expands our agency and ability to affect change using the design or redesign of artifacts, systems, and experiences.

Hum goes on to examine imagery and perception, citing Thomas Nast as an example of the positive effects imagery can have on perception. Nast was seen as the "Father of the American Cartoon"[16] and "created political cartoons that advocated for cultural inclusiveness and racial tolerance as the foundation for a racially integrated, progressive America."[17] His work was published in *Harper's Weekly* for eighteen years and was acknowledged by President Abraham Lincoln, who stated, "Thomas Nast has been our best recruiting sergeant. . . . His emblematic cartoons have never failed to arouse enthusiasm and patriotism, and have always seemed to come just when these articles were getting scarce."[18] His work was an early and positive example of designers' potential and ability to advocate for change. More recently, design has seen a surge of people in academia, industry, and the broader society looking to make a difference within their own practice and communities. Designers have the power and agency to mitigate and dismantle racialized designs if they remain conscious of and critically examine traditional and colonial ways of designing.

A more contemporary example using imagery to combat racialized design is French photographer JR, who places photos to draw attention to complex social issues—but instead of telling the viewer how to think, the photos are meant for them to question their own ideologies. His project titled *Giants* on the border of Mexico and the United States, constructed in Tecate, Mexico, is an example of his positive societal impact.[19] It was placed during a time when the border wall between Mexico and the United States was being politicized for political gain. JR explained that he is compelled to bring a human conversation into areas of the world that are political conflict zones. When he was scouting for a location on the border to place a photo, he met a family with a little boy who was looking at him from his crib. He asked the family if he could take a picture of the little boy and use it in his work on the border wall. The mother said she would consider it when she saw the rendering of what it would look like. When JR came back to show her his idea, the mom said, "I hope this will help people see us differently than what they hear in the media, that they will stop talking about us like criminals or rapists. I hope in that image they won't only see my kid. They will see us all."[20] The photo JR and his team placed on the border wall is of the little boy; he looks to be peering over the wall, curious as to why the wall even exists. The mom expands on her thoughts in a video, saying, "In a place that nobody considers, and he made it stand out, seeing the same faces that live here, that no one looked at until he made them big."[21]

RACIALIZATION AS PROCESS

Sociologist Robert Miles describes *racialization* as "a dialectical process by which meaning is attributed to particular biological features of human beings, as a result of which individuals may be assigned to a general category of persons which reproduces itself biologically. . . . The process of racialization of human beings entails the racialization of the processes in which they participate and the structures and institutions that result."[22] Miles explains how the social construct of race is the participation in cultural norms that create racialized groups based on the biological function of genetics. He explains that these social constructs created the means for systems to be created whereby people are treated inequitably. This harks back to the normalization and protection of whiteness that allows for the mistreatment of Black people, Indigenous people, and people of color in various systems. Miles's scholarly work focused on the term *racialization* beyond the binary perspective of white and other. Through the acknowledgment of social constructs, we are able to create a space for discourse on identity.[23]

Understanding racialization as a process has helped guide our courses and workshops, especially around conversations of agentic action and institutional racism (further explored in chapter 5). Participants who have just entered the work sometimes have a hard time separating and intersecting with how racism shows up in their personal actions. Discussing how racialization is a process leaves room to explore racism as more than using a racial slur or burning crosses. Most of the time, it is not a blatantly conscious act; rather, it took years and years of implementation and normalization for racism to become normalized—a process. While there are definite times in which the institution and personal actions intersect, breaking down racism in this way helps to make sense of how each of us exist in our society today.

In the definition of *racialization* we have introduced in this research study, we were explicit in using the word as a verb and an adjective. This division helps us highlight the actions that uphold inequities and a shared language to discuss the experiences of Black people, Indigenous people, and people of color interacting with inequitable systems.

RACIALIZED HISTORICAL CONTEXTS

The most broadly accepted version of history is inextricably linked to those who have had the power to shape it. It conveys that much like the disabled body is the subject of disability, so too is the Black, Indigenous, or person of color's body the subject of racism. The ideas and ideologies that have shaped the dominant culture in our society were intentionally created, perpetuated, and normalized by those in power to keep themselves in power. Globally, colonial settlers overused the writing of history to craft historical narratives about the past that gave certain identities more power or privilege than others (e.g., white people, Christians, cisgender people, men).

These problematic historical narratives have long functioned in Eurocentric and Westernized cultures, stripping power and agency from underserved and underinvested communities. The written history from a homogeneity narrative was true across many academic fields, but particularly the disciplines that comprise the natural sciences—once considered "value-free."[24] The world has been anything but value-free. Science has been tainted with capitalistic and egotistical motivations. As historians Joyce Appleby, Lynn Hunt, and Margaret Jacob insisted in their historiographical 1995 text *Telling the Truth about History*, "Understanding the challenge to truth in an age in full revolt against inherited certainties means going back in time to discover how and when science became an absolute model for all knowledge in the West."[25] The natural sciences play a pivotal role in crafting and sustaining these narratives, which are supported by mass media organizations. These organizations often pay "scientists" to lie to the public in hopes that "the masses" will predominantly strive toward sustaining their beliefs within these structured normalcies.

One prevalent example of this kind of deception that quickly became racialized is the development of the body mass index (BMI) system. Margaret T. Hicken from the University of Michigan's Institute for Social Research explains that BMI was "designed to examine the biological, social, and environmental correlates of adult physical and mental health. . . . The inequalities in obesity, particularly those that proxy visceral adiposity,[26] may then result in a cascade of health, social, and economic consequences that burden non-White adults with decreased life chances compared to White adults."[27] The "racist roots" of BMI and "the way it furthers the oppression of and discrimination against"[28] Black people, Indigenous people, and people of color exemplifies how it was designed to uphold the racialized design of Eurocentric beauty standards and norms. This false sense of normalcy, which disability studies specialist Lennard J. Davis argues "has always existed," is socially ingrained in us, creating a toxic binary—between the ideal and nonideal, the normal and the abnormal—which is socially, culturally, and physiologically dangerous to billions of people.[29] The result of the sustenance of this toxic binary has deprived millions of communities across the globe of their basic human rights. This unattainable standard of normalcy has been socially constructed and perpetuated to make people of color feel as though they will never be able to look good enough without the latest trend or with regard to the issues of BMI, ideal body type, and weight.[30] The toxicity of the binary relationship between a desirable BMI and an undesirable BMI is a carefully crafted and intentionally designed invention that creates social norms and—in opposition—*the other* through the carefully calculated retelling of past events.

The power held in the historian's pen can completely erase the nuances and truths that constitute our past and inform our current realities. As the creators of the Racism Untaught toolkit, we sought to emphasize the power of storytelling to alter and overcome the effects of warping or erasing these socio-culturally rooted nuances and truths. We provide participants with the opportunity to carefully consider three questions: (1) Who writes the stories?, (2) Who benefits from the stories being told from that perspective?, and (3) Who is missing from the stories?

In 1893, Ida B. Wells stated this quote as part of an address she gave to the Women's Era Club. "Those who commit the murders write the reports. . . . The victims were black, and the reports are written to make it appear that the helpless creatures deserved the fate which overtook them."[31] The effects of history are designed intentionally to create social norms that systemically oppress people of color and can be positively affected using anti-oppressive design interventions. For designers to contribute to design responsibly, they must understand their ability to influence rhetoric in the public domain, not only from a visual perspective but also from a systemic perspective.[32] The Racism Untaught framework begins by giving participants a racialized design prompt—an artifact, a system, or an experience—via which designers have the power and privilege to positively change our society. It is imperative to explore examples of racialized design to incorporate anti-racist and anti-oppressive outcomes into diverse and inclusive pedagogical and industry processes. This exploration ensures that designers understand the implications of design within our culture and communities. These racialized design examples are given to ensure that participants who engage with the framework will see the importance of acknowledging that racialized design is both a historical and current issue. We curated examples of the three categories as a resource for designers and educators to use with the Racism Untaught framework. We recognize the ways the identifiers in our research intersect, collide, and layer with each other. We see the value of acknowledging this complexity to further understand racialized design.

ARTIFACTS

WHY ARTIFACTS?

The first design category is *artifacts*—objects showing human workmanship or machine modification.[33] We have artifacts all around us, daily. Historians seek out artifacts to understand how people interacted and communicated values to one another. They are a hint to what we value in our culture.[34] David Pilgrim is an applied sociologist and founder and curator of a twelve thousand–piece collection of racist artifacts at the Jim Crow Museum located at Ferris State University in Grand Rapids, Michigan. Pilgrim was interviewed in 2015 and was quoted as saying, "I've always said that if you show me the things that a society produces, I can tell you a lot about their attitudes, tastes, and values—which may also shape attitudes, tastes, and values in the future. If you hate a group of people, it's going to show up in the images that you have of that race or ethnic group. When you draw a picture of a person of that race, you're going to draw them a certain way[...] The stereotypes and all the other stuff just become expressions of that hatred."[35]

Dr. Pilgrim was invited to speak at North Central Michigan College by then-president Cameron Brunet-Koch, and he brought over 150 artifacts with him. "(Pilgrim) provided us some pretty specific examples that were very hard to hear and look at, but that is exactly what people in our community need to be exposed to. We need to be challenged to not accept things as presented by the media or groups of people, but to really ask some challenging questions to try to clarify intent and to start eliminating things that really don't meet our own value system."[36]

In 2016, the *New York Times* published an article titled "Confronting Racist Objects," which stated, "It's important to see how a seemingly harmless toy can affect the way we see people who are not like us."[37] The article showed nine historically racialized artifacts people purchased and why they bought the items. A few examples include a Jemima figurine, intended to reflect the feelings of Black women who were content working as slaves in white family homes.[38] The person who purchased this self-identified as African American and stated, "I was indeed liberating them from the clutches of their 'owners' (usually white people) and bringing them home to rest in a household that would hold them in high esteem."[39] A second item was a piece of sheet music purchased by a person who self-identified as Chinese Filipino. The cover of the music sheet was an illustration of a presumably Chinese man carrying a rickshaw with a white man dressed as a hunter sitting inside of it: a racist interpretation of colonialism in which Chinese people were only capable of providing service to people in the white communities. A third item is a black paper face mask held up by a stick that features a racist caricature of a Black man created for a restaurant. The Black individual who owns it acknowledges the harm it does to have these artifacts in the public domain: "I feel sick when I look at it. I've never shown it to my students. There's a risk of re-brutalizing the people on whom these artifacts are based. I don't think we're fully equipped as a society to rehabilitate some of these things."[40] These artifacts are a representation of how racialized artifacts can impact a person's identity and the lived experience for people of color.

HOW DESIGN PLAYS A ROLE IN THE CREATION OF ARTIFACTS

Designers play a large role in the creation of artifacts, both analog and digital, that are placed in the public domain. Frequently those artifacts have intended and unintended consequences. We see this in product design, interface design, architecture, interior design, and fashion design; these are only a few examples where our culture is shaped by artifacts and placed on display for people to interact with. In the ideate step of the framework, we currently have over forty-five cards of artifacts for participants to select from. Langdon Winner argues the politics of artifacts in his book *The Whale and the Reactor.* He states, "Material artifacts can be seen as constitutional phenomena; intricate blends of technē and politeia; the interweaving of useful devices, technical systems, philosophical ideals, institutional arrangements, and civic practices that together express the quality of life in any political society."[41] He is questioning not only the weight artifacts carry within our culture but our ideals and responsibility as creators of these artifacts and the ideals of the consumer. The philosophical ideals held by our dominant culture show up as artifacts in our everyday lives. As designers, we play a role in the racialized artifacts that are approved, produced, placed, and purchased in the public domain.

LOOK
LIKE YOU
GIVE
A DAMN

WHOOPS

RE-CIVILIZE
YOURSELF

Figure 2.2. Example artifact:
Nivea ad recreation.

RACIALIZED ARTIFACT EXAMPLES

We have intentionally focused this research study on contemporary examples of racialized design. We have done this to ensure people see elements of racism as both historical and contemporary forms of racialized design. A recent example includes a Nivea advertisement from 2011 with the image of a Black man whose hair is cut short, representing a clean-cut and professional visualization (see figure 2.2). In his right hand, the man is holding an older version of himself with an afro which he is getting ready to throw. The ad reads, "Re-Civilize Yourself," implying that a Black person's natural hair is uncivilized. After community outrage, the ad was retracted, and Nivea posted an apology, stating: "Thank you for caring enough to give us your feedback about the recent 'Re-civilized' NIVEA FOR MEN ad. This ad was inappropriate and offensive. It was never our intention to offend anyone, and for this we are deeply sorry. This ad will never be used again. Diversity and equal opportunity are crucial values of our company."[42]

Another example of a racialized artifact is coveted by large communities of fans at sporting events: the mascots of sports teams who depict marginalized populations of people. The National Congress of American Indians (NCAI) has continuously made a clear statement since 1968 about ending the harmful and derogatory stereotypes seen in team mascots and brand representations.[43] The NCAI began a campaign to educate people about the harmful and stereotypical depiction of Indigenous populations in the media and at sporting events. While there have been changes and updates to existing mascots, no new mascots that depict racial stereotypes have been created since 1963. In 2005, the National Collegiate Athletic Association (NCAA) created a new policy to remove mascots depicting Native Americans.[44] The University of Illinois retired its mascot, Chief Illiniwek, in 2007; however, the chief can still be found at sporting events and on campus more than a decade after its removal. Stanford University officially removed its "Indian" mascot in 1972, but it was not until 1996 that the bookstore agreed to stop selling merchandise that depicted it. It was not until September 2018 that California State University retired its Prospector Pete mascot that symbolizes the treatment of Native Americans during the gold rush era in the United States.[45]

During the international uprisings that occurred after the murder of George Floyd, the Washington, DC, football team changed its name from a derogatory term specific to Native Americans to the Washington Commanders. In 2013, the team owner, who bought the team in 1999, said he would never change the team name.[46] However, civil rights and Indigenous rights groups have been advocating for this change for decades. This time, the pressure to change the name included additional pressure from sponsors. "Nike, FedEx and PepsiCo each received letters signed by 87 investment firms and shareholders worth a combined $620 billion asking the companies to sever ties with the [football team] unless they change their controversial name."[47] This statement was released to the public on July 1, 2020. The team announced on July 3, 2020, that it would no longer use the derogatory term as its name and would be going by Football Team until a new name had been decided upon.[48] While there has been progress in regard to sports teams moving away from racist depictions in their brand representation, designers need further education about their responsibility to ethically guide discussions during the rebranding process on the betterment of identities depicted by universities and major league teams.

SYSTEMS

WHY SYSTEMS?

The second design category is *systems*—organized sets of doctrines, ideas, or principles usually intended to explain the arrangement or working of a systematic whole.[49] There are also systems around us every day; these systems can be visible and invisible. Our interaction with these systems results in a pattern of behavior that becomes a cultural norm. Donella Meadows talks about systems in her book *Thinking in Systems*. She explains complex systems that exist around us and how we, as complex systems ourselves, interact with other complex systems: "We have built up intuitively, without analysis, often without words, a practical understanding of how these systems work, and how to work with them."[50] Therefore, if we were to break down a system, and rebuild it, how would we make sure to dismantle the intuition of bias and racism in our systems? How are we creating interventions in the design process to ensure we are creating new systems in inclusive and equitable ways? As designers who are focused on dismantling systems of inequality, such as racism, sexism, homophobia, and ableism, how do we require people to pause and question the status quo? Even when we are deliberately working to dismantle systems of inequality and designing for good, we need to decolonize our design process in order to develop systems that are anti-racist and anti-oppressive.

HOW DESIGN PLAYS A ROLE IN THE CREATION OF SYSTEMS

Designers must understand the needs of their users to design an effective system. We utilize ethnography, moving between observing and designing, to ensure we are designing with a diverse set of voices. This process includes a network of people actively engaged with a system through usage and development who are seeking to change the system. For the book *Design Anthropology*, editors Wendy Gunn, Ton Otto, and Rachel Charlotte Smith put together a group of scholars and industry practitioners who are working together with designers and anthropologists in codesign spaces.[51] The authors recognize the value designers bring to a collaborative work environment when analyzing a system: "We resort to squeezing it into words. Designers have used mood boards, targeted collections of imagery, as a way of absorbing the material and visual surroundings at a particular moment and as a way of pointing toward a possible trajectory; a way of making sense of the present while also carving out a space for exploring the future."[52]

Part of a designer's work is to visualize invisible systems of oppression. In turn, the developed visuals help viewers to know, analyze, and reimagine a new way of doing. We acknowledge the importance of working with the field of design as a site of cultural production, a field with the agency to work collaboratively to affect cultural change. "Design is not a politically or socially neutral space. Concepts are increasingly phenomena that mediate what kinds of relationships individual people, citizens, consumers, and users have with governments, corporations, and international bodies."[53] When we work to dismantle designs that support systems of oppression, it is important to build sustaining relationships with the community we work in to disrupt the status quo. Instead of designing what we think a community needs, this enables the team to truly create a sustainable and lasting positive impact with the community.

RACIALIZED SYSTEM EXAMPLES

Historically, systems are designed to create a way of working that affects everyone, either negatively or positively. Langdon Winner pointedly reflects on the development of bridges erected in New York City as one example of systemic racism. Robert Moses, an urban architect, developed the public transportation system in New York City. His associate, Lee Koppelman, says Moses deliberately built the bridges with low clearance to prevent city buses from going under them

Figure 2.3.
Example system:
transportation
bridge system
recreation.

(see figure 2.3), thus limiting the Black and brown communities, who primarily use public transport, from entering certain areas of the city, including Jones Beach. Moses developed Jones Beach specifically for people who could afford car ownership.[54] Koppelman was quoted as saying, "The old son of a gun had made sure that buses would never be able to use his goddamned parkways."[55] He not only purposely developed these structures but implemented this public transportation into policy, defining a systemic form of inequality that exists to this day. Winner stated these artifacts, systems, processes, and policies all have politics and continue to shape our culture and become "a part of the landscape" or viewed as "unseemingly meaningless." In this research study, we have identified the transportation system as a form of racialized design.

Another example of urban transportation as a system of oppression exists in Cleveland, Ohio. In 1976, Sixth Street in the Shaker Heights neighborhood installed "traffic diverters" or roadblocks. Cleveland Historical outlines the historical timeline of the barricades. The original explanation given for why the roadblocks were implemented was that it was at the request of neighborhood residents to prevent accidents and traffic jams. Six roadblocks and barriers were set up in 1976 near new neighborhoods that were predominantly Black and African American because of "black migration into the suburbs during the 1960s."[56] They were installed and meant to remain for only 180 days as a trial. The roadblocks were positioned right along, or close to, the border of these neighborhoods. The placements of the roadblocks were identified as being racially driven. The Black community called the barriers and roadblocks "the Berlin Wall for black people."[57] In 1979, two of the six barriers became permanent, resulting in community upset and litigation. In 1985, a common pleas court hearing ordered the removal of all six barriers. Later in 1985 the Ohio Supreme Court overturned the 1985 order and said the neighborhood was "legally able to keep the barricades where they were permanent.[58] Today, more than forty years later, two barricades still exist. These types of systemic choices affect our culture, both explicit and implicit. People in power, whether they are making decisions in urban transportation, community zoning, planning, or criminal justice systems, have implicit biases, which are embedded in the choices being made. These decisions directly affect communities with Black people, Indigenous people, and people of color. According to the NAACP, though African Heritage and Latinx populations make up 32 percent of the US population, they comprised 56 percent of all incarcerated people in 2015.[59] Racialized design continues to perpetuate a system of oppression that has limited opportunity and access for marginalized communities for many years.

EXPERIENCES

WHY EXPERIENCES?

The third design category is *experiences*—things personally encountered, undergone, or lived through.[60] Personal experiences have proven to be a key element in empathy-building across a variety of disciplines. Storytelling is an integral part in understanding each other. The Harvard School of Public Health studied the personal experiences of discrimination in partnership with National Public Radio (NPR) in the spring of 2017. In their findings, they reported that 51 percent of Black Americans have experienced racial slurs, 52 percent have experienced negative assumptions made about their race, and 42 percent have experienced racial violence.[61] For students of color, racist experiences affect their complete well-being (mentally, physically, and emotionally), and they can experience struggles with time management, work, class, or difficult assignments.[62] It is imperative for people who experience racism to share these experiences in a safe space. These safe environments could foster collaboration with individuals who have experienced either forms of racism or forms of "otherness," and with the wider population. Together they can help develop innovative solutions with the potential to provide clarity on racialized experiences. Because people of color experience racism daily, design should push to create experiences in an anti-racist way.

Experiences are one of the most common prompts we use with our industry and community partners during the Racism Untaught workshops. The experiences are collected through a survey that is a part of the pre-workshop activities (discussed at length in chapter 1). We anonymize the prompts to ensure that one person cannot be connected to who shared it and who was involved in the incident. Once the prompts are shared, we introduce the design research process and work collaboratively to create new narratives in their shared spaces. Through the shared racialized experiences of participants in our pre-workshop survey, participants use their shared experiences as their racialized prompts. They can contextualize, analyze, reimagine, and produce outcomes, with the impact as their first consideration. Sharing these experiences and the stories of everyday racism provides the opportunity to break down how racism shows up in their lives each day.

Figure 2.4. Example experience: Black student success recreation.

HOW DESIGN PLAYS A ROLE IN THE CREATION OF EXPERIENCES

As designers, we are tasked with framing user experiences. We use the design process to simplify everyday tasks or intentionally complicate experiences by hindering choices or perpetuating discriminatory societal norms. Experiences can be designed to be racialized, intentionally or unintentionally, based on the bias of the individual(s) taking on the role of the designer(s). The privilege held by designers should be used in such a way that it allows for the inclusion of a variety of voices before decisions are made. The world we interact with is connected to our interpersonal experiences. These experiences shape our point of view and the way we interact with the world.[63] If we do not understand the constructs of our social identities, then we will continue to experience the world from the perspective of monoculturalism.

RACIALIZED EXPERIENCE EXAMPLES

One example of a racialized experience is that of a Black person, Indigenous person, or person of color walking on the campus of a historically white college or university (see figure 2.4). The lived experiences of students who identify as a Black person, Indigenous person, or a person of color are often not acknowledged or considered in the development of academic spaces, services, cocurricular planning, or program development. Even without these considerations, they are expected to learn and academically succeed at or above the level of their peers. The makeup of our institutions of higher learning, despite mainstream culture, have been designed to uplift, empower, and represent the white mainstream experience in teaching, relationships, economics, and so on.

A second example of racialized experience is the fraught relationship between law enforcement and the Black, African American, and Black diaspora communities. Police brutality is only one element of systemic racism. According to a 2021 report from Mapping Police Violence, Black people are 2.9 times more likely to be killed by police than white people in the US.[64] Although this statistic is daunting, it does not even touch the other communities of color that are victimized by police. The system of policing negatively affects community trust, disproportionately affects communities of color, and leaves communities vulnerable to trauma and a lack of justice.[65] This experience was purposefully created and designed by a system that devalues human lives, particularly those in marginalized communities. Governing bodies have allowed this experience to continue despite the call for a national redesign that includes police abolition and the offering of new systems of intervention that heal, resolve conflict, and empower communities to work together.

Despite the weighted conversations around policing, Pepsi decided to bring the issue to its commercial platform. In an advertisement Pepsi created, it placed Kendall Jenner amid a gathering of protestors who, although portrayed here as mainly white, are often in reality communities of color.[66] Jenner walks through the crowd to the other side, where there is a line of police officers in stoic poses. Her hand is outstretched to give a soda to a police officer, who accepts this apparent peace offering. The protesters erupt in joy and the visual tension between the police and the people dissipate. A *New York Times* article said that the commercial "shows attractive young people holding milquetoast signs with nonspecific pleas like 'join the conversation.' The protesters are uniformly smiling, laughing, clapping, hugging, and high-fiving. In the ad's climactic scene, a police officer accepts a can of Pepsi from Kendall Jenner, a white woman, setting off raucous approval from the protesters and an appreciative grin from the officer."[67] In other words, Jenner, the white savior, can lead this movement for communities of color and easily solve the traumatic histories and negative impacts of police in our communities with a capitalistic soda. When confronted with how the advertisement landed for folks, Pepsi responded with a statement from its chief executive, Indra Nooyi: "'This has pained me a lot because this company is known for diversity, and the fact that everybody who produced the commercial and approved the commercial did not link it to Black Lives Matter made me scratch my head. I had not seen that scene,'

Nooyi said. 'And I take everything personally. The minute I saw people upset, I pulled it. And you know what, it's not worth it. There were people on both sides, but at the end of the day, our goal is not to offend anybody.'"[68] The design of this commercial, which might have very well have been well-intentioned, trivialized the experience of people of color. By minimizing the experiences of Black and brown folks and simplifying the issue to a soda solution, Pepsi's design works against the activism focused on the system of policing and these traumatic experiences. To begin to discuss the systems at play around police brutality takes careful consideration and a well-thought-out design to help heal and break down the negative histories and impacts within communities of color.

INDUSTRY CASE STUDY

Large Corporate Institution, Train-the-Trainer

RETHINKING THE CORPORATE DESIGN PROCESS: INDUSTRY EXPERIENCE IN TRAINING RACISM UNTAUGHT FACILITATORS

ORGANIZATION
Train-the-trainer sessions over Zoom using digital workboards (see figure 2.5), seven two-hour sessions, online, fall 202.

TEAM
Facilitators: Lisa Elzey Mercer and Terresa Moses.
Trainees: Four individuals from the same company. Trainees were guided through the framework to be trained as facilitators of the Racism Untaught framework within their prospective organization of six hundred employees. The racial makeup of the group was three people of color and one white person.
Participants: The participants in this case study are the organization's six hundred employees they will be training.

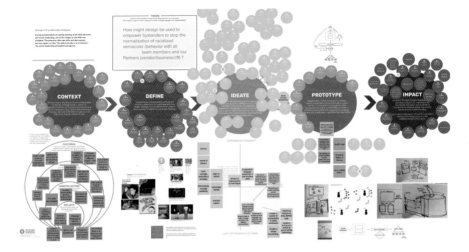

Figure 2.5. Industry case study workboard. Digital workboard by participant group.

⊙ ONBOARDING ACTIVITIES: TWO HOURS

During the first session of the Racism Untaught train-the-trainer program, we began with a land acknowledgment and introductions, including prompts and questions, such as name and pronouns, department (area of work), and "Why did you say yes to this training?" Trainees were guided through activities to explore their social identities, and we helped them become equipped to help members of their organization explore their identities. We then moved forward with an introduction of Racism Untaught as a framework to help identify racialized design and use the design research process to assist in cultivating anti-racist design approaches in project-based learning environments. Next, we discussed definitions for racialized design and the design categories—artifacts, systems, and experiences—providing participants with examples in each category. We then reviewed the analog and digital toolkits with participants. The analog toolkits are available via PDFs; participants can print out materials as needed. The digital toolkit is available via an online collaborative whiteboard platform.[69] We then used the online collaborative whiteboard platform to craft a community agreement or community alliance with the trainees. Because the trainees were breaking up the workshop into multiple sessions, we encouraged them to review the community agreement or community alliance at the beginning of each session. We have found this simple reminder helps participants reaffirm the physical or conceptual space we are building for conversations on race and racism. After finalizing the community agreement using the online collaborative whiteboard platform, we introduced and explored important terms that the trainees should know. These terms included *racism, humility, transparency, trauma* (versus *discomfort*), *positionality, intersectionality, power, privilege,* and *dominant culture.* We then guided trainees through the unpacking of their own social identities, asking them to consider the impact of the identities they hold in social groups. They used a table of social groups to mark the identities they held and to help them begin to contextualize how their power, privilege, and marginalization affected their everyday experiences, especially in the context of their organization. Our two lead questions during this activity were: What identities are at the forefront of your mind or the ones you lead with most? How do your identities shape how you move about the world?

We emphasized the importance of group work while using the toolkit and framework, in turn supporting the fact that it is important that group members are self-aware of their own strengths and how they might show up in collaborative group spaces. From our work as educators in the classroom and other collaborative spaces, we have found that to appreciate social identities and differences in a collaborative way, the trainees should engage in self-assessments to help clarify their personality traits and ways of working. We listed self-assessments we believe can be used for that purpose, allowing participants to choose which evaluations their organization might have more access to. These included but are not limited to the CliftonStrengths assessment,[70] the True Colors assessment,[71] the DiSC assessment,[72] the Social Change Ecosystem,[73] and the Crystal profile.[74] Before ending the first session and sending the trainees off with homework, we went over what we as facilitators share with participants approximately one week before the workshop begins. We entitle this shared informational document Racism Untaught + [insert partner name]. It includes important links and pre-workshop activities, such as the pre-workshop survey, the community agreement online activity, the Socio-cultural Identities worksheet, the workshop facilitator's slide deck, the shared Social Identity Profile slide deck, the Racism Untaught worksheet (which includes a map of the design research process and levels of oppression), the workshop digital report-out slide deck, and the cards from the workboard document (which includes all the language from the workboard; see chapter 1 for more detailed descriptions).

The homework assigned for session two (four days away) was for participants to complete their individual assessments using a free online resource called Crystal Knows, explore Deepa Iyer's Social Change Ecosystem,[75] and to come to the next session prepared with any questions about the previous session.

◀ CONTEXT: TWO HOURS

The second session began with a review of the previous session and the community agreement. Next, we explored the design research process again, noting that we would be covering the first step, context.

THE PROMPT: A RACIALIZED EXPERIENCE

To help trainees work through the toolkit, we ask them to think about an instance of racism that has happened within their organization. This allows participants to solve for an actual instance of racism close in their circle of influence rather than a fictitious scenario, adding a layer of complexity and closer proximity to the issue at hand. The trainees recounted a complaint that had circulated among employees in the organization. The prompt they chose to work with stated: "During a presentation at a group meeting of all white directors and senior leadership, one of the images on the slide was pixelated. The presenter, who was white and also seemed nervous, spoke out that 'the slide looks like it is in Chinese.' All of the senior leadership laughed and agreed. This experience is a strong example of bias against foreign languages."

THE CARDS

After reading through the prompt, we instructed the trainees to decide which elements of racism applied to the prompt in order to help them further contextualize what happened in this racialized experience. On their digital whiteboard, they began to discuss the prompt in terms of which elements they agreed represented the experience. Some of the cards the trainees pulled include the following:

- *Xenophobia:* An extreme or irrational fear or distain of people from different countries. *Rationale:* Ignorance or lack of understanding supports irrational fear. The subject's nervousness (in the prompt) supported their bias against the Chinese language, using it to negate attention, perhaps away from their own perceived failings during the presentation.
- *Nativism:* Policies or systems favoring native inhabitants as opposed to immigrants. *Rationale:* Because the United States' primary language is English, many citizens are supported in their discrimination against foreign languages due to systemic policies that favor English-speaking inhabitants.
- *Linguistic oppression:* Discriminatory judgments about a person's wealth, education, social status, or character, based on an individual's language, vernacular, or accent. *Rationale:* Degrading the Chinese language by comparing it to a pixelated (or confusing) image reinforces discriminatory judgement about individuals who use the Chinese language.
- *White ally fatigue:* A term that expresses the tiredness of white people who feel "stretched thin" while standing in solidarity with Black people, Indigenous people, and people of color who have suffered all their lives. *Rationale:* The white people in the room did not correct the discriminatory joke; rather, they laughed it off, standing in solidarity with the joke and the bias the joke perpetuated.

THE LEVELS OF OPPRESSION

In the second part of step one, the trainees worked together with the levels of oppression model to further contextualize the experience of oppression that showed up within the prompt they provided. They were asked to consider how and where, at different levels, oppression was introduced, reinforced, and perpetuated within the model. The following are examples of how the trainees chose to break down the levels of oppression as related to their racialized prompts:

- *Beliefs:* Personal beliefs, ideas, and feelings that perpetuate oppression. *Rationale:* Chinese people and their language is hard to understand (incorrect).
- *Agentic action:* When oppressive beliefs translate into oppressive behavior. *Rationale:* The discomfort of the presenter is mitigated by racist humor.
- *Institutional:* Structural oppression that results from agentic oppressive behavior. *Rationale:* Leadership positions in this organization are held predominantly by white, English-speaking individuals.
- *Cultural:* Systems of norms, values, beliefs, and trusted systems of acquiring truth that preserve, protect, and maintain oppression. *Rationale:* Asians and Asian languages are often used as comic relief in entertainment.

The homework assigned for session three (three days away) was to review the context cards that we did not get through in this session and to come to the next session prepared with any questions about the previous session.

◑ DEFINE: TWO HOURS

The third session began with a review of the previous session to address any questions that arose. We then began to review the define step by reviewing *theories*, which we described as a lens through which to look at racialized design, and *methods*, which we described as ways of gathering data. This provided trainees with the opportunity to understand the variety of qualitative and quantitative research methods available for them to further contextualize and analyze the prompt. The group chose the following methods and theories, although they only worked through the popular media search for the purposes of this training:

- *Group threat theory:* A sociological theory that proposes that the larger the size of an out-group, the more the corresponding in-group perceives it to threaten its own interests, resulting in negative attitudes toward the outgroup
- *Culture of prejudice:* The theory that prejudice is embedded in our culture
- *Case studies:* A research method involving an up-close, in-depth, and detailed examination of a subject of study (the case), as well as its related contextual conditions
- *Popular media search:* Searching popular forms of media to gain further context

Next, the trainees engaged in the popular media search, pulling articles, reports, videos, and imagery to help contextualize their prompt. The trainees were then guided through the process of creating a thesis question using this guiding question as an example: "How might design be used to [action] in order to [create change] with [stakeholders]?" Through brainstorming and discussion, the trainees crafted the following thesis question, which they used to guide them in creating an anti-racist approach for their racialized experience: "How might design be used to empower bystanders to stop the normalization of racialized vernacular/behavior with all [company name] team members and our Partners (vendor/business/cft)?"

The homework assigned for session four (four days away) was to come to the next session prepared with any questions about the previous session.

◀ IDEATE: TWO HOURS
THE CARDS

After reviewing the previous session, the trainees continued their work, moving on with the third step, ideate. We explained to the trainees that this grouping of cards was meant to spark ideas and avenues through which they might affect positive change as an answer to the thesis question they created. Each card fell within one of the three categories of design described earlier in the chapter. The trainees were encouraged to use all three categories of design in the ideation process. We even encouraged the groupings of artifacts, systems, and experiences that might work together in a design approach. Some of the cards the trainees chose are as follows:

- *Campaign:* A connected series of operations designed to bring about a particular result. This term fell within the artifact section of design.
- *Education:* Generally referring to schools that provide information to students. This term fell within the system section of design.
- *Experience design:* The connectedness of everything in a process. This term fell within the experience section of design.

QUADRANT MAP

The second part of the third step created opportunities for more specific ideas and for measuring the implementation of those ideas using the quadrant map. Each trainee created a list of ideas based on the areas of design they pulled from the ideate deck of cards. Trainees were encouraged to write down all their ideas, which they placed on individual sticky notes. Trainees then placed their sticky notes on the quadrant map to gain a better understanding first of how far their idea would take their stakeholders from oppressive thought to anti-oppressive action, and then how far the idea moved culture norms from good intentions to positive impact. In addition to their crafted thesis question, participants were encouraged to consider how they might be intentionally anti-racist in their new design approach.

The trainees decided on a mixed media art installation that would focus on stories of racial injustice using photography, audio storytelling, and visual words of marginalized groups. The stories would focus on multicultural language that would educate through play and global social interactions. With this installation, the trainees would build in opportunities to build courage, including practice, role playing, and demonstrations. They would also implement policies that supported a process of multilingualism for use within the organization's processes; a system of accountability within their leadership; a reporting system to keep Black people, Indigenous people, and people of color safe; and practices that redefined wrongdoing to support growth and the validation of experiences.

The homework assigned for session five (two days away) was to come to the next session prepared with any questions about the previous session.

◀ PROTOTYPE: TWO HOURS

During this fifth session, trainees were guided through the fourth step of the toolkit, prototype. We introduced the three different levels of prototypes: low, mid, and high fidelity. During the session and during facilitated workshops, participants are only prompted to complete a low-fidelity prototype, although they were asked to review all the prototype cards in this step.

The low-fidelity prototype is the initial, raw presentation of an idea. The trainees began to outline and prototype the idea(s) that were the most promising from the ideate step. They started this process by dreaming big as we encouraged ideas that should know no limits. The trainees talked through processes and visuals to craft an idea that could be easily recognized. This happened using process maps, sticky notes, concept boarding, and sketches. Through their work, they entitled their idea "So, This Happened." Their prototype showed how users might walk through a visual and tactile system that tells the stories of colleagues to help them understand differing experiences. At the end of the installation, there would be opportunity for discussion and an analysis of their reactions. Depending on the story being introduced, there was a certain call to action that users could take with them in their journey to understanding others' experiences and their own biases.

The homework assigned for session six (five days away) was to come to the next session prepared with any questions about the previous session (see figure 2.6).

◀ IMPACT: TWO HOURS

During the sixth session, the trainees were guided through the fifth step, impact. The trainees were asked to select the cards they were most interested in implementing to further understand the impact of their idea. In this step, we reminded all trainees that the framework was iterative and nuanced. Understanding the impact of their work would guide their design process and would likely require more ideation and prototyping to ensure that they were working toward a positive impact. Some cards that the trainees pulled during this step include the following:

- *Competencies plan:* Planning for the outcomes needed to make innovation initiatives successful

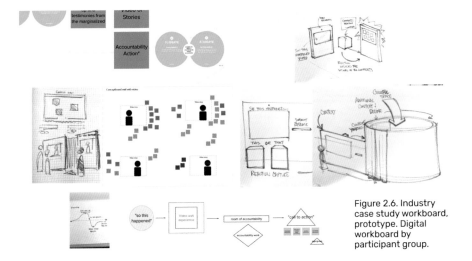

Figure 2.6. Industry case study workboard, prototype. Digital workboard by participant group.

- *Gamified survey:* An interactive and/or game-like way of polling users to gather data on attitudes, opinions, and/or beliefs of sections of a population
- *Strategy plan workshop:* Creating organizational strategies and aligning them around one or more proposed solutions—such as policy changes

The homework assigned for session seven (seven days away) was to come to the next session prepared with any questions about the previous session.

◖ OFF-BOARDING: TWO HOURS

During the seventh session, we worked with the trainees to go over the entirety of the workshop so that they felt ready to facilitate the toolkit with their colleagues. This meant fielding questions, discussing problems that might arise during facilitation, and reviewing their access to the Racism Untaught framework and templates. We also went over additional elements of sexism in case they decided to add those as a nuanced layer in the context step—however, the participants were keen to discuss racism, which seemed to be a hard topic for many colleagues.

Next, we discussed the intentionality of workshop groups and potential schedules they might use in crafting their eight-hour sessions. They ultimately decided on breaking up their workshops into three sessions, of two, three, and three hours each. We also scheduled our quarterly check-ins to navigate any issues that might come up. The first quarterly meeting happened right after their first workshop. Finally, we discussed intentional ways of integrating Racism Untaught into their current institutional design processes and offered a map to assist them. And we ended with intentional questions: What do community partnerships look like in these processes? How will you respond to or support the ideas being generated from the workshops?

❹ CHALLENGES

One of the challenges that trainees brought up regarding identity was the pushback they might receive when trying to engage with social identity work within their organization. They also spoke to the deflection or microinvalidation of racialized experiences. All the trainees in this session were aware of the social identities they held, and so we discussed ways to leverage those within workshops when addressing problematic behaviors. Because this group was made up of designers, they were elated to begin using the toolkit in a customizable way to assist in their decision-making.

This group of trainees has since continued their use of the Racism Untaught toolkit, training the intended 600 employees and beginning to train 1,200 more vendors and partners.

INTERSECTIONALITY IS A LENS THROUGH WHICH YOU CAN SEE WHERE POWER COMES AND COLLIDES, WHERE IT INTERLOCKS AND INTERSECTS. IT'S NOT SIMPLY THAT THERE'S A RACE PROBLEM HERE, A GENDER PROBLEM HERE, AND A CLASS OR LBGTQ PROBLEM THERE. MANY TIMES, THAT FRAMEWORK ERASES WHAT HAPPENS TO PEOPLE WHO ARE SUBJECT TO ALL OF THESE THINGS.

—Kimberlé Crenshaw[1]

POSITIONALITY

When participants use the Racism Untaught framework and toolkit, it is necessary for them to gain an understanding of their positionality in the context of race, racism, and other forms of oppression to better understand their design outcomes. We define positionality as the place in which our social identities are situated in the broader context of oppression and other socio-cultural constructs. The context of positionality supports their understanding of how we perpetuate and uphold systems of oppression that shape the everyday lives of Black people, Indigenous people, and people of color. Often, participants have not engaged in conversations about their social identities nor in activities that allow them to analyze and deconstruct them. Before the positionality exercise, participants could not identify how their privileged/benefiting social identities created easier paths, access, and opportunities. These statements made it clear that many participants had not thought about how their identity affects what they can and cannot do. Although deconstructing one's social identity may be hard for those in the dominant culture(s), we have received feedback from participants about the social identity activities, with comments such as, "Yes, it's very eye-opening. Especially when we all spoke about our own social identities. It helped me begin to understand what some of my coworkers are going through every day."[2] We have found exploring personal identity in addition to introducing the following concepts in our onboarding process to be a strong foundation for the Racism Untaught framework.

Recognizing positionality is a lifelong process that entails understanding privilege, power, and marginalization. The social identities that an individual holds are *contextually framed*, meaning that the space and time in which an individual presents themself has a significant impact on how they are perceived, how they perceive others, and who holds power within that context. We have come to understand the norms of the *dominant culture* in the United States as a culture whose values, language, and ways of behaving are imposed on one or more subordinate cultures through economic or political power.[3] As Margaret T. Hicken of the University of Michigan's Institute for Social Research and her colleagues explain, "Racism does not require explicit intent or personal dislike on the part of its dominant actors. Rather, it is woven into our social structure and institutions, allowing for unequal life experiences and chances based on the socially-constructed racial group membership categories."[4] In the United States, these interwoven dominant roles within particular social identity groups are—specifically—white, male, cisgender, Christian, and English-speaking. All of these are embodiments of dominant social identities that have long held and continue to hold and wield power and privilege. Brazilian educator and advocate for critical pedagogy Paulo Freire emphasized the absoluteness of this power: "In cultural invasion (as in all the modalities of antidialogical action), the invaders are the authors of, and actors, in the process; those they invade are the objects. The invaders' mold; those they invade are molded. The invaders choose; those they invade follow that choice—or are expected to follow it. The invaders act; those they invade have only the illusion of acting, through the action of the invaders."[5] So, in this case, those in the dominant culture, white, are the authors and invaders who create the mold—systemic racism—and Black people, Indigenous people, and people of color are expected to mold to and follow the rules of white supremacy.

Designers need to recognize the dominant culture and its effects on our creative outputs. Internationally recognized designer and trailblazer Dr. Cheryl D. Miller emphasizes this point when she states, "In Graphic Design practice, this magnet to only see the dominant culture prevails—it still does. That's why diversity in design and diversity, equity, and inclusion (DEI) trends are pushing back. White default is the opposite of full regard for the palette of population."[6] The recognition of social norms—or, as Miller states, "defaults"—is directly linked to how we might begin to design for social good. Ezio Manzini, the founder of the DESIS Network, explores a similar idea in his work at the intersection of design and social innovation. He acknowledges the dominant culture globally in his book *Design, When Everybody Designs*: "The dominant world, still the reference for many, that shapes the main economic and institutional structures and that draws from its history of success the conviction that its continuity in time is inevitable."[7] His work has supported the development of over fifty labs, with projects focused on social impact, social innovation, and sustainability that work to break down the narrative of the dominant culture.

THE CONCEPTS

We provide definitions in this research study to ensure all participants work from a shared understanding of the concepts we introduce (more on this in chapter 4). We begin with the concept of *racism*, defining it as the social construct of race as the primary determinant for the racially dominant culture to uphold conscious or subconscious beliefs, actions, and/or benefits that support systemic racial prejudice and oppression through power and privilege (prejudice + power over + privilege = racism); that is, the ideology that the white race is superior to people of color, at least in the United States. We emphasize that Racism Untaught was not created to prove that racism exists in design but to reveal how deeply racism affects many aspects of the societal foundation and framework within which design decision-making occurs. In short, we work to sensitize workshop participants about approaches and methods for creating and operating design approaches guided by perspectives framed with an anti-racist lens.

INTERSECTIONALITY, POWER, AND PRIVILEGE

Participants begin by critically examining the various social identities recognized by the dominant culture in their society. Then they use this knowledge to further contextualize how and why social identities intersect and how the intersectionality of those social constructs operate within the socio-cultural norm. Almost all people on our planet are affected by various aspects of how they perceive themselves—and how they are perceived by others in their society—according to how specific aspects of their identities intersect with each other. These intersections can fuel unique types of discrimination. For example, people who live in the United States who could be categorized as Native American, gay, and hearing-impaired could be forced to confront discriminatory public policies and social behaviors. As a result, the intersection of these three identities could be perceived as "undesirable" or "less than." Intersectionality becomes an apt descriptor for how and why race, class, gender, ethnicity, and other individual characteristics have been categorically used throughout much of the world's history to ensure that marginalized and historically underinvested communities remain that way. In short, intersectionality helps ensure that the socio-cultural perceptions of those with intersecting identities, residing in the margins of the margins, will continue to find their paths away from normalized limitations. Kimberlé Crenshaw—a scholar in the field of critical race theory, a professor at Columbia Law School, director of the Center for Intersectionality and Social Policy Studies, and a cofounder of the African American Policy Forum think tank—coined the term *intersectionality*, specifically referring to economically disadvantaged Black women. "Black women are subsumed within the traditional boundaries of race or gender discrimination these boundaries are currently understood, and that the intersection of racism and sexism factors into Black women's lives in ways that can be captured wholly by looking at the race or gender dimensions of those experiences separately."[8] Intersectionality goes beyond exclusively examining socio-cultural identities that intersect and instead focuses on the identities that tend to be oppressed due to social normalcy within a given society.

We also define *power* and *privilege* for participants; however, we remind participants to leave room for context and nuance when using these terms to define social identities. We define *power* as earned authority granted through social structures and conventions that affords given individuals and groups access and control over people through the intentional planning and operation of institutions and systems (e.g., management, human resources, and executive-level leadership). We define *privilege* as unearned personal, interpersonal, cultural, and institutional rights or benefits that provide or contribute advantages, favors, and benefits to members of dominant groups in a society at the expense of members of target groups within it from whom these rights and benefits are withheld. (In this context, targeted groups are defined by race, gender, sexuality, ableness, ethnicity, etc.) Both power and privilege give dominant groups the upper hand across multiple societal contexts; through these means, they can affect and control public policy, educational initiatives, who gets to live where, and who gets to pursue the most desirable and profitable career paths. Recognizing this upper hand does not negate the challenging work that many individuals engage in to fuel their careers and attain their life achievements. Rather, this recognition is intended to help many types of people—including those who use our Racism Untaught toolkits in workshop settings—to understand that these social constructs make it harder and add more work for individuals in the marginalized categories of the targeted social groups living within a given society.

HUMILITY, VULNERABILITY, AND TRANSPARENCY

We acknowledge that humility and vulnerability are keys to having productive conversations among participants in the workshops within which the Racism Untaught toolkit is utilized. It is important that both the facilitators and participants do not claim to be or assume others to be experts on the topic of racism, especially if that assumption is based on cultural identity. There exists a toxic expert culture, especially across academia, that has often hindered our ability to work in a transdisciplinary manner[9] that could help us—and our workshop participants—learn new ways of thinking (i.e., to engage in so-called higher-learning activities). The work of unpacking racism is heavy and often hard to do, but it is necessary if we hope to move our organizations and classrooms forward regarding how racism—or exclusion—is addressed when coupled with planning and operating design processes necessary to do this effectively. New language is being developed in and around these topics every day, and this is directly and indirectly affecting how these topics evolve. Because of this, we ask participants to be willing to acknowledge when they do not know or cannot effectively articulate an answer to a question or a prompt and suggest that it is imperative they do their own research so that further misconceptions or miseducation does not occur.

It is beneficial for facilitators and participants in courses where we use the Racism Untaught framework to be transparent about recounting their own histories and to offer these up willingly. Doing this helps create a space within which others can be freely allowed to share their own histories. We have found that one effective way to talk about your past is by using the "Where I Am From" poem by George Ella

Lyon[10] to help workshop participants articulate how their identities are shaped by things, events, and incidents that transpired in their pasts. We have participants create their own version of this poem, critically assessing where cultural bias is present in their social upbringing. We also recommend having participants create a visual element or collage with their poems to present to their design team. This will allow for a long and deep look into their past and the critical assessment of racialized design in their background. Transparency grants people who have never talked about these subjects the grace to learn and grow from their mistakes. Absolutely no one is perfect, and, in fact, the Racism Untaught toolkit reveals to participants that everyone plays a role in the perpetuation of racism.

TRIGGERS AND DISCOMFORT

Racialized design is so deeply embedded in the global culture that it is important to recognize that racialized trauma will exist for Black people, Indigenous people, or people of color who choose to participate in the workshops within which Racism Untaught is used. One way we have learned to plan for the cultural taxation that participating in our workshops may cause is by offering racial affinity spaces within which Black people, Indigenous people, or people of color can work with each other. We have found this intentional space helps shield these participants from feeling the pressure of having to teach white colleagues about their racialized experiences. It is imperative to be sensitive to these traumas and to have a plan of action if participants feel triggered into feeling uncomfortable.

Remember that there is also a difference between being triggered and being uncomfortable. Being triggered entails intense emotions linked to a traumatic experience that cause a response such as fight, flight, freeze, or fawn.[11] Trauma can show up when you least expect it, so using a community agreement is a terrific way to help validate and repair harm. Being triggered is often confused with the feeling of discomfort that individuals within the dominant groups tend to feel when confronted with issues dealing with systems of oppression they benefit from. Crystal Raypole gives an example of coming to understand this matter better in the following excerpt from the article "What It Really Means to Be Triggered" in *HealthLine*: "There's no doubt these topics can be unpleasant, offensive, or distasteful. But it's important to understand the distinction between discomfort and trauma. For a lot of people, these topics won't cause flashbacks, dissociation, or other distressing emotional experiences."[12] In order to grow, participants should lean into this discomfort with topics they do not usually discuss, especially when they hold power and privilege in that context.

CREATING SPACE

In each workshop and course, we verbally acknowledge that all the participants are learning new concepts, how to use these new concepts, and a shared language (further explained in chapter 4). We therefore ask them to be open to changes in their and their group mates' thinking, and to be flexible when new knowledge is uncovered or constructed. The importance of community agreements lies in the crafting of a collective agreed-upon culture that allows for the power of vulnerability and accountability. Tarana Burke emphasizes this point in her book written with Brené Brown, *You Are Your Best Thing*, stating, "Place and space matter. Being vulnerable in places and spaces where we are 'not supposed to be,' or where our truth has never been spoken and our vulnerability has never been seen, is powerful. Being seen and compelling others to witness the violence of white supremacy invites accountability. It injects truth into a façade. This truth-telling is a powerful step in dismantling White supremacy, putting cracks in it."[13] Marta Elena Esquilin from Bryant University in Smithfield, Rhode Island, and Mike Funk from New York University have written about the importance of community building and the value of crafting and then abiding by engagement agreements. They have provided over twenty classroom and meeting guidelines to create an intentional space within which conversations focused on diversity, equity, and inclusion can occur.[14] We asked Racism Untaught workshop and classroom participants to join us in the development of a community agreement by starting with these five prompts: (1) engage in conversations in ways that honor each other, (2) speak from your own lived experience, (3) think beyond binaries, (4) foster a space for vulnerability and humility, and (5) acknowledge, validate, and repair harm. Each of these areas are outlined in more detail ahead.

ENGAGE IN CONVERSATIONS IN WAYS THAT HONOR EACH OTHER
One of the first concepts in our community agreements is to engage in conversations in ways that honor each other. For us, this means a variety of layered and nuanced notions that include listening actively, seeking to understand, keeping time in mind, and intentional communication. Graham D. Bodie et al. describe active listening as imperative to the functioning of continued communication in their article "The Role of 'Active Listening' in Informal Helping Conversations." They state that importance lies in "both nonverbal and verbal behaviors [which] function to demonstrate attention, understanding, responsiveness, and empathy; to encourage continued expression of thoughts and feelings; and to aid in relational maintenance."[15] We would add that in addition to what active listening offers during times of communication, it is particularly important to communicate this way as tensions are likely to be high when participants and teammates are walking headfirst into the discovery of oppression and their positionality within those systems. We like to remind people to seek to understand first before allowing their own defensiveness or assumptions about one another to dominate the space. Having conversations about potential harm we have caused by not recognizing our privileges in the context of oppression can be a hard pill to swallow, so coming to a complete understanding of each other's stories allows for time to digest the nuanced relationships among thoughts, intentions, and impacts. In addition to these nuances, we like to bring up the very real privilege of using time and how overusing time can cause others to feel unheard, often perpetuating bias in who deserves to speak and who is worth being listened to. Speaking to each other takes time, and in honoring our space together, we want to be intentional about how we use time in our sessions.

Finally, we open discussion on what it means to honor each other. We personally like to use the word *honor* because terms like *respect* have often been weaponized against those who do not hold the dominant cultural identity. Honoring implies intentionality in the ways we perceive one another. It is a term that is higher than a surface-level respect or the obligation of respect due to social constructs. We prefer its usage because it allows participants to explore how they feel most honored as their true selves and how they might honor each other regardless of status or perceived status.

SPEAK FROM YOUR OWN LIVED EXPERIENCE

Speaking from your own experience is a tactic that deters the assumptions of how others feel, should feel, act, and should act. It removes the chance that we may accidentally speak for someone else and in turn cause harm due to our own assumptions. The act of speaking for ourselves is also an empowering one, providing an opportunity for ownership of one's actions or lack of actions. It is a way in which we can be held accountable for the choices that we, and we alone, make. It is a colonial idea that we know exactly what others feel due to our own lens and perspective in our society. But it is this positionality that should actually encourage us to lean in to empathy to help us understand others.

Owning one's own story is also a form of reparations and counter-storytelling. Because history is crafted by the dominant culture, many individuals do not have the opportunity to tell their stories. Speaking from your own experience is just one small way of righting this wrong that we have all been socialized to believe is the truth. There are many stories to be told, and so we should allow space for those stories, empowering one another to add to the workshop and broader cultural narrative.

THINK BEYOND BINARIES

We ask participants to consider how so much of United States history (and that of other colonized areas of the world) has been intentionally crafted to perpetuate the biases and the binary foundations, or systems, necessary to keep the dominant culture that operates within it in power. In the context of this discourse, binary foundations or systems may be described by this definition offered by women's and gender studies scholars Milian Kang et al.: "Black and white. Masculine and feminine. Rich and poor. Straight and gay. Able-bodied and disabled. Binaries are social constructs composed of two parts that are framed as absolute and unchanging opposites. Binary systems reflect the integration of these oppositional ideas into our culture. This results in an exaggeration of differences between social groups until they seem to have nothing in common."[16] We ask participants to investigate how an individual's own positionality is shaped and sustained by that history. It is also important to understand that social, cultural, and political power and privilege—and the lack of these in our societies— are not inherently binary. It has become increasingly easy for those in power to use digitally facilitated communications systems to severely limit what could be a wide variety of social, cultural, political, economic, ethical, and values-based metrics for guiding our perceptions of ourselves and each other. This results in individuals and population groups around the world being denied opportunities to be perceived, and to perceive themselves, as possessing unique and richly nuanced personal and societal identities. When all the identifiers that make us not only different but also socio-culturally relevant and authentic because we are different are erased, we force ourselves to live in incredibly one-dimensional, static situations. In turn, this gravely stifles our abilities to envision futures that improve rather than inhibit, that facilitate rather than suppress.

Myopically crafted history that attempts to erase what a given society has identified and framed as nonideal races, genders, sexualities, abilities, and so on from its past to guide its present retains a status quo that is both toxic and willfully ignorant. If these negative limitations are to be overcome, it is imperative to recognize the diverse nuances with which historically formed and framed identities are imbued. This tends to go against what so many who have been educated in school settings across the US have been taught. As a system to guide societal organization, the binary is a colonial, purist, and white supremacist concept that does not allow room for depth, distinction, or gray areas (the lack of which are exemplified in the binary between "good" and "evil").[17] This hinders our willingness and ability to fully, or even nominally, understand so many of the societal complexities within which people living around the world must live their daily lives. To unpack our own positionality, we stress that all people must bring their full selves to the table, which must include all the components, or parts, that may perpetuate systems of oppression, along with all of the parts that are striving for justice.

American author and professor bell hooks, known for her writings that interrogate the intersectionality of race, capitalism, and gender, stated, "It seems to me that the binary opposition that is so much embedded in Western thought and language makes it nearly impossible to project a complex response."[18] This inability to express social complexities is what Nigerian American author and feminist Chimamanda Ngozi Adichie refers to as "the danger of a single story."[19] She warns that single stories produce and sustain limited and limiting stereotypes about what people are and what they have the potential to become. All too often, these stereotypes and social tropes play outside roles that eventually define whole communities, tribes, nations, and even continents of people. To understand the power and danger of the single story, it is important to make the distinction between the past and history.[20] *The past* is what occurred, whereas *history* is that which is written about the past, in the way that historians—who often write as informed by specific social, cultural, economic, ethical, and political perspectives—attended to it. What we know about the past tends to be informed from a certain, often quite biased perspective. If we were to trust most of what historians have written about how and why particular civilizations and the societies that comprised them evolved over time, many marginalized communities would be rendered virtually nonexistent. The cause of this is their purposeful erasure from so many of the historical canons we use to inform us about the past that have been directly affected by the often myopically restricted lenses through which the individual documenting the past chooses to look.

History often becomes a means to weaponize various aspects of the past because there is no truly objective, unbiased worldview. Thus, it can never completely provide accurate retellings of the past without being affected by the influence of capitalism and what has become the toxic normalcies of our consumer-constructed culture. A power dynamic will always exist that creates meanings for and about past events as told by those who wield power in a particular society to influence types and levels of oppression—individual, agentic, institutional, and cultural[21]—within the broader context. There is no way to avoid the problematic tendencies of history as it is written. Those in power have dictated the stories of the past that are told. It is these power structures that hold the blame when the narratives of marginalized communities are erased from history. It is no wonder that when stories of the oppressed are brought to light, those in the dominant group try to suppress those narratives. It is much easier to remember a history crafted to keep one in power than to understand those who were oppressed in the making of that history. As Freire points out: "There is no history without humankind, and no history for human beings; there is only history of humanity, made by people and (as Marx pointed out) in turn making them. It is when the majorities are denied their right to participate in history as Subjects that they become dominated and alienated."[22]

FOSTER A SPACE FOR VULNERABILITY AND HUMILITY

When participants are interacting with the framework, either virtually or physically, we ask them to extend grace to one another. The grace to make mistakes, acknowledge those mistakes and move forward. This extension creates a space for vulnerability and humility to exist. We do not often have the opportunity to talk with one another about the topics of race and racism in a space that provides a shared language. Participants often share their lived experiences, and this is why we also ask participants to hold each other's stories close. This sort of vulnerability requires bravery. So if a person shares a story in a Racism Untaught workshop, we remind participants not to ask that person, in a different environment, to share the personal lived experience out of context. We acknowledge the value of creating an equitable and vulnerable space when working with the framework, to ensure that diverse individuals and population groups can thrive. In the book *Culture, Class, and Race*, the authors acknowledge that it is easier to discover how to be vulnerable and humble "in an arena where mistakes are welcomed and forgiveness is practiced. We refer to it as a place of grace, where things are allowed to emerge, where people are not judged for revealing who they are and what they are about. Relationships are built and maintained by knowing yourself and sharing it with others. Discovery conversation requires this perspective."[23]

ACKNOWLEDGE, VALIDATE, AND REPAIR HARM

When we are faced with a problematic, negative, or uncomfortable comment, we recommend that the participants slow down and take a pause. While it would be easier to walk away from that experience or just not say anything, it is important that we are willing to use every opportunity to learn from one another. For instance, consider the aforementioned active listening technique, seeking to understand. One way of doing this is by starting with questions to ensure we understood the true meaning of what was said and give the opportunity for the speaker to begin to analyze what they truly meant and if what they said is what they truly believe. "Questions have the uncanny ability to break patterns and tunnel a path of opportunity. Being skilled at asking questions about values, beliefs, and assumptions allows examination of the origins of such, which allows us to ascertain if those values, beliefs, and assumptions continue to serve us well. Careful scrutiny can determine which values, beliefs, and assumptions are root causes of damaging conversations in which we've engaged. At that crucial revelation, we can make the moral choice to change."[24] This provides participants with the opportunity to construct meaning from what they are saying and to decide if they truly believe what they are saying or if there is an opportunity to unlearn something and then learn a new way of thinking.

SOCIAL IDENTITIES

Understanding their own positionality against and within the context of racism and racist ideologies can help students and participants unlearn how we perpetuate and bolster systems of oppression that shape the everyday lives of Black people, Indigenous people, and people of color around the world. The recognition of positionality is a lifelong process of conscious knowledge cultivation and construction that entails attempting to understand privilege, power, and marginalization. Specifically, we learned how important it was to immerse participants of the toolkit in an onboarding process that would increase their understandings of how their positionality could affect the dynamics of any design team of which they were a part, as well as the roles they could play in advocating for anti-racist design decision-making. It is important for each person to begin to unpack their own identity and socialization so we can be aware of the bias (conscious and unconscious) that is part of the lens through which we move through the world—and design with! One example is for white participants to answer, When did you begin to realize you were white? What did it mean?

This area of research investigates how participants of the Racism Untaught framework and toolkit construct knowledge in a workshop setting about how their predetermined social identities were and are created and perpetuated by the numerous factors that constitute the culture within which they live, as well as how these identities then affect the way individuals engage in design processes that can evolve within their respective communities. The onboarding process is necessary to effectively implement the operation of the Racism Untaught toolkit in a workshop setting, as well as the activities rooted in examinations of social identity that we have implemented in specific situations to help prepare toolkit participants to engage in open conversations about race, racism, and racialized design. One of the primary goals of this undertaking has been to sensitize diverse populations in particular communities about the often biased and illegal treatment some individuals and groups in those communities experience based on how they are perceived racially.

BREAKING DOWN SOCIAL IDENTITIES

The Racism Untaught toolkit was designed to be utilized by small groups of participants (four to six) over two to eight hours (or a course of approximately sixteen weeks). We begin these workshops and courses by asking participants to engage in activities that walk them through a process designed to help them acknowledge their social identities. As they do this, they begin to build an understanding of the roles they each play in forming their own social identities and those of fellow community members and how these roles are affected by oppressive socio-cultural, political, and economic systems (among others). Engaging in the process of articulating and navigating their own stories as these transpire and then acknowledging the historical contexts within which they have evolved provides participants with the perspectives necessary to analyze the roles they play in upholding various systems of oppression. Jan Stets and Peter Burke, social scientists at Washington State University, study the way people perceive themselves and others and how these perceptions guide an individual's social identity. They offer the following insights on how society impacts self-perception: "Individuals are born into an already structured society. Once in society, people derive their identity or sense of self largely from the social categories to which they belong. Each person, however, over the course of his or her [or their] personal history, is a member of a unique combination of social categories; therefore, the set of social identities making up that person's self-concept is unique."[25]

The activities of acknowledging both a particular social structure and the roles one plays within it activate a form of self-identity rooted in what Stets and Burke refer to as "the psychological significance of a group membership."[26] These activities are engaged with before participants are introduced to the racialized design challenge, or prompt, that they will use to guide their critical analyses as the workshop progresses. This constitutes the first step that operates within the Racism Untaught framework. It has become an important activity for participants to complete prior to working with the rest of what comprises the Racism Untaught toolkit.

Initiating this activity entails providing participants with a list of just over thirty social identities that are accompanied by descriptions of the roles they play or occupy within it. We then ask participants to select five social identities from the categories they are comfortable sharing. Those identities include the "big eight": race, gender, sexual orientation, class, ethnicity, ability (or ableness), age, and religion. We acknowledge that there are many social identities that we do not list and that social identities are heavily informed by social ideologies and practices that operate within a particular culture. This has been especially evident in the international workshops we facilitated and manifests itself in how participants often provide context to frame the roles (privileged or marginalized) that reside or "operate" within each social identity category.

International participants assign different meanings to some social groups, encouraging a more nuanced discussion. The social identity groups listed for participants to select from are subdivided into the roles of privileged/powered or marginalized, which are designated positions or groups in many societies the world over. In the cultural norms in the United States, these roles take on particular meanings and are governed by culturally dominant identities. For example, one social identity group (or what we call a *group classifier*) that is listed is race. We provide the following articulations for the roles that operate within that social identity group: white people are listed under the "beneficiary/beneficiaries" group heading, and Black people, Indigenous people, people of color, and biracial/multiracial people are listed under the "involuntary benefactor(s)" groups heading. An example of the table we offer to communicate these categorizations is shown in figure 3.1. An example of a completed worksheet by the authors are in figures 3.2–3.7. Participants are presented with a worksheet that includes the categorical distinctions per social group identity that exists across a spectrum of privilege, power, and oppression. This worksheet is titled Socio-cultural Identities: Historical Invented and Constructed Classifications.

The only requirement for engaging in this activity is participants being asked to select the social group identity of race and then select whether they are in the beneficiaries or involuntary benefactors roles that comprise that group. As they engage in these selection processes, participants are afforded opportunities to discuss race in the design challenge that they will soon be prompted to undertake to ensure they have analyzed their own perception of race before participating in broader discussions about racism. Once they have completed these processes, participants are invited to choose four additional identities from the list of thirty-two that they can then discuss with their group.

MAKING INTENTIONAL ANTI-RACIST CHOICES

In addition to having hard conversations, we routinely ask workshop participants to consider these questions: (1) How does the knowledge or unawareness of our own identities affect the way we design? (2) What identities are at the forefront of your mind or the ones you lead with most? (3) How do your identities shape how you move about the world? We also ask workshop participants to consider how and why these questions affect how they perceive and how they might need to reperceive the artifacts, systems, and experiences they utilize and perhaps support on a day-to-day basis. One example of the work designers have begun to question centers on artist and designer Eric Gill, one of the most respected artists and designers of the twentieth century—who was also a convicted pedophile.[27] His work is included in the permanent displays of multiple museums, including the Ditchling Museum of Art + Craft[28] and the European headquarters of the United Nations at the Palais des Nations in Geneva. Designers continue to use the typefaces he designed, Perpetua and Gill Sans. The BBC asked the question, "Can the art of the pedophile be celebrated?"[29] Would this same difficulty not apply to forms of racialized design? It is critical that we identify invisible forms

Figure 3.1. Social identity worksheet.

of oppression that exist in design and ensure the acknowledgment of cultural habits that are considered invisible and that ultimately perpetuate various forms of oppression.[30]

These considerations are true for both the pedagogical approach to design and are exclusively inherent to the traditional practice of design. The design research process is not inherently inclusive.[31] Therefore, design interventions that question the colonial slant of design pedagogy are imperative to the progress of the contemporary practice of design. Tony Fry—principal designer at the Edge of the World; adjunct professor at the Creative Exchange Institute, University of Tasmania, Australia; and a visiting professor at Universidad de Ibagué, Tolima, Colombia, and Hong Kong Polytechnic University—writes, "How can a designer be designed to provide care via the designing of things that ontologically care? . . . It requires an understanding of design's implication in the state of the world and the worlds within it. To gain this understanding means fully grasping the scale and impact of design as an ontological force of and in the world in its making and unmaking."[32] It is vital to acknowledge the experience people bring to their design practice and provide them with the space to explore how their social identity will be present in their process of making. This inherent way of working requires an iterative process at the foundation of their practice to ensure an individual's skills and their own design practice are evolving and overlapping with the understanding of their positionality.

The continual, iterative nature inherent in the process of developing design interventions is important because meaning and language shift across time and space. As Freire writes, "As times change so do attitudes and beliefs."[33] His book *Pedagogy of the Oppressed* describes the importance of people's continual work toward an understanding of inclusive language. The Racism Untaught framework provides participants with an ever-growing and evolving set of terms to critically analyze forms of racialized design. To further anti-racist design decision-making, we address the toxic binary of power and privilege by creating space to discuss and acknowledge harm. This can be done through restorative design and a practice of transformative justice.[34] Students respond in a positive way to critically analyzing forms of racialized design and are motivated to work toward reimagining design approaches.

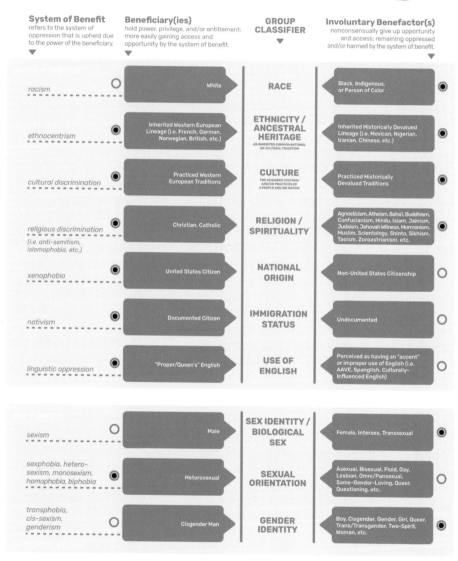

Figure 3.2. Lisa Elzey Mercer's social identity:
social + national and sex + gender.

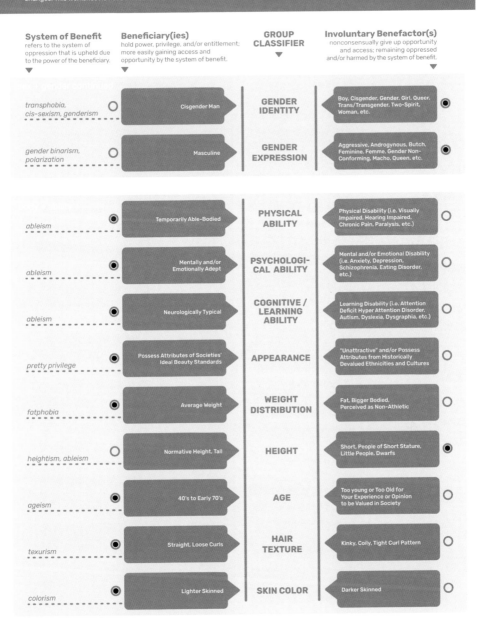

INSTRUCTIONS + DISCLAIMER
Use these worksheets to explore your socio-cultural identities and your positionality in the context of systems of oppression. Fill in the empty circles next to the beneficiary or involuntary benefactor that applies to your socio- cultural identity. **Note:** Be sure to consider context when using these guides; identity is nuanced, lives at a variety of intersectional experience, and does not live within a binary. Much like the Racism Untaught framework, this worksheet is iterative and will change as our language and culture of liberation changes. This worksheet is not exhaustive of all socio-cultural identities.

System of Benefit
refers to the system of oppression that is upheld due to the power of the beneficiary.

Beneficiary(ies)
hold power, privilege, and/or entitlement; more easily gaining access and opportunity by the system of benefit.

GROUP CLASSIFIER

Involuntary Benefactor(s)
nonconsensually give up opportunity and access; remaining oppressed and/or harmed by the system of benefit.

transphobia, cis-sexism, genderism — Cisgender Man — **GENDER IDENTITY** — Boy, Cisgender, Gender, Girl, Queer, Trans/Transgender, Two-Spirit, Woman, etc.

gender binarism, polarization — Masculine — **GENDER EXPRESSION** — Aggressive, Androgynous, Butch, Feminine, Femme, Gender Non-Conforming, Macho, Queen, etc.

ableism — Temporarily Able-Bodied — **PHYSICAL ABILITY** — Physical Disability (i.e. Visually Impaired, Hearing Impaired, Chronic Pain, Paralysis, etc.)

ableism — Mentally and/or Emotionally Adept — **PSYCHOLOGI-CAL ABILITY** — Mental and/or Emotional Disability (i.e. Anxiety, Depression, Schizophrenia, Eating Disorder, etc.)

ableism — Neurologically Typical — **COGNITIVE / LEARNING ABILITY** — Learning Disability (i.e. Attention Deficit Hyper Attention Disorder, Autism, Dyslexia, Dysgraphia, etc.)

pretty privilege — Possess Attributes of Societies' Ideal Beauty Standards — **APPEARANCE** — "Unattractive" and/or Possess Attributes from Historically Devalued Ethnicities and Cultures

fatphobia — Average Weight — **WEIGHT DISTRIBUTION** — Fat, Bigger Bodied, Perceived as Non-Athletic

heightism, ableism — Normative Height, Tall — **HEIGHT** — Short, People of Short Stature, Little People, Dwarfs

ageism — 40's to Early 70's — **AGE** — Too young or Too Old for Your Experience or Opinion to be Valued in Society

texurism — Straight, Loose Curls — **HAIR TEXTURE** — Kinky, Coily, Tight Curl Pattern

colorism — Lighter Skinned — **SKIN COLOR** — Darker Skinned

Figure 3.3. Lisa Elzey Mercer's social identity: sex + gender and body + ability.

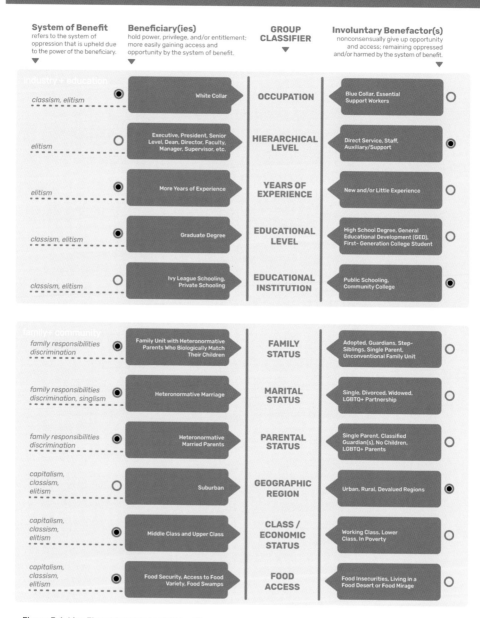

Figure 3.4. Lisa Elzey Mercer's social identity:
industry + education and family + community.

SOCIO-CULTURAL IDENTITIES

historically invented and constructed classifications

Terresa Moses's Socio-cultural Identity Profile

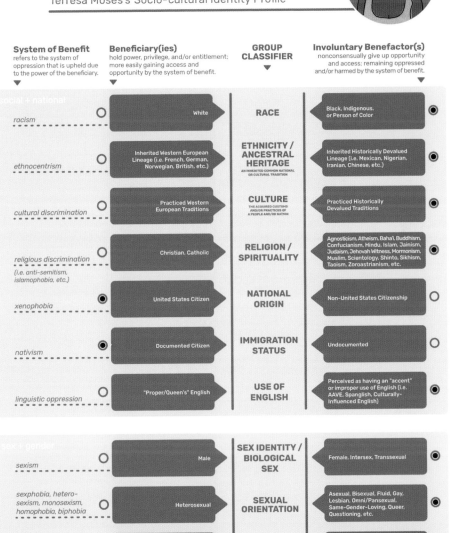

Figure 3.5. Terresa Moses's social identity:
social + national and sex + gender.

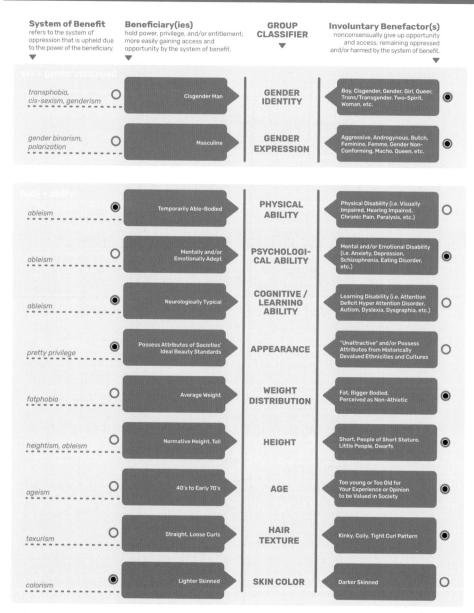

System of Benefit	Beneficiary(ies)	GROUP CLASSIFIER	Involuntary Benefactor(s)
refers to the system of oppression that is upheld due to the power of the beneficiary. ▼	hold power, privilege, and/or entitlement; more easily gaining access and opportunity by the system of benefit. ▼	▼	nonconsensually give up opportunity and access; remaining oppressed and/or harmed by the system of benefit. ▼

sex + gender continued

transphobia, cis-sexism, genderism	○ Cisgender Man	GENDER IDENTITY	Boy, Cisgender, Gender, Girl, Queer, Trans/Transgender, Two-Spirit, Woman, etc. ◉
gender binarism, polarization	○ Masculine	GENDER EXPRESSION	Aggressive, Androgynous, Butch, Feminine, Femme, Gender Non-Conforming, Macho, Queen, etc. ◉

body + ability

ableism	◉ Temporarily Able-Bodied	PHYSICAL ABILITY	Physical Disability (i.e. Visually Impaired, Hearing Impaired, Chronic Pain, Paralysis, etc.) ○
ableism	○ Mentally and/or Emotionally Adept	PSYCHOLOGI-CAL ABILITY	Mental and/or Emotional Disability (i.e. Anxiety, Depression, Schizophrenia, Eating Disorder, etc.) ◉
ableism	◉ Neurologically Typical	COGNITIVE / LEARNING ABILITY	Learning Disability (i.e. Attention Deficit Hyper Attention Disorder, Autism, Dyslexia, Dysgraphia, etc.) ○
pretty privilege	◉ Possess Attributes of Societies' Ideal Beauty Standards	APPEARANCE	"Unattractive" and/or Possess Attributes from Historically Devalued Ethnicities and Cultures ○
fatphobia	○ Average Weight	WEIGHT DISTRIBUTION	Fat, Bigger Bodied, Perceived as Non-Athletic ◉
heightism, ableism	○ Normative Height, Tall	HEIGHT	Short, People of Short Stature, Little People, Dwarfs ◉
ageism	○ 40's to Early 70's	AGE	Too young or Too Old for Your Experience or Opinion to be Valued in Society ◉
texurism	○ Straight, Loose Curls	HAIR TEXTURE	Kinky, Coily, Tight Curl Pattern ◉
colorism	◉ Lighter Skinned	SKIN COLOR	Darker Skinned ○

Figure 3.6. Terresa Moses's social identity: sex + gender and body + ability.

INSTRUCTIONS + DISCLAIMER
Use these worksheets to explore your socio-cultural identities and your positionality in the context of systems of oppression. Fill in the empty circles next to the beneficiary or involuntary benefactor that applies to your socio-cultural identity. **Note:** Be sure to consider context when using these guides; identity is nuanced, lives at a variety of intersectional experience, and does not live within a binary. Much like the Racism Untaught framework, this worksheet is iterative and will change as our language and culture of liberation changes. This worksheet is not exhaustive of all socio-cultural identities.

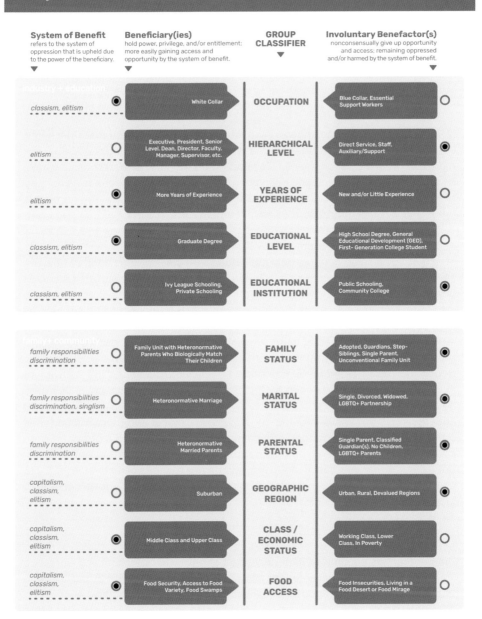

Figure 3.7. Terresa Moses's social identity: industry + education and family + community.

During each workshop, participants often expressed their desire for more time during each segment of the operation of the toolkit, particularly during the onboarding process. We have answered this request by discussing the plethora of opportunities that exist to continue their personal work toward understanding their positionality. We hope that participants in Racism Untaught workshops continue the lifelong journey of understanding their positionality to make well-informed and anti-oppressive design decisions. The onboarding process is often seen as a welcome beginning to conversations on race and racism. This process has helped participants become vulnerable and more aware of their own implicit and explicit biases, allowing them to engage in open dialogue about how their design decisions impact Black people, Indigenous people, or people of color.

We encourage readers to engage in an introspective practice so that they might come to better understand how and why their power, privilege, and specific marginalizations exist as they do. Facilitating the number of workshops we have has taught us that gaining and cultivating understanding is integral to leveraging the power of design processes and the outcomes they yield to counter numerous types and levels of oppression. We have found that when participants engage with self-assessments, it has been an effective way to understand how they "show up" and are perceived (by others and by themselves) in social spaces. These kinds of activities can also begin to help individuals and small groups analyze how the socialization of cultural norms contributes to how they show up and are perceived, internally and externally. We have also found that these kinds of activities are also important for educators, because there is often unchecked power held by instructors that can make for a toxic educational environment within which students are not inclined to learn. We would also encourage readers to explore how the traumas of systemic racism can manifest themselves in our bodies. Books such as *My Grandmother's Hands: Racialized Trauma and the Pathway to Mending Our Hearts and Bodies* by Resmaa Menakem[35] may also prove useful as guides for information and coping strategies regarding these issues. The work of anti-racism is not easily initiated, much less sustained, and there will be times during which well-intentioned efforts may unintentionally do more harm than good, but be encouraged: you may not be an expert on racism—or anti-racism—but as a designer or a design educator, you have a responsibility to at least try to use your power to affect the good of humanity, whether your efforts occur on a local, regional, national, or international scale.

ONBOARDING

Onboarding has become an imperative part of both the classroom and workshop learning experience. This segment allows for brave vulnerability as participants begin to discover more about themselves in the context of systemic oppression. Although participants feel vulnerable during these activities, we have noticed that this intentional time develops a sense of community and connection with their peers. Author bell hooks emphasizes the role vulnerability takes in the creation of a community, stating, "We can allow them to experience their vulnerability among a community of learners who will dare to hold them up should they falter or fail when triggered by past scenarios of shame—a community that will constantly give recognition and respect."[36] Ahead, we dive into specific activities and exercises we use during the classroom and workshop onboarding experience.

EXPLORING YOUR SOCIO-CULTURAL IDENTITY

Before we introduce the materials and racialized prompts to participants, we provide them with a worksheet that explores their socio-cultural identity (see figure 3.1). We encourage participants to explore all five socio-cultural identity areas: social + national; sex + gender; body + ability; industry + education; and family + community. Each worksheet explores one of the identity areas. The instructions and disclaimer on each worksheet are as follows: "Use these worksheets to explore your socio-cultural identities and your positionality in the context of systems of oppression. Fill in the empty circles next to the beneficiary or involuntary benefactor that applies to your socio-cultural identity. *Note:* Be sure to consider context when using these guides; identity is nuanced, lives at a variety of intersectional experiences, and does not live within a binary. Much like the Racism Untaught framework, this worksheet is iterative and will change as our language and culture of liberation changes. This worksheet is not exhaustive of all socio-cultural identities." Our worksheets emphasize that each area, or group classifier, is a historically invented and constructed classification. We have four columns total, each representing a different label—system of benefit, beneficiary/beneficiaries, group classifier, and involuntary benefactor(s)—which participants use to help them visually see their own positionality in each group classifier. *System of benefit* refers to the system of oppression that is upheld due to the power of the beneficiary. *Beneficiaries* hold power, privilege, and or entitlement, more easily gaining access and opportunity from the system of benefit. The *group classifier* refers to the specific historically invented and constructed classification of identity. And the *involuntary benefactor(s)* who nonconsensually give up opportunity and access remain oppressed and or harmed by the system of benefit.

For instance, the group classifier of race uses racism as a system of benefit upheld by the beneficiary, white people, and the involuntary benefactors, Black people, Indigenous people, and people of color (see figure 3.8).

As explained previously, participants are prompted to select five social identities; one of them is race because they are participating in a workshop focused on racism and should understand their positionality within that context. Once the participants have completed the worksheet, they are asked to place their five selected identities on the Social Identity Profile slide. In addition to their selections, they are asked three questions about each identity, including: (1) Which identities are you most aware of? (2) Which identities do you think about the least? (3) Do others perceive you this way? This slide is referenced during the first activity of the workshop. In small groups, participants are asked to share their five identities with each other and keep in mind the two following questions during their discussion: (1) What identities are at the forefront of your mind or the ones you lead with most? (2) How do your identities shape how you move about the world? After this step is complete, we often hear participants state, "I appreciated talking about social identities with my colleagues because we do not often have these conversations with each other."[37]

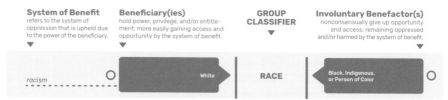

Figure 3.8. Socio-cultural identities: historical invented and constructed classifications: close-up of race. Social identities.

COLLABORATIVE COMMUNITY AGREEMENT

We provide participants with the opportunity to add their ideas to our community agreements (explored in more depth in the "Creating Space" section of this chapter). We direct them to an online collaborative whiteboard containing the five main areas of the community agreement (see figure 3.9). We ask participants to add one to three sticky notes per area. We provide examples of our own sticky notes that explain what that main area means for us. We also provide a link to a video with tips on using the online collaborative whiteboard platform. This step was not only to emphasize language and meaning in each area of the community agreement, but also to help familiarize participants with the online collaborative whiteboard platform before they attended the workshop.

WORKSHOP SURVEY

We ask workshop participants to complete a short survey to confirm attendance and to help us in gauging the learning levels of attendees. The information we collect helps us create the groups and anonymize the prompts (which participants provide) that we ultimately use for the workshop. Survey prompts and questions include the following:

- Email.
- First and last name.
- We recognize that there are many categories that make up your social identity. While these categories are extremely important to the identities we each hold, during the Racism Untaught workshop we want to provide resources to folks specifically within marginalized racial groups during the workshop. Please help us do so by answering the following question. How do you identify? *Depending on the participant's answer (Black, Indigenous, person of color, or white), the survey takes them to another question. All participants answer the same question, but only those who identify as Black, Indigenous, or a person of color see the next question.*

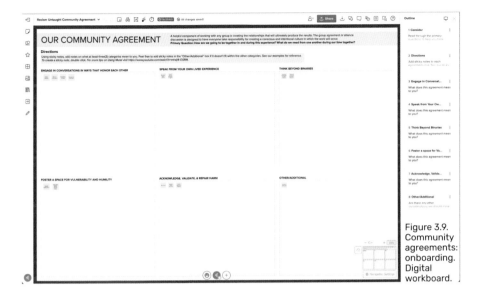

Figure 3.9. Community agreements: onboarding. Digital workboard.

- *Only if the participant identified as Black, Indigenous, or a person of color:* Participating in anti-racist workshops or trainings is often culturally taxing for racially marginalized individuals, who are often made to teach their white colleagues about the everyday racism they experience. We'd like for this workshop to be a positive experience for all participants. Would you like to be part of a breakout room that includes exclusively people who identify as a Black person, Indigenous person, or a person of color? *Participants answer with a yes or no. Overwhelmingly, they answer with yes.*
- *We list the community agreement as explained in the "Creating Space" section of this chapter, after which we ask:* Have you read the community agreement? Participants must check the Yes box to complete the survey.
- Do you need clarification on any points made in the community agreement? *Participants have the option to write in an answer or leave it blank.*
- During this workshop, we will be discussing and creating design approaches for real instances of racism at your institution/organization. We define *racism* as "the social construct of race as the primary determinant for the racially dominant culture to uphold conscious or subconscious beliefs, actions, and/or benefits that support systemic racial prejudice and oppression through power and privilege." To that point, are there any instances of racism that you have experienced or observed at your institution/organization that you feel comfortable writing about and that we can analyze in order to

create design approaches? Please tell your story without using specific names; these experiences will be shared without any personal identifiers. *Participants have the option to write in an answer or leave it blank.*

We use this survey to craft racialized prompts based on the answers in the last question. These real-world prompts are integral to the framework and internal design process, but also key to realizations about the realness of racism.

ONLINE COLLABORATIVE DOCUMENT

Specifically for workshops, we provide participants with a link to an online collaborative document entitled Racism Untaught + [enter organizational partner's name]. This document includes the date and log-in/location information for the workshop, our names or any additional facilitators' names, our phone numbers to contact us with any immediate group concerns to ensure anonymity, and numerous links for the duration of the workshop. Those links include the following:

- *Workshop online collaborative whiteboard links:* These links are activated on the first day of the workshop and lead participants to their specific group's digital working space.
- *Workshop facilitator presentation deck:* This is the slide deck the facilitators will present from during the workshop.
- *Socio-cultural Identities worksheet:* This is a written document that explores all five socio-cultural identity areas (Sociological + National, Sex + Gender, Body + Ability, Industrial + Educational, and Familial + Communal).
- *Social Identity Profile deck:* This is the slide deck participants use to create the social identity profiles they share with their group members during introductions.
- *Racism Untaught worksheet (and worksheet in large print):* This worksheet includes a breakdown of the Racism Untaught framework and the levels of oppression. It is available for each participant to print and take notes on (see figure 3.10).
- *Workshop digital report-out slide deck:* This slide deck is available for each group to report their progress through the workshop and their final ideas. It is only available during the eight-hour workshops.
- *Cards from the workboard in list form:* This online collaborative document is available for participants during online workshops in case they are having any issues using the online collaborative whiteboard.

ADDITIONAL CLASSROOM ONBOARDING ACTIVITIES

During the workshops, we only get a short amount of time to explore social identity and community agreement. During classroom learning experiences, we utilize approximately two weeks to onboard students on their positionality and a

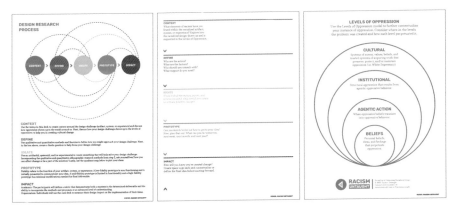

Figure 3.10. Racism Untaught handouts.

better understanding of race and racism. We use some of the following activities for classroom onboarding:

- *Introductory slides:* We instruct students to create short presentations about themselves. The participants are allotted four slides, each with a prompted question they can answer using text or images. Students have about twenty minutes to create the presentation and two minutes to present.

- *Racism Untaught bingo:* Students are instructed: "Find someone to talk with and choose a topic to discuss from one of the squares. Initial each other's sheet, then find a new person with whom to discuss a new topic." A bell is rung every two minutes to signal students to move to the next person and topic. Adapted from Kathy Obear, *Alliance for Change Consulting*, for the purposes of the class, there are six questions on the bingo sheets, which ask participants about concepts tied to their levels of comfort and nervousness when discussing issues about race, how well they understand racism, and their awareness of their own socialization to whiteness.[38] A short discussion is facilitated after the game to glean from student answers and ask questions.

- *"Where I'm From" poem:* In this adaptation of George Ella Lyons's community-based "I Am From Project,"[39] students are prompted to talk about their past in a way that critically analyzes their positionality and learned biases (see "Where I'm REALLY From"[40]). In addition to the poem, students are asked to craft a visual collage about themselves that they will present to the class as a projected image while they read their poem.

- *Can you find it?:* In this activity, students are instructed to find examples of racialized design that they can discuss during the next session. These examples of racialized design prompt conversation about racism in everyday life.

- *Guest speakers:* It is imperative that you are not the only voice during the classroom learning experience in order to validate and emphasize the importance of positionality. We bring in four to six guest speakers each semester to lead discussions and critique work with students.
- *Journaling and journey maps:* Participants end their onboarding with discussions on their new realizations about racism. They are provided the opportunity to journal about their learning experiences in a document that they eventually turn into a visual journey map.

COLLABORATIVE AND PARTICIPATORY DESIGN

We included six case studies in this book to explore how the Racism Untaught framework helps people working in collaborative and participatory design spaces to dismantle systems of oppression. We acknowledge that the work of anti-racism starts with the individual's journey of understanding their social identities and how they intersect with systems of oppression. The immediate next step in the framework is how they can begin to dismantle the system of racism in a collaborative workspace. It is important to take the time to nourish and build lasting relationships with individuals that can help to hold you accountable on your journey. We, as a culture, uphold an imperialistic and colonial thought that knowledge production by one person, by one individual, is the most important. Author adrienne maree brown emphasizes collaboration in her book *Emergent Strategy*: "The practice of collaborative ideation is about sharing that process as early as possible. This is not to say there is no space for individual creation . . . But how do we disrupt the constant individualism of creation when it comes to society, our shared planet, our resources?"[41] Typically, we place greater value on ideas produced by one person than ideas produced in community with one another. We each live and work in spaces where we are influenced by the people and things around us. We are influenced by our interactions with one another and with events that happen at the local, national, and global level. Audre Lorde emphasizes this point in her book *Sister Outsider* when she states, "Without community there is no liberation, but community must not mean a shedding of our differences, nor the pathetic pretense that these differences don't exist."[42] We must place as much value on *lived experience* (the knowledge gained from everyday lives) as we do on *learned experience* (the knowledge gained through formal education), doing so collaboratively.

We have seen the Racism Untaught framework support a group of participants in thinking and connecting on anti-oppressive ideas in a space where they are able to hold each other accountable for the impact of their outcomes. They are learning a new language, and new ways of thinking, and doing that supports a meaningful dialogue with one another. This space fosters the necessary relationships to create anti-oppressive work. John Thakara, a writer, curator, event producer, and visiting professor at Tongji University, wrote in his book *In the Bubble*, "The 'we' here is important. In a world of complex systems and constant change, we are all, unavoidably, 'in the bubble.' The challenge is to be both in the bubble and above it, at the same time—to be as sensitive to the big picture, and the destination we are headed for, as we are to the smallest details of the here and now."[43] A group setting provides participants with a space for discourse that elevates each other's work and ideas, which ultimately creates a strong foundation for innovation.

In the book *Decolonizing Methodologies: Research and Indigenous Peoples* by Linda Wuhiwai Smith, she acknowledges the changes to the research agenda of Indigenous peoples since she first wrote this book over twenty years ago in 1999. However, in the second edition of this book, published in 2021, she explains that there is still so much that offends: "It appalls us that the West can desire, extract and claim ownership of our ways of knowing, our imagery, the things we create and produce, and then simultaneously reject the people who created and developed those ideas and seek to deny them further opportunities to be creators of their own culture and own nations."[44] She acknowledges two different paths to making headway on an Indigenous research agenda: "The first one is through community action projects, local initiatives and national or tribal research based around claims. The second pathway is through the spaces gained within institutions by Indigenous research centers and study programmes."[45] The pathways invite us to be more intentional in a collaborative process. She recognizes that the movement of working collaboratively also presents new "problems and tensions." She poses the questions: "How do we avoid being complicit with colonization and colonizers, how do we break away from categories that slice and box up complex realities while at the same time we do not end up 'blunting the edge of the only knife we have' to communicate our experiences of violence?"[46] In our work, we have been asked to consider how providing elements of racism as terms perpetuates Western ideologies that are applied to that experience. We acknowledge the nuances that exist in creating terms that work to dismantle binary oppositions when working in community with one another, but we also see great value in being able to communicate and validate experiences with one another through this shared language. Without a shared language in a collaborative environment, we are not able to validate a specific experience, which then means we are not able to actively dismantle what we have no name for. Our hope is that this framework does not support a binary or dualistic opposition but is actively disrupting the status quo.

COMMUNITY CASE STUDY
Social Workers

YOU'RE TAKING OUR JOBS: SOCIAL WORKERS FROM CALIFORNIA

ORGANIZATION
Conducted an eight-hour workshop on Zoom, over two consecutive days, four hours each day using digital workboards (see figure 3.11).

TEAM
Facilitators: Lisa Elzey Mercer and Terresa Moses.
Participants: Sixty-six individuals total (twenty-nine from academia, twenty-six from government agencies, seven from non-government agencies, and four from the private sector). The group focused on in this case study had seven participants (four from government, two from academia, and one from the private sector) and will be referred to as "the group." This case study will only feature one group's progress. The racial makeup of the participants was twenty-nine people of color and thirty-seven white people.

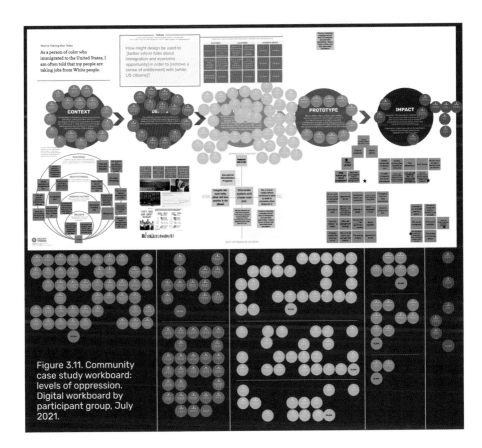

Figure 3.11. Community case study workboard: levels of oppression. Digital workboard by participant group, July 2021.

◀ ONBOARDING ACTIVITIES: PRE-WORKSHOP ACTIVITIES

Participants were provided with an email inviting them to the workshop to share space with us in the workshop. However, we asked them to complete a few onboarding activities approximately one week before the workshop began. We shared a document that had all the activities the participants were to complete. We entitled this shared informational document Racism Untaught + [insert partner name] which includes important links and pre-workshop activities such as the pre-workshop survey, the community agreement online activity, the Socio-cultural Identities worksheet, the workshop facilitator's slide deck, the shared Social Identity Profile slide deck, the Racism Untaught worksheet (which includes a map of the design research process and levels of oppression), the workshop digital report-out slide deck, and the cards from workboard document (which includes all the language from the workboard; see chapter 1 for more detailed descriptions).

◀ INTRODUCTION AND ONBOARDING: FIFTY-FIVE MINUTES

During the first session of the workshop, we read aloud a land acknowledgment, statement of unity, and community agreement. We acknowledged the additional agreements that the participants added in the pre-workshop activity. We provided participants with a link to an online collaborative document that included our names, our phone numbers to contact us with any immediate group concerns to ensure anonymity, and numerous links for the duration of the workshop.

◀ CONTEXT: ONE HOUR AND FIVE MINUTES

PROMPTS

In the survey for workshops conducted with industry and academia, we asked participants if there were any instances of racism they had experienced or observed that they felt comfortable writing about. We asked them to tell the story without using any personal identifiers to ensure that the story did not identify anyone personally. Before the workshop, we ensured that we anonymized those answers so that no one person could be directly associated with what was shared in the survey. These were used as prompts during the workshop. The workshops we have conducted often end with participants asking how the ideas that result from the workshop could be implemented in their workspace. This workshop had ten different prompts for ten different groups, and each of the prompts depicted real racialized experiences. When the participants were broken into their groups, they were also provided with links to the digital workboard that corresponded with the group number they worked with. The group prompt explored in this particular case study was as follows: "As a person of color who immigrated to the United States, I am often told that my people are taking jobs from white people."

CARDS

Once participants in the group read the prompt, they took turns and read aloud each context card to decide as a group if the element of racism applied to the prompt. If it did, they moved the card up to the context circle; if not, the card remained where it was. A few of the cards they selected included the following:

- *Xenophobia:* An extreme or irrational fear or disdain of people from different countries. *Rationale:* It is relevant to this prompt because of the displaced dislike of someone we most likely do not know, and we rely on negative depictions of immigrants in the media as a reference.
- *Othering:* To view or treat a Black, Indigenous, or person of color as intrinsically different from and alien to oneself, also known as exclusion. *Rationale:* The idea that immigrants could not fit into the work culture and should not be hired to work as colleagues.
- *Nativism:* Policies or systems favoring native inhabitants as opposed to immigrants. *Rationale:* Nepotism hiring, when we only hire people we know and who are from the same or very similar social groups as those the dominant culture belongs to.
- *Systemic racism:* Inequalities rooted in the system-wide operation of a society that exclude members of particular racial groups from significant participation in major social institutions. *Rationale:* This term shows how racism is perpetuated in our hiring systems, including recruitment, hiring, retention, and promotion practices.

LEVELS OF OPPRESSION

In the second part of step one, the group worked together with the levels of oppression model to further contextualize the instances of oppression that showed up within the prompt they had been given (see figure 3.12). They were asked to consider how and where, in the different levels, oppression is introduced, reinforced, and perpetuated:

- *Beliefs:* Personal beliefs, ideas, and feelings that perpetuate oppression. *Rationale:* People of color are lazy and will not fit into the culture of our workspace.
- *Agentic action:* When oppressive beliefs translate into oppressive behavior. *Rationale:* Accusing people of color who are immigrants of taking jobs away.
- *Institutional:* Structural oppression that results from agentic oppressive behavior. *Rationale:* Institutionally, this shows up in human resources policies and immigration laws.
- *Cultural:* Systems of norms, values, beliefs, and trusted systems of acquiring truth that preserve, protect, and maintain oppression. *Rationale:* Depiction of the types of jobs immigrants have in movies or in the media that are focused on labor and service.

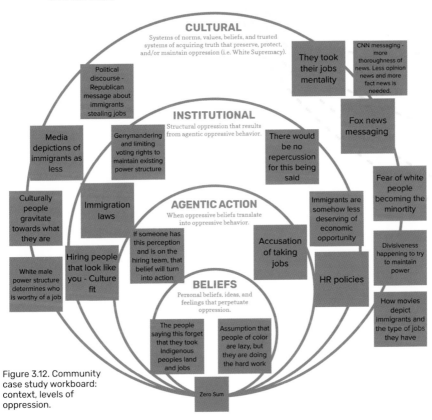

Figure 3.12. Community case study workboard: context, levels of oppression.

◀ DEFINE: ONE HOUR AND FIVE MINUTES

The groups were asked to begin by reviewing the cards in the define step. This provided participants with the opportunity to find value and understanding in the number of qualitative and quantitative research methods available for them to further contextualize and analyze the prompt. The group chose the following methods:

- *Intersection theory:* A theory that suggests we cannot separate the effects of race, class, gender, sexual orientation, and other attributes. This is a theory.
- *Narrative identity theory:* A framework that investigates how individuals form an identity by integrating their life experiences into an internalized, evolving story of the self that provides the individual with a sense of unity and purpose in life. This is a theory.
- *Case studies:* A research method involving an up-close, in-depth, and detailed examination of a subject of study (the case), as well as its related contextual conditions. This is a method.

Figure 3.13. Community case study workboard: define. Participants selected research collected from the popular media search they conducted as a group.

Once this was done, participants were asked to conduct a popular media search, a method for participants to search popular forms of media to gain further context on their prompt. Participants were encouraged to discuss the findings with each other, pull quotes from articles, and take screenshots of the articles or images used (see figure 3.13).

The question participants created from what they learned from secondary sources was: "How might design be used to better inform folks about immigration and economic opportunity in order to remove a sense of entitlement with white US citizens?" When participants created their question, they began by using a breakdown we included to the right of the question, a space on the digital workboard separated into three different areas. It prompted them to consider: What *change* do they want to happen? What *actions* need to happen for that change to occur? *Who* needs to be involved for those changes to be sustainable? Each participant's voice was needed in this section to ensure the question was created collaboratively (see figure 3.14).

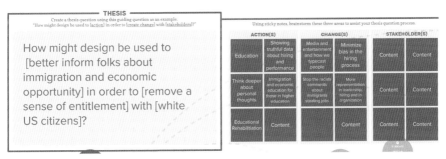

Figure 3.14. Community case study workboard: define. Participants' thesis question.

◀ IDEATE: THIRTY-FIVE MINUTES IN SESSION ONE, FIFTY MINUTES IN SESSION TWO

THE CARDS

The ideate step contains the most cards, divided into the three identifiers in this research study: artifacts, systems, and experiences (further explored in chapter 2). Participants were prompted to review the cards in this step (see figure 3.15). They were asked to consider how they could create a combination of these ideas to create a system that would help answer their question. Some of the cards the participants chose were the following:

- *Role playing:* The acting out of the part of a particular person or character—for example, as a technique in training or psychotherapy. This term fell within the experience section of design.
- *Book:* A written or printed work consisting of pages glued or sewn together along one side and bound in covers. This term fell within the artifact section of design.

- *Community support:* Services that support community well-being, such as after-school activities for children. This term fell within the system section of design.

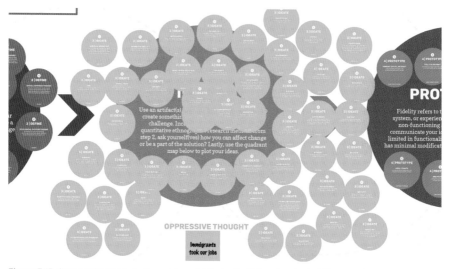

Figure 3.15. Community case study workboard: ideate. Participants selected these cards.

QUADRANT MAP

The quadrant map is an intervention meant to prompt conversation on ideation in collaborative spaces. Participants were asked between sessions to write down their ideas for answering the question they had created based on everything they had completed in the workshop so far (see figure 3.16). Each participant wrote down an idea. However, the group wanted to include their prompt on the quadrant map with a sticky note that read, "Immigrants took our jobs," and placed it as an intentional oppressive thought.

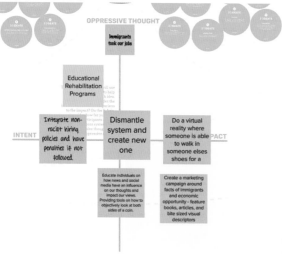

Figure 3.16. Community case study workboard: ideate. Participant ideas.

Once the participants returned for the second session, their ideas were listed on a sticky note and the groups were placed back into their breakout rooms to discuss where the sticky notes should be placed on the quadrant map. Often, the participants noticed that a combination of ideas was truly the only way to achieve impact. We as facilitators often mentioned in this step that the phrase "that wasn't my intention" is overstated and that we need to work toward understanding the impact of the designs we place into the public domain.

◉ PROTOTYPE: ONE HOUR AND TEN MINUTES

In this step of the framework, we introduced three different levels of prototyping, low-, mid-, and high-fidelity prototypes. During the eight-hour workshop, participants did not have time to complete the mid- and high-fidelity prototypes, so they were asked to focus on making a low-fidelity prototype. They were asked to review all the prototype cards in this step (approximately thirty cards).

The low-fidelity prototype is the initial, raw presentation of an idea. The participants developed two sketches and a flow chart with sticky notes to present their ideas (see figures 3.17 and 3.18). Their ideas included hosting listening sessions to hold space for community members to discuss race and racism and to learn from each other. They created two questions that would lead the listening sessions: (1) What scares you about immigration? (2) What are your biggest fears concerning immigration? Some of the items the groups listed for the community listening sessions were offering a space to amplify articles focused on the benefits of immigrants, hiring community members with knowledge in this specific area to guide conversations, providing fact sheets, watching movies focused on issues of immigration to prompt discussion, and working with immigrant interest groups, elected officials, and candidates to influence policy.

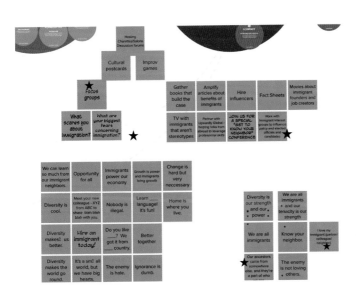

Figure 3.17. Community case study workboard: prototype. This is the work developed by the group to communicate its ideas.

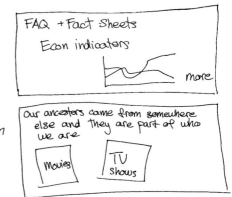

Diversity is our Strength + Power

I love my immigrant partner

:-) :-)

We are all immigrants and our tenacity is our Strength

Book recommendation

Know your neighbor
Join a Charette

Culture postcard

FAQ + Fact Sheets
Econ indicators

more

Our ancestors came from somewhere else and they are part of who we are

Movies

TV Shows

Figure 3.18. Community case study workboard: prototype. This is the sketches of low-fidelity visuals developed by the group to communicate its ideas.

◀ IMPACT: FORTY-FIVE MINUTES

The group was asked to select the impact cards they were most interested in implementing to further understand the impact of their idea. In this step, we reminded all participants that this framework was iterative. When we further understand the impact of our work, we can do more research to help us ideate the prototyping of more ideas and to ensure that we are working toward a positive impact. They selected the following:

- *Listening sessions:* Similar to a focus group, this is a type of facilitated discussion with a group of people aimed at collecting information about their experience and/or experiential knowledge.
- *Vision statement:* This shows and tells a comprehensive outline of what the organization will bring to the wider community.
- *Strategy plan workshop:* This creates organizational strategies and aligns them with proposed solutions, such as policy changes.

FINAL PRESENTATION: FORTY-FIVE MINUTES

◀ In the final presentation, the participants in the group presented the work they completed together. We asked that only one or two individuals from each group present to ensure they meet the time limit of five minutes. The groups were provided with a slide deck and were asked to fill in the five slides per group, one slide per step of the framework (see figure 3.19). There was an introductory slide for each group that included the group's prompt.

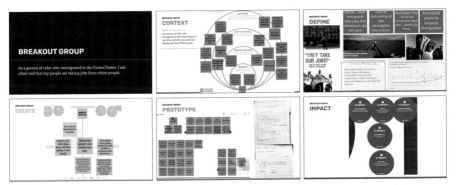

Figure 3.19. Community case study workboard: presentation. Participants presented the work they completed in the eight-hour workshop.

◐ CHALLENGES

Participants are often hesitant about committing to an eight-hour workshop focused on race and racism, but at the end of the workshop participants often state they wished it was longer. This workshop was very similar, and we reminded participants that they have their whole lives to learn more about their social identities and how those identities uphold or perpetuate systems of oppression. The following are quotes from the participants about their experience during the workshop :

> It was very refreshing to have open conversations and be comfortable (talking about racism). Lately, it hasn't felt like you can do that in a work setting. It was refreshing. The first exercise opened the door for conversations that made everybody very comfortable and at ease. We were able to roll up our sleeves and tackle this (racism) in an open and respectful manner. I really enjoyed it, Thank you.[47]

> I wanted to share that even though I consider myself very knowledgeable on this topic, it is fascinating to see the complexity of racism. There are definitions now compared to a couple of years ago they clearly defined the cost of a lot of people's behaviors. The takeaway is that I wished those who are critical and in the media use the term so loosely that they really would take the time to really look into what (racism) really means and how it affects people's lives. They talk about it so loosely by saying, "(Teachers) are trying to teach critical race theory, and they are screwing with education." They are talking about it (racism) in a way that is completely unrelated to what it really is and what it does to a community and our society because it affects everybody at all levels.[48]

I really appreciate being able to do this work in small groups. I was able to really hear other people's perspectives and also see the struggle that I'm having with some of the terminology and verbiage, that it's not just me. This has been really helpful to have these conversations, so I thank you so much I really appreciate this.[49]

I appreciated the facilitation and how you both guided us through some intense tools that allowed us to unpack the nuance and complexity of these issues that we generally don't have a vocabulary for. We also had space for imagination in support of getting us from seeing what's happening to the point where we were able to think through various ways of doing something about it.[50]

RACISM DOES NOT ALWAYS LOOK THE SAME. IN OUR DEFINITION OF RACISM WE NEED TO INCLUDE PREJUDICE, DISCRIMINATION, BIAS, AND BIGOTRY. THESE ARE ALL MANIFESTATIONS OF THE SAME ROOT PROBLEM—RACISM

4

SHARED LANGUAGE

THE ROLE OF LANGUAGE IN CONTEXTUALIZING

The ability to identify and discuss designs that have supported the overgeneralization of historically marginalized communities is imperative to guide a social shift in the design community. This thread of research originated from our facilitation of more than thirty workshops (over two hundred hours) attended by over two thousand participants. When discussing racism, we are often missing the language that would help us create connections for the relationships among racialized design, how we interact with it, and how it shapes our relationships with each other. Having a shared language to discuss the nuances of racism when we work in a collaborative design process is imperative to progress. Suppose this was missing in a human-centered space, where we are intentionally working to collaborate and design with each other. In that case, we would not be able to develop outcomes that dismantle oppression.

Over the past few years, we have worked to iteratively develop the cards, the workboard, and other design interventions that make up the Racism Untaught framework. Through participants' verbal and written comments and feedback, we have learned the immense value of how a shared language can dismantle forms of racialized design. Over time, participants have shared with us the ways they were learning and the important factors they took with them after participating in our workshops. We heard this through the oral accounts of the participants' shared experiences, how participants interacted with the framework, and how they reimagined forms of racialized design using the framework. As we iteratively worked to shape the framework, we learned how a shared, more precise language validates the lived experiences of people of color and how a more ambiguous language highlights the alienation, trauma, and lack of community that can be the result of a racist experience. When we are working to dismantle systems of oppression, we need to work in a team environment with the tools to discuss racism directly and accurately. This chapter outlines the value of a shared language to discuss forms of racialized design.

In our discussions with participants, we often hear people explain the use of a derogatory word by saying, "To me, that word means . . . " But the structure and meaning of every word, including derogatory words, are pulled from the context of our culture and seen through our individual lens. When we hear any word, we typically think of the definition held by the dominant culture. For example, if we think of a term of endearment that we commonly hear in our culture, such a word typically conveys or conjures feelings of love and a form of care. When we think of a term of degradation, it typically conveys or conjures feelings of hate or fear. Until recently, few words known by the dominant culture have provided a shared language to discuss the nuances of racism, essentially gaslighting the experiences of Black people, Indigenous people, and people of color, limiting the ability to process and understand a personal experience with racism openly and effectively. Language provides people with the agency to self-validate a positive or negative lived experience and validates each other's lived experiences. Linguistic anthropologists study cultures through language and see that language is "not just a passive means of referring to or describing phenomena in the world, but creates social relations in cultural contexts."[2] Through Racism Untaught, we are shifting culture in both design outcomes and in participants' relation to the dominant culture.

Over the past two years, since the murder of George Floyd, we have seen an increase in a language in our dominant culture that is more widely available to us to identify, acknowledge, and describe various forms of racism. In 1963, James Baldwin wrote in *The Fire Next Time*: "For the horrors of the American Negro's life there has been almost no language. The privacy of his experience, which is only beginning to be recognized in language, and which is denied or ignored in official and popular speech."[3] We have mentioned previously that culture, time, and place shift language. A shared language allows us to recognize and acknowledge the lived experiences of Black people, Indigenous people, and people of color in our communities with cross-cultural tools that positively influence communication. Audre Lorde explained it this way: "The transformation of silence into language and action is an act of self-revelation."[4] When we are making decisions to be anti-racist, we are working to transform not only the dominant culture but also ourselves. We are working to create a culture of awareness with a shared language that acknowledges the nuances of racism and other forms of oppression.

In the book *Atlas of the Heart*, Brené Brown analyzes our relationship to language: "Having access to the right words can open up entire universes. When we don't have the language to talk about what we're experiencing, our ability to make sense of what's happening and share it with others is severely limited. Without accurate language, we struggle to get the help we need. . . . Language shows us that naming an experience doesn't give the experience more power, it gives us the power of understanding and meaning."[5] We have come to recognize that creating shared language empowers participants who may have felt powerless and unvalidated in their racialized experiences. Brown also notes that limited language exists to express feelings when she asks, "What does it mean if the vastness of human emotion and experience can only be expressed as mad, sad, or happy?" She continues to wonder, "What about shame?"[6] The same holds true for racism. If we rely on the media and Hollywood portrayals of racism to exemplify what racism is, then we will have a limited and narrow idea of what it is, who it affects, and how it shows up in the world around us. We might think that a racist person is one who wears a white hood, carries a tiki torch, or aligns themselves with cultural ideologies that politicize racism. In truth, and in addition too, people who uphold racialized ideologies exist covertly in our everyday lives and shape our everyday experiences.

We are often asked, "What is the difference between someone who says they are not racist and someone who says they are anti-racist?" Someone who states they are not racist is ignorant of or unwilling to acknowledge how the social constructs they identify with support oppression. They are unwilling to understand the benefits they receive due to the system of racism. Someone who says they are anti-racist is a person who is actively working to dismantle systems of oppression. They understand how they benefit from the oppression of others and actively work against that system. This can look different for everyone. This could be protesting, crafting new policies, supporting companies owned by people of color, or reading more books written by Black people, Indigenous people, and people of color. As we broaden our lived experiences, we will begin to learn and have a more enriched understanding of language that explains the nuances of racialized artifacts, systems, and experiences. For instance, shared language can begin to help us understand the stereotypical and harmful language "about inequality that made 'black' the virtual equivalent of 'poor' and 'lower class,' thus creating a distinctive idiom that has no parallel in other Western democracies."[7] We need language to accurately share experiences and uncover racialized wrongs so that we can dismantle forms of racialized design in a more precise way.[8]

Another example of shared language and its effects on our culture is one that describes the harm that many women experience. Although this harm has happened since women were able to join the workforce, it was not until 1975[9] that the term *sexual harassment* was coined by Cornell University feminist activists to specifically describe the intimidation and exploitation women were experiencing, providing a term that had not previously existed for this shared experience.[10] This shared knowledge and way of speaking created a collective understanding for a group of people to validate and talk about their experiences. A shared language also helps overcome hermeneutical marginalization—that is, "the injustice of having some significant area of one's social experience obscured from collective understanding."[11] Matching an experience with a term enables an individual to understand mistreatment and then take measures to prevent that experience from happening again.

In her book, Brené Brown shared a quote from philosopher Ludwig Wittgenstein: "The limits of my language mean the limits of my world."[12] We have seen workshop participants respond in joyful ways when given the ability to match an experience with an element of racism in the context step. The cards that contain the elements of racism are the cards that participants will often try to take when we conduct an in-person workshop. We had one participant ask if they could take the set of cards with them to keep in their desk at work. This way, when they experienced racism, they could take a card out of their desk and say, "This [insert element of racism] is what you are doing right now."[13] The empowerment of being able to identify a racist experience and then immediately process it with the correct term provided that person with more agency and self-advocacy. Brown mentions the importance of being able to create connections through language when we are processing information. This is exactly what excited the participant.[14] We see this time and again with participants who identify as Black, Indigenous, or people of color.

Through the use of shared language, we often see a sense of enlightenment among participants who identify as white. We hear this when white participants say things such as, "I didn't know there were so many words that describe the nuances of racism. If I am missing this [insert element of racism], what else am I missing?" Language can provide us with a validating community of witnesses or those who have experienced racism themselves. We are able to deconstruct white supremacy and systems of inequality with language. "Breaking down power and privilege by acquiring language and recognizing shared narratives enables us to see and name inequity and shame."[15] Feelings of isolation and alienation by people of color are perpetuated by only validating the binary perspective in our culture (more about the binary in chapter 3). We are not either good or bad, racist or not racist; we do not have all the power or no power; and we do not have all the privileges or no privileges. Language allows us to break down the binary and dualistic perspectives of racism. The ambiguity of racism often makes participants feel uncomfortable when exploring racism. It is okay—in fact, it is normal—to feel uncomfortable in the space of discovering and learning a new language that allows us to engage in conversations on race and racism in a real way. Language is important; "words mean things. The things they mean can have an insidious effect on how we see the world, ourselves, and each other."[16]

Brown goes on to describe language as "a portal to meaning-making, connection, healing, learning, and self-awareness. Having access to the right words changes everything." It is important to contextualize, to build a shared understanding of identifying the elements of racism that are present in a designed artifact, system, or experience because it validates the lived experience for Black and brown people, and it is an important part of dismantling systems of oppression. Dr. Susan David, Harvard Medical School psychologist, discusses with Brown the importance of understanding our emotions. She explains that when we do not validate or listen to each other's experiences, we are essentially saying, "My comfort is more important than your reality."[17] She further explains that when we are not able to listen to each other without trying to change the narrative of someone else's experience, it stops us from "truly understanding what it is that they are experiencing in a more nuanced, precise, and effective way."[18] As a result of the generative research we have conducted in our workshops, we have come to recognize the words that more accurately identify racial trauma and the frustration experienced by Black people, Indigenous people, or people of color who do not have the words to express their harm. Not being able to describe our lived experiences in words has an impact on the mental health of people who, daily, are not able to put words to their lived experiences.

Audre Lorde discusses this idea in her book *Sister Outsider*: "What are the words you do not yet have? What do you need to say? What are the tyrannies you swallow day by day and attempt to make your own, until you will sicken and die of them, still in silence?"[19] In this book, she has titled one chapter "The Transformation of Silence into Language and Action," in which she speaks to the experience of Black women in our culture who have been "rendered invisible through the depersonalization of racism."[20] She acknowledges the importance of words and shared language to discuss racism without fear and to draw attention to those whose voices are silenced.

In many institutions, we interact with buzzwords like *diversity*, *decolonization*, and *equality*, which each skirt past the more nuanced issues of racism that exist. When this happens, it enables our culture to be apathetic and ignore the real issues of oppression. Diversity, equity, and inclusion are institutional buzzwords associated with planning and doing social-justice-centered work. They are palatable words that many organizations use to avoid the uncomfortable conversations that would happen if they admitted their organization was systematically affected by overt or more insidious manifestations of racism, sexism, homophobia, ableism, and so on. These palatable buzzwords problematically conflate racism and sexual harassment with "bullying." This kind of downplaying is a barrier to both progress and the uncovering of oppressive systems that further perpetuate the marginalizing nature of systems—systems that have been designed and operationalized to affect how we live, work, and play.

THE ETHICS OF DETERMINING A SHARED LANGUAGE

The use of a shared language provides collaborative partners with the opportunity to focus on multiple elements of racialized design and reimagine new solutions and changes in patterns while working together to disrupt the continuum of overgeneralization. If we continue to work with a vague perspective of racism, it allows Black people, Indigenous people, and people of color to be painted with broad strokes of understanding and for systems to perpetuate inequality. A change in design would provide a strong foundation for developing work that is able to recognize both visible and invisible forms of racialized design. Often people explain design as problem solving. Ezio Manzini speaks to design as problem solving: "This interpretation of what design can do, though important and widely expressed, is not the only one: we can also talk about design while moving away from this approach, oriented toward problems to solve, and focus on a definition that highlights its role in the field of culture, and therefore of language and meaning."[21] This is such an important part for designers to remember, that in order for cultural shifts to take place, "the constants—media, language, repertoire, appreciative systems, overarching theory, and role frame— are also subject to change. They tend to change over periods of time, longer than a single episode of practice, although events may trigger their change."[22]

This cultural change also requires designers to be aware of and have more knowledge of racialized design. The ethics of using a shared language to make sense of a racialized form of design depends on the social cognition connected to an artifact, system, or experience. This social cognition does not depend solely on an individual's understanding but on the "shared intention of social group members who constitute a particular institution." Social groups discuss whether an idea can be believed or denied based on our observations of what something is.[23] How, then, do designers conclude that a design is perpetuating the overgeneralization of a historically oppressed community? Racism Untaught provides the design community with language and interventions that seek to understand the social experiences of those who encounter racialized design firsthand and need to communicate their knowledge of a lived experience.[24]

A designer makes an artifact, system, or an experience. Sometimes they make the outcome; more often, they make a representation of it—a plan, program, or image, often an idea to be constructed by others. They work in particular situations, use particular materials, and employ a distinctive medium and language. Typically, what they are making is complex. There are more variables than can be represented in a finite model. Because of this complexity, the designer's actions or decisions tend to, happily or unhappily, produce consequences other than those intended. When this happens, the designer may take account of the unintended changes they have made in the situation by forming a new appreciation and understanding and by making new choices. They shape the situation in accordance with their initial appreciation of it, which requires reflection.[25] It is imperative for designers to learn a process they can incorporate into their making that results in responsible design, where they are critically contextualizing an artifact, system, or experience. Manzini acknowledged the value of "finding a language that enables us to talk about the function and form, the utility and beauty, not only of material objects but also of relationship systems."[26]

By doing this, not only do we develop a shared language, but we are also able to focus on the impact of the outcomes we deliver. This will move us past the status quo of the design research processes and require that we think more deliberately about the processes we are engaged with and whether we are producing outcomes that are equitable and innovative. "In our case, these conversations occur between various social actors who are all interested in achieving the same result (for example, in resolving a problem or opening a new possibility), and who follow an innovative path to achieve it, breaking with established ways of thinking and doing things."[27] Participants in our workshops often end up asking how their group-created anti-racist design approaches will be implemented in their work environments. The framework provided them with a language for talking about the systems of oppression that exist around them and the interventions provided with the tools to more accurately dismantle those systems of oppression.[28] One participant in our workshop shared with us, "I think a shared language for DEI and anti-racist work is really important for a company/organization to all understand and adopt. It's a hard topic for some and going through this workshop can help people navigate how to talk about it and start thinking about how to make changes."[29]

As a society, we continue to create racialized design while arguing the need to be "untaught" racism. This contradiction or cognitive dissonance results in our blaming others for racist incidents while distancing from social justice movements. The fear of engaging leads us to do nothing, which sets us up to actively perpetuate systems of oppression. It is our hope that Racism Untaught can help rectify this disconnect and positively impact our communities in order to develop new and inclusive design at any level. This effort is necessary to redesign how individuals engage with and create artifacts, systems, and experiences to break down systemic racism. We have begun creating additional cards focused on sexism and ableism to work toward an intersectional conversation on oppression. The goal is to extend the framework's shared language to include homophobia, transphobia, cissexism, the gender binary, ageism, and other forms of oppression. We will continue to research and develop tools that participants can use to identify racialized design and critically assess anti-racist design concepts while developing space for a dialogue on racism and racialized design. These conversations require a safe and brave space to allow participants to speak to their own experiences with racialized design or convey knowledge and validation of these experiences. These types of conversations are imperative to guide the social shift in collaborative design environments.

DEVELOPING AND LEARNING A SHARED VOCABULARY

In our work, we emphasize impact over intention. Words have and communicate deliberate meanings within given societal contexts, and being specific about the words participants choose to use is essential to the design process. Clarity helps individuals to contextualize and not make assumptions. During the onboarding step, participants can process their positionality within their group (explored in depth in chapter 3). It is helpful to understand that our reactions will be informed by our lived experiences before we begin to reimagine an artifact, system, or experience that perpetuates oppression. For instance, when participants talk about their racial identity versus their ethnicity, it is an important opportunity to uncover areas of privilege and power associated with their experiences. Understanding the complexities of participants whose racial identity differs from their ethnicity can be hard for some, so taking time in this process of unlearning racial biases is important. Purposeful language used throughout onboarding sets participants up to be intentional throughout the design process. It also helps people understand how meaning can shift depending on a context, time, and culture. Being sensitive to how we express ourselves and how we accept the expression of others helps everyone in the research process feel comfortable making mistakes and learning from one another.

The context cards that outline elements of racism create a shared understanding of racialized designs and how this shared language became an essential thread of research. We ask participants to use the terms in this deck (see figure 4.1) to create context around the identifier they have been given and discuss how forms of oppression are perpetuated and supported in the world around us, and to indicate which elements are relevant to the identifier, why they are relevant, and which are not (further explored in chapter 1). Through the execution of courses and workshops, we acknowledge the need for a foundation of a shared language in the practice of design. A foundation that provides participants with the ability to identify and discuss racialized design is valuable. It enables participants to responsibly contribute to design and acknowledge their agency to influence rhetoric in the public domain. Using the framework, participants apply the design research process to identify racialized design and critically assess anti-racist design approaches.

Initially, our intention behind running the workshop numerous times was to iteratively improve the design interventions we had developed. We intentionally ran the first workshop at a conference with like-minded designers and researchers—people who conduct research to critically analyze and reimagine systems of oppression or as a form of activism. We did this to make sure all the words in the framework, especially in the first step, were as comprehensive as possible. We included five blank cards in each deck for each step of the process so that participants could write words and definitions they thought were missing. We began to run the workshop at conferences that had a more contemporary view

Figure 4.1. Context step showing shared language. A close-up of the Racism Untaught toolkit step titled *context*, which has been used with a group of participants in a workshop to analyze a racialized prompt.

of design and with a broader set of topics. This helped us refine the words and definitions even more. We continued to add words and create and apply our own definitions based on these conversations. In the first prototype of the framework, we had approximately thirty words. The framework now has approximately seventy-five words.

As we mentioned previously, once a workshop is complete, there are usually a few participants who ask for or take a copy of the first deck of cards. This applies to both white people and people who hold racially marginalized identities. Black people, Indigenous people, or people of color want to take the cards due to a feeling and sense of empowerment and validation, whereas white people who wanted these cards hoped to use them to learn about racism, how they might see their own racialized actions, speak up when seeing others take racialized action, and dismantle racialized design. Both groups were seeking a shared language to speak more accurately of their own social experiences with racialized design, as oppressed and oppressor. The following ten terms are examples of cards in the context step of the Racism Untaught framework specific to racism:

- *Aversive racism:* A form of implicit bias in which a person persistently avoids interaction with other racial and ethnic groups
- *Blockbusting:* The convincing of white property owners to sell their houses at low prices by promoting fear that racial minorities will be moving into the neighborhood
- *Cultural erasure:* Forcing non-Western cultural groups to adopt Western culture, including; attire, the English language, Christianity, and Western birth names, etc
- *Exoticism:* Objectifying, othering, sexualizing, and/or dehumanizing Black, Indigenous, women and femmes who hold racially marginalized identities who do not align or fit within Eurocentric beauty standards, also known as *racialized sexism*
- *Implicit bias:* The subconscious beliefs about members of social and cultural groups
- *Intent over impact:* Prioritizing well-intended actions over the negative impact they might have on a individual who identify as a Black person, Indigenous person, or person of color
- *Microinvalidation:* An interaction that passively excludes or negates the experiences, feelings, and experiential reality of a Black person, Indigenous person, or person of color (e.g., "You have good hair, so you are not really Black").
- *Nativism:* Policies or systems favoring native inhabitants, as opposed to immigrants
- *Redlining:* The racially influenced and systematic denial of various residential services, including access to specific neighborhoods, through selectively raising of prices
- *Xenophobia:* An intense or irrational fear or distain of people from different countries

THE INTERSECTIONALITY OF THE FRAMEWORK

We acknowledge the value of intersectionality when discussing different forms of oppression and how they intersect with each other. We have begun running workshops using the cards focused on different elements of oppression. The reason we began with racism is that it was evident through observation that participants were more comfortable talking about other forms of oppression over the topic of racism. The additional elements we have added are focused on sexism and ableism. Kimberlé Crenshaw speaks to the importance of overlapping marginalized identities: "Intersectionality is a lens through which you can see where power comes and collides, where it interlocks and intersects."[30]

SEXISM

We define *sexism* as a person's sex classification being the primary determinant for the male-dominant culture to uphold conscious or subconscious beliefs, actions, and/or benefits that support systemic patriarchy and oppression through power and privilege (prejudice + power over + privilege)—for example, male over female or intersex individuals. The following ten terms are examples of cards in the context step of the Racism Untaught framework specific to sexism:

- *Body shaming:* Humiliating someone by criticizing their body shape or size
- *Commodity feminism:* The way it appropriates feminist ideology for capitalistic purposes, typically emptied of their political significance and offered back to the public in a commodified form
- *Gender role expectations:* Assumed roles socially attached to a person's biological or perceived sex or gender (e.g., secretarial roles, cooking, cleaning)
- *Intersectional feminist:* A lens of viewing how various forms of inequity and marginalization operate together and exacerbate experienced sexism
- *Male-centric language:* Language that assumes men are the majority or norm when referring to a particular occupation or group of people; also known as *gendered language* (e.g., "Hi, guys" or "Doctors are male, and nurses are female").
- *Misogynoir:* A term coined by Moya Bailey, referring to misogyny directed toward Black women, with an emphasis on the intersectionality of bias
- *Mom-shaming:* Bullying mothers for their parenting choices in micro- and macroaggressive ways
- *Patriarchy:* A society that has been systematized to support men in power at the expense of woman, femmes, and nonbinary individuals
- *Rape culture:* A society, community, and/or environment in which rape and sexual violence against women are normalized
- *Unsolicited body comments:* When an individual feels compelled to comment on another person's appearance; usually these comments are received by women

An example of a prompt we have used for participants who are analyzing the intersection of racism and sexism is a commercial by Heineken developed in 2018. The thirty-second commercial shows a bartender slide a bottle of Heineken down the bar. It passes a Black woman with a dark skin tone, a Black man with a dark skin tone, and a second Black woman with a dark skin tone, before it stops in front of a woman with a light skin tone. The commercial ends with the statement, "Sometimes, lighter is better."[31] This ad promptly received backlash after being released into the public domain. A few cards that would be associated with this prompt from the elements of sexism are gender role expectations, body shaming, and commodity feminism (each defined in the preceding list).

ABLEISM

We define *ableism* as the conscious or subconscious beliefs, actions, and/or benefits that place value on people's bodies and minds based on societally constructed ideas of normality, intelligence, excellence, desirability, and productivity. Ability is seen as the primary determinant of human capacities and those without disabilities are viewed as inherently superior (prejudice + power over + privilege)—for example, able-bodied over disabled individuals. The following ten terms, created in partnership with educator, disability activist, and designer Jennifer White-Johnson, are examples of cards in the context step of the Racism Untaught framework specific to ableism:

- *Ableist metaphor:* A disabled person's type of body and/or brain used synonymously for brokenness, awfulness, mediocrity, or ignorance (e.g., "the governor is willfully blind to the crisis" or "the prisoners' cries for help falling on deaf ears")
- *Access barriers:* Any obstruction that prevents or limits a disabled person from being integrated into structures, systems, environments, or social situations
- *Compliance culture:* Adhering to established norms that take the form of external laws, internal policies, and values meant to put an end to unwanted behaviors by associating those behaviors with negative, harmful, and violent stimulus (e.g., beatings, electric shock, deprivation techniques, prolonged restraint, seclusion, forced exercise and labor, forced medication or chemical restraint, and/or verbal abuse)
- *Disability burnout:* The exhaustion that disabled individuals feel on a day-to-day basis or when living within an ableist society and system
- *Disability delegitimization:* Invalidating the expressions and viewpoints of disabled people by suggesting that characteristics of their group impair their ability to adequately understand or respond to discourse about issues that affect them
- *Disability simulations:* An exercise in which a nondisabled person simulates a disability for a day, shown to promote harmful stereotypes about disabled people rather than improving awareness (e.g., a nondisabled person wearing a blindfold or using a wheelchair for a day)
- *Eugenics:* Unscientific and racially biased policies and/or practices that arrange (re)production of the human population to increase heritable characteristics that are normalized as desirable—justifying the treatment of disabled people and other marginalized populations

- *Euphemistic phrase:* A term or set of terms used to avoid labeling the disabled community in order to avoid offense or shaming (e.g., special needs, handicapable, handicapped, differently abled)
- *Internalized ableism:* Aspects of oppression that a disabled person believes to be true and will often enforce on other disabled people; often co-occurs with self-hatred
- *Neurotypical:* A shortened term for *neurologically typical,* describing individuals whose ways of thinking and processing information are considered "normal" by the standards of their society (e.g., anyone who does not have a mental, psychiatric/psychosocial, learning, cognitive, intellectual, or developmental disability)

An example of a prompt we have used for participants who are analyzing the intersection of racism and ableism is: "Students of color are less likely than their white peers to be identified [i.e., diagnosed] and to receive special education services, despite demonstrating similar levels of academic performance and behavior, even when attending the same schools."[32] So although Black and brown students are placed in classrooms for learning differences at a higher rate, they remain undiagnosed. Their behavior is more likely to be seen as disruptive rather than the behavior being indicative of a learning difference. A few cards associated with this prompt from the cards that hold the elements of ableism are neurotypical, eugenics, and access barriers (each defined in the preceding list).

FOCUSED DIALOGUE TO SUPPORT ETHICAL SOCIAL INNOVATION

These workshops allow for more focused dialogue and provide more discussion on social innovation, ethics, and responsible design. We have participants who come in ready and eager to work with us, as well as participants who are ready to challenge our ideas. We welcome both and work to guide the conversation in a shared space. We have had participants who challenged the examples of racialized design we provide and some of the definitions we use. We are happy to have this dialogue and support participants in joining the conversation to work together to create a shared understanding. It is rewarding to see people empowered by the knowledge of shared language and to see how this helps shape the conversation about racism in a direct manner.

ACADEMIC CASE STUDY

Graphic Design, University of
Illinois, Urbana-Champaign

LIFE'S A BRIDGE: ANTI-RACIST APPROACHES TO THE TRANSPORTATION SYSTEM OF ROBERT MOSES

COURSE
ARTD 451: Ethics of Designer in a Global Economy
sixteen-week course, in-person, fall 2019

TEAM
Facilitator: Lisa Elzey Mercer.
Participants: Sixteen undergraduate students; four groups of four students each. Only one group is focused on in this case study. Students were guided through the framework as a group, but there were specific steps in this case study, such as the final deliverable, that were completed by one student in the group, who will be referred to as the *lead participant*. The racial makeup of the class was six students of color and ten white students. The racial makeup of the group was two students of color and two white students.

◀ ONBOARDING ACTIVITIES: TWO WEEKS

The course began with onboarding activities that helped participants get to know each other. This included activities such as personality assessments, a fill-in-the-blank-style poem, and a presentation from each participant focused on their personal life and their design goals. The personality assessments allowed for intentional conversations about how the participants showed up in the space and may be perceived by their group members. The poem prompted the participants to include artifacts, traditions, guardian and familial characteristics, traits, and mementos. The visual presentation allowed the students to use their creativity to create a collage about their hobbies, aspirations, and industry experience.

The onboarding process also included deep discussions of the concepts of racism, intersectionality, privilege, and power. Dr. Jan Carter-Black, professor of social work at the University of Illinois, visited the classroom to lead a discussion on the lens we use to identify racism and how that lens influences our understanding. It was important that participants understood how these concepts are nuanced—not binary—and that the context in which we all exist affects our lived experiences. The course provided participants with a space to ask questions and hold conversations focused on race and racism, given that these are not typical conversations racially privileged participants have in their everyday lives. The participants also used onboarding to develop a community agreement on how to honor their shared space together and create expectations of each other and how they would hold themselves accountable to those expectations (discussed further in chapter 3).

◀ CONTEXT: ONE TO TWO WEEKS

THE PROMPT: A RACIALIZED SYSTEM

Robert Moses was a prominent urban architect in New York City from the 1920s to the 1970s. He developed the public roadways and transportation system to intentionally favor white, middle-class people. Moses stated that "whites of upper and comfortable middle class would be free to use the parkways for recreation and commuting."[33] He developed a bridge system that discouraged public transportation by building bridges with nine-foot clearances, making the highway system impassable by twelve-foot-tall public buses. By doing so, he excluded people who primarily use public transportation from specific areas of New York City—mainly Black people, Indigenous people, people of color, and people from lower socioeconomic statuses. This transportation system is a strong example of a systemic social inequality that is still in existence today.

THE CARDS

During the first part of step one, participants began by identifying elements of racism that they believed applied to the racialized prompt. When the participants selected an element of racism, they discussed as a group whether they agreed on the use of that element to describe their prompt. Participants were required to briefly explain why the term applied and to explain why it may not have applied.

This group selected over eighteen elements of racism. A few the group identified are as follows:

- *Segregation:* The separation of racial groups by way of artifacts, systems, and experiences. *Rationale:* Moses designed the bridges at a shorter height to intentionally exclude people of color who primarily used public transportation from going to specific areas of New York City.
- *Institutional racism:* The racial discrimination that results from an individual's actions of a prejudiced institution or society. *Rationale:* Moses argued for this form of urban architecture to be voted into public policy, which then made it easier for other cities to perpetuate similar, if not the same, systemic racism.
- *Redlining:* The racially influenced and systematic denial of various residential services, including access to specific neighborhoods, through the selective raising of prices. *Rationale:* The bridge system segregated communities, providing greater access to white people of upper- and middle-class status while excluding people of color.
- *Systemic racism:* Inequalities rooted in the system-wide operation of a society that excludes members or particular racial groups from significant participation in major social institutions. *Rationale:* The highway systems Moses created systemically disadvantaged communities of color.

THE LEVELS OF OPPRESSION

Participants worked together with the levels of oppression model to further contextualize the instances of oppression that showed up in the transportation system that Robert Moses created. They considered how and where oppression is introduced, reinforced, and perpetuated within the model. Participants chose to break down the levels of oppression as related to their racialized prompt in the following ways:

- *Beliefs:* Personal beliefs, ideas, and feelings that perpetuate oppression. *Rationale:* Moses believed "that Black and white people were incapable of coexisting."[34]
- *Agentic action:* When oppressive beliefs translate into oppressive behavior. *Rationale:* Moses intentionally built the bridge's clearances substantially lower on the Southern State Parkway to create a barrier that would keep Black and brown communities, who mostly use public transit, away from Jones Beach.
- *Institutional:* Structural oppression that results from agentic oppressive behavior. *Rationale:* As the chairman of the Long Island State Park Commission, Moses supported the development of racist policies to uphold Jim Crow Laws of segregated spaces.

- *Cultural:* Systems of norms, values, beliefs, and trusted systems of acquiring truth that preserve, protect, and maintain oppression. *Rationale:* This normalized transportation system is still in existence today and continues to affect the everyday lives of Black and brown people, and low socio-economic populations.

◖ DEFINE: FOUR TO FIVE WEEKS

During the second step, the participants were instructed to write an individual annotated bibliography and a group literature review. Each participant in the group was required to write at least five hundred words within the collective literature review. This group consisted of four participants, and the literature review had approximately 2,200 words. This literature review helped provide cultural context specific to the time period in which the bridges were built. Here is an excerpt from the literature review:

> While we primarily are aware of Robert Moses for the lingering impact his bridge designs have had on some communities, the scope of his reach in public transportation was far wider than the public bus system. Moses had a hand in every form of public transportation New York City has developed, and like the bridges that remain, the struggling subway system stands as a modern reminder of his former power within the city government and disinterest in public transportation as a concept. During the 1930s and 40s, the New Deal was being enacted to help citizens rise up from the impact of the Great Depression and to help cities build up their infrastructure, and Robert Moses was taking advantage of this in New York with his established power to push through projects at breakneck speed. As the country grew out of the depression, the idea of a person owning their own car as an American goal started to become part of the culture's ideology. Moses bought into this idea as well and pushed New York away from public transportation by building bridges that wouldn't accommodate public buses, an intentional move against people who were too poor to own their own vehicles. His construction projects had incredibly negative impacts on over a dozen low-income and non-white communities that can still be seen to this day.[35]

The annotated bibliography included a list of citations to books, articles, and documents, both peer-reviewed and not, followed by a brief descriptive and evaluative paragraph. This gave the participants opportunities to understand how their racialized prompt and similar prompts were being talked about, analyzed, and theorized.

The question they developed from what they learned from secondary sources was: "How might design bring awareness to the transportation system that was made to negatively impact people of color and lower economic class in order to compel community members to take action and create a movement for change with New York residents?"

In addition to the collective literature review and the individual annotated bibliographies, each participant added to their group's collective research proposal. The proposal outlined two options that each participant could engage with to conduct primary research—either two methods, or one method and one theory. Each participant began working on their methods and/or theories to further contextualize the racialized prompt. The define step included cards of methods and theories that might be used to help participants explore further. The lead participant chose the following methods:

- *Personas:* Defining user personalities in order to explore concepts centered on them (see figure 4.2)
- *Hero's journey:* A narrative arc format that validates ideas and provides an opportunity for the audience to identify with the struggles of the hero and the journey
- *Journey maps:* Plotting the path users take within certain experiences (see figure 4.3)

The lead participant explained, "I specifically focused on research that helped me understand the struggles individuals from different social and economic classes go through from the bridges. We tracked different ways and times money is lost (in their daily travels), and the design opportunities through the journey maps. Surveys were sent out to understand other ways people struggled with public transportation and how they dealt with it."[36]

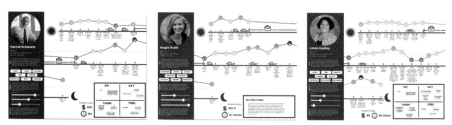

Figure 4.2. Academic case study. Three personas include a journey map, an empathy map, and a heuristic analysis of the journey.

At the end of the define step, participants gave a thirty-minute research presentation on the secondary and primary data they collected and what they learned from each other in the process. The presentation reinforced the idea that while participants conducted their research methods individually, discussing the research they conducted helped to provide insight into the factors they each learned. These discussions provided them with additional information from which they could draw in the next step, ideate.

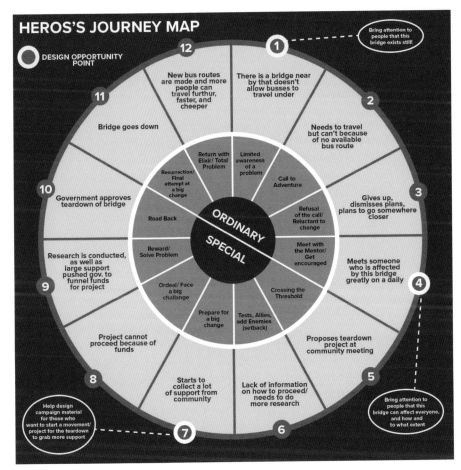

Figure 4.3. Academic case study. A hero's journey to teach people about the transportation system that Moses developed.

◉ IDEATE: ONE TO TWO WEEKS

THE CARDS

During the first part of the third step, participants shuffled through the ideate cards to help them think of avenues through which they might affect positive change given the racialized design they were assigned. Each card fell within one of the three categories of design explained in chapter 2. The participants were encouraged to use all three categories in the ideation process. Some of the cards the lead participant chose were as follows:

- *Gamification:* The process of adding games or game-like elements to encourage participation and productivity. This fell within the artifact section of design.
- *Transit/transportation:* A system of buses, trains, and so on, running on fixed routes, on which the public may travel. This fell within the system section of design.

- *Experience design:* The connectedness of everything in a process. This fell within the experience section of design.

QUADRANT MAP

The second part of the third step created opportunities for more specific ideas and for measuring their implementation using the quadrant map. Each participant created a list of ideas based on the areas of design they pulled from the deck of cards. Participants were encouraged to write down all of their ideas, omitting none, which they placed on individual sticky notes. Participants then placed their sticky notes on the quadrant map to gain a better understanding of first how far their idea would take their stakeholder from oppressive thought to anti-oppressive action, and then how far the idea moved culture norms from good intentions to positive impact.

The lead participant decided that an educational and awareness approach would be most impactful. They chose to approach their design challenge using gamification to break down the experience of using public transportation with the restriction of the bridges. The participant wanted the game to exemplify the time and money one would lose traveling on public transportation. It was hoped that this interactive way of learning would move stakeholders to anti-oppressive action.

◀ PROTOTYPE: FOUR TO FIVE WEEKS

During this step of the toolkit, the participants created the idea(s) that were the most promising from the ideate step. Prototypes occurred in three steps, each one growing in functionality and applying the factors garnered from user testing completed between each prototype stage. The lead participant explained the prototype step as follows: "I combined a hybrid of the games [the Game of Life and Chutes and Ladders], to have the players experience a journey while inflicting specific pain points through the game board to mimic the systematic problems of the bridges and how they affect everyone. Moments in the game, the players have fun building their interesting stories, but encounter moments where they are stuck with financial struggles or unexpected privileges that benefit the players."[37]

Low-fidelity prototype. This is the initial, raw presentation of an idea. Initially, the research included playing the game to ensure the mechanics of the game worked and see if the goal of the game was reached. It became clear that the game needed to include different privileges and powers for it to be a more accurate representation of the ways public transportation negatively affects the lives of people of color (see figure 4.4).

Mid-fidelity prototype. This prototype had limited functionality but presented enough interactions and possibilities for participants to play the game. The lead participant added three sets of themed cards (life, career, and education) to the game that participants were prompted to select by the tile they landed on. This prototype was tested with peers in the class and with people outside the class (see figure 4.5).

High-fidelity prototype. Minimal changes, if any, were needed to this prototype. It was one step away from the final deliverable. The gaming pieces all supported a more accurate representation of public transportation (see figure 4.6).

Figure 4.4. Academic case study. Low-fidelity sketch of the game Life's a Bridge.

Figure 4.5. Academic case study. Mid-fidelity sketch of the game Life's a Bridge.

Figure 4.6. Academic case study. High-fidelity sketch of the game Life's a Bridge.

◀ IMPACT: ONE WEEK

The lead participant included a briefing manual with the game. The briefing manual prompted participants into further conversation about power and privilege. The lead participant stated, "Privilege operates on personal, interpersonal, cultural, and institutional levels and gives advantages, favors, and benefits to members of dominant groups at the expense of members of target groups." The manual prompted players with questions such as: What were the outcomes of the game? How did this game make you feel? How do you think this game reflected real life? Did any cards stick out to you? Why? What things in your life do you think you have over- looked at that could be a form of power or privilege? The briefing manual was inspired by and could be measured using the selected impact cards:

- *Cohort model of accountability:* A group of individuals who hold themselves or a particular person responsible, often equated to answerability, blameworthiness, liability, and the expectation of account-giving
- *Listening sessions:* Similar to a focus group, a type of facilitated discussion with a group of people aimed at collecting information about their experience and/or experiential knowledge
- *Gamified survey:* An interactive and/or game-like way of polling users to gather data on the attitudes, opinions, and/or beliefs of sections of the population

RUBRIC

The grading for this case study included work from each step of the iterative process the student utilized. The rubric breaks down the whole project into these categories:

- *Understanding—30 percent of grade:* The research the lead participant conducted was strong and was used thoughtfully in the creation of a gamified experience that represented the day-to-day interaction of people of color with the transportation system.
- *Application, critical thinking, justification—45 percent of grade:* The prototyping of this game was thoughtful in each step. The research conducted between the low-, mid-, and high-fidelity prototype stages provided the lead participant with specific improvements necessary to produce a game that was both usable and helped players understand the systemic racism in public transportation.
- *Create deliverable—25 percent of grade:* The final deliverables for this case study included a game board, game pieces, a box to hold the game pieces, and a custom box that held the entire game.

CHALLENGES

When the participants began the course, the onboarding activities invited them to share with each other their own identities and their lived experiences with one another. In one group in this course, two participants of color and two white participants were in a group together. This group was able to hold space for conversations that were not typically had in a design course. One conversation was focused on language and the assumptions one student of color experienced by being asked, "Do you speak English?" and "Where are you from?" The two white participants were surprised that these assumptions were made, and this provided an opportunity to share and learn from each other.

The challenge for participants who were given a system as a prompt was that they were often curious about how they were going to visualize or develop an outcome from their research. This was a large conversation in the ideation step of this course. The benefit of working in a group was the opportunity for participants to come together in discussions and learn from each other to integrate the ideas they generated together into their individual project.

FINAL REPORT: ONE WEEK

During the final week of this course, the participants presented their final outcomes and a designed process book. The process book included all the work they completed during the sixteen-week course. The book included a journey map (see figure 4.7), a visualization of the prompted journal entries, which outlined the learning process through the course. The participants also created a final presentation that reviewed a summary of their work throughout the course and was presented in front of invited academic guests.

Journey Map

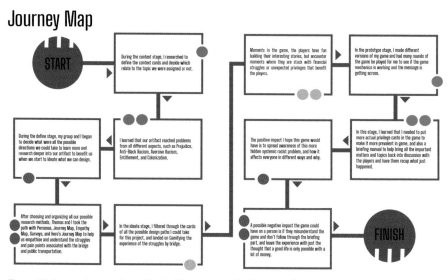

Figure 4.7. Academic case study. Student journey map for the semester.

Participants often step away from this class appreciating the opportunity to discuss racism and ethics in relation to design. Students relay their understanding and see great value in moving past good intentions and focusing on the impact their designs that are placed into the public domain have. The following are direct quotes from class participants:

> The stage [context] made me realize how deep institutional racism is and how individuals, at any step of the way, could have stopped these ads from being released. It also made me realize that institutional racism isn't just the institution or CEO itself, but the individuals that make up the institution. I was surprised by how many elements of racism fit into our artifacts such as colorism, white washing, institutional racism, cultural erasure, etc.[38]

> When my group and I started this project months ago, I was unsure about what route I would take to design a project where I felt that could have the most effective change the way people view microaggressions and othering in our society. At the end of this project, I look back and think about all the hard work and research my group members and I have completed to create impactful projects. I am very happy with the way that my website turned out, and I am excited to see how this project could possibly turn into something that I do on the side.[39]

> I've never had the opportunity to have discussions like this and haven't been educated much about these topics outside of the internet. Our group is the only one that has an experience to base our project off of. It's interesting to see the difference between the context cards we chose in comparison to other groups. We have all of our context cards sorted out and I think the conversations that we had about them were incredibly rewarding and educational for me.[40]

> I think this was a very beneficial and unexpected class because I did not think that we would be talking about racism in class. Thinking of the beginning, I noticed how different I felt around my peers when we first started talking about racism. Before, I had felt a bit cautious because I wasn't sure what others might think about this subject. However, as we went along the class, I felt more comfortable sharing my ideas for our projects with my peers. I think that through this, I got to learn a lot about how others approach design.[41]

OPPRESSION IS NOT MERELY THE PROVINCE OF CORRUPT GOVERNMENTS AND TYRANTS; NOR IS IT ALWAYS COMMITTED BY POWER HUNGRY CONSPIRATORS. MODERN OPPRESSION IS THE RESULT OF THE ACTS OF NUMEROUS INDIVIDUALS, EACH OF WHOM MAY OR MAY NOT INTEND TO OPPRESS OR EVEN TO HARM

5 ANTI-OPPRESSIVE INTERVENTIONS

There is a continually growing number of scholars whose work is focused on using the design research process to create a positive impact on complex social issues. We see great value in the existence of multiple routes to liberation (discussed further in chapter 6). In the development of a collective voice, we strengthen a collective culture that is working to dismantle the status quo in the design research process. The paths include but are not limited to (1) the development and implementation of inclusive pedagogical practices, (2) creating and maintaining relationships in the community that support sustainable community engagement, and (3) analyzing and dismantling industry practices that produce racialized design and introduce it into the public domain. Paulo Friere was a philosopher and a leading advocate in the development of inclusive pedagogy. In his 1968 book *Pedagogy of the Oppressed*, he acknowledges the importance of exploring the difference between an academic understanding of a human condition versus the personal knowledge of having lived through an experience: "This condemnation of human suffering must happen so that we can protect the intellectual coherence needed to help others comprehend the critical difference between studying hunger as anthropological tourists and experiencing it, between deploring violence and surviving it, and between the false benevolence of 'giving voice' and being institutionally forced into voicelessness."[2]

More recently, scholars have viewed the notion of *knowledge development* in various ways: "The position around the idea that colonialism has a direct effect on knowledge gained and disseminated comes from a postcolonial perspective. This perspective recognizes that institutions in power have structured systems—like our educational system—to perpetuate specific notions to keep white men as the authority on knowledge gained and disseminated."[3] *Postcolonial theory* is the attempt to disrupt colonial power; it theorizes a postcolonial world: "Post-colonial theory looks at issues of power, economics, politics, religion, culture, and how these elements work in relation to colonial hegemony (western colonizers controlling the colonized)."[4]

We look to our peers who are developing and disseminating similar work and the interventions developed by them that add to the discourse of working to dismantle racism with language, ways of working, and the development of anti-racist curricula. We want to share with those who we have engaged with in conversations or whose scholarly disseminations have helped us shape our ways of working and thinking.

The first work we would like to highlight is the 1619 Project, created by Pulitzer Prize winner Nikole Hannah-Jones and launched in 2019. The project was disseminated by the *New York Times Magazine* and works to reframe the shared history in the United States "that placed slavery and its continuing legacy at the center of our national narrative [and] offered a revealing new origin story for the United States, one that helped explain not only the persistence of anti-Black racism and inequality in American life today, but also the roots of so much of what makes the country unique."[5] The project was an educational curriculum intentionally shared in 2019 because it commemorated the four hundredth anniversary of the first twenty enslaved Africans' arrival in the colony of Virginia. It is a part of the history of the United States that is not often shared, discussed, or acknowledged. "I wanted people to know the date 1619 and to contemplate what it means that slavery predates nearly every other institution in the United States. I wanted them to be transformed by this understanding, as I have been."[6] It places the first enslaved Africans and the economic value they held at the center of what shaped the United States.

Dark Matter University is an "anti-racist design justice school collectively seeking the radical transformation of education & practice toward a just future."[7] It is looking for immediate change in the practice of design education toward an anti-racist model. It seeks to explore dominant narratives that have been centered and the inequalities that have contributed to "global extraction, racial capitalism, and colonialism."[8] It provides five principles it is focused on: (1) new forms of knowledge and knowledge production, (2) new forms of institutions, (3) new forms of collectivity and practice, (4) new forms of community and culture, and (5) new forms of design.[9]

Sasha Constanza-Chock, the director of research and design at the Algorithmic Justice League, wrote a book published in 2020 titled *Design Justice*. They highlighted the important role design has in centering historically marginalized voices: "In essence, it's a call for us to heed the growing critiques of the ways that design . . . too often contributes to the reproduction of systemic oppression."[10] The book includes a list of ten design principles, the first being, "We use design to sustain, heal, and empower our communities, as well as to seek liberation from exploitative and oppressive systems."[11]

Lesley Ann-Noel is an assistant professor of art and design at North Carolina State University. She identifies as an Afro Trinidadian design educator and is focused on the practice of design through emancipatory, critical, and antihegemonic lenses and on decolonizing design by focusing on the experiences of people who are often excluded from design research. In her 2020 article "Envisioning a Pluriversal Design Education" for the Design Research Society Pluriversal Conference, she looks at the emerging pedagogy of design education for "'vulnerable' countries, using definitions by the United Nations."[12] She asks this series of questions: "I've often wondered what design education should look like for someone from a small non-industrialized context? How can design and design education in these places use, like the athletics program in Jamaica, their varied culture and contexts to create relevant design curriculum to serve their populations? How do we create a global view in design education that is not a hegemonic Western view, and a repeat of curricula from the West?"[13]

Jacinda Walker developed the organization designExplorr. Its mission "aims to diversify the design profession by expanding access to design education for youth and raising awareness for corporate organizations. This work is accomplished through collaborations that develop youth activities, coordinating diversity building initiatives, and connecting stakeholders to resources."[14] Walker is an advocate for youth and is proud to mentor design students on their portfolios and professional and career planning. Her goal is to provide design education to youth who have been historically marginalized and provide them with a pathway to a career that incorporates their interests and love of creative making with tools.[15]

Antionette Carroll founded the company Creative Reaction Lab in the summer of 2018. Its mission is to "educate, train, and challenge Black and Latinx youth to become leaders designing healthy and racially equitable communities."[16] They are looking to change the dominant narrative that only adults in positions of power and with specific titles have the power to "challenge racial and health inequities."[17] Their audience is youth, educators, and youth alumni. They have distributed over $200,000 to youth interested in redesigning education for racial equity and social healing, artwork for equity, a community design apprenticeship program, and a youth creative leadership fund and fellowship.

DEVELOPING INTERVENTIONS

We created the Racism Untaught toolkit to disrupt the status quo and dismantle the colonial elements within the design research processes. Because we understand that we are designing for complexity, we wanted to dismantle traditional ways of doing and thinking within our research. Reimagining elements of the design research process was meant to ensure we were putting emphasis on the iterative nature of the framework to negate sequential, waterfall, or prescriptive design practices. We wanted to remove the design savior complex that sees communities as clients rather than cocreators. We knew that we also needed to address how we as designers show up regarding our identity and create ways where we might intentionally look at how our biases affect our impact (outlined further in chapter 3). How might we use the design research process to provide opportunities for people to analyze how privilege and power play a role in the ways we make decisions and further collaborate on design development?

Interconnectedness was a concept we had to understand if we were going to create truly equitable and inclusive collaborative design spaces. The nuance and connection to broader systems of oppression that both we and our end users hold had to be considered. We wanted to enable flexibility in the process and critical moments of conscious considerations. As stated by the community members of the Inclusive Design Research Centre at OCAD University, "Design processes need to take into account the interactions of various systems with complex and unique humans, as well as the external social, cultural, economic and technological forces that exist for each of us."[18] Our uniqueness makes collaborating an exciting and education-filled process, but our uniqueness also creates a sense of urgency in designing for systems that affect all of us. Karen Potts and Leslie Brown speak about uniqueness and the elements we should take into consideration as designers when considering how we are connected to systems of oppression. They ask us to "believe in your capacity for 'agency'—that is, your capacity to act and alter the relations of oppression in your own world. Most of us can recognize oppression when it occurs or when we are being oppressed ourselves, but can we also recognize the complicity that each of us have in creating and sustaining oppression over others?"[19] We hope that the interventions in the Racism Untaught framework bring these considerations to the forefront, being ethically intentional about our power in the design research process.

Another issue we hoped to negate is that of disjointed incrementalism. Because we are reimagining large systems, it is often the norm to address what is burning rather than address the larger or foundational issues that started the fire in the first place. John Mathers speaks to this hurried or rushed ideology of action in their article "Design Intervention," stating, "In the phenomenon sometimes known as 'disjointed incrementalism,' solutions to problems are frequently bolted on, one after another, in firefighting mode, without examination of the underlying structural hindrances that may be the real issues. Where major reforms are implemented, they are often brought in too big too quickly, without being tested at a small scale."[20] We have found that when designing for social justice, those in power tend to want quick, easy fixes to a huge, nuanced, and wicked problem. Design interventions can help us understand issues more clearly before we choose to act on our own assumptions of what might be going wrong. Design has to become more comfortable in addressing complex issues because we are complex human beings situated in complex systems. Great care should be taken when we design for our communities so that we do not perpetuate even more harm than if we did nothing at all.

We continued to structure how we and participants using our framework could keep their design outcomes equitable. We did this first through working in a collaborative environment (referenced in chapter 3), learning a shared language (referenced in chapter 4), and developing intentional design interventions that invite participants to take pauses in their work. Our goal is that participants of the framework might be more intentional in their application of the design research process, from the beginning to the last step—which, for us, is not actually a last step at all, but rather a chance to measure impact and continue the iterative process when designing for social change. The integration of design interventions into the Racism Untaught framework was to work toward structural and cultural changes when focused on social innovation for complex social issues.[21]

The design interventions we have created so far include the cards (explained in further detail in chapter 1), the levels of oppression, the thesis question structure, and the quadrant map. We continue to explore design interventions that could further promote the facilitation of anti-racist thinking and innovative creative making. We acknowledge that the design interventions that we have integrated into the Racism Untaught framework may require adaptations when we consider additional forms of oppression. Additional refining and innovation will be needed to ensure that the framework will eventually be able to guide participants through analyzing a wider variety of identifiers and the effect design has on those who hold intersectional identities.

THE LEVELS OF OPPRESSION

The first step of the framework introduced in chapter 1 includes not only the elements of racism, sexism, and ableism, but also a diagram of concentric circles visualizing the levels of oppression. This diagram allows for further contextualization of the instance of oppression or prompt the participants are working to create an anti-racist design approach for. The diagram has four different levels, each of them intertwined with one another, emphasizing the interconnectedness of the four levels. We worked with our advisory team to create a visualization and definitions that would easily help the participants understand how each level works cohesively to uphold the system of oppression (see figure 5.1).

The first level is entitled *beliefs*, which we defined as personal beliefs, ideas, and feelings that perpetuate oppression. At this level, participants are instructed to consider foundational ideologies that we as individuals hold that would lead to

Use the **Levels of Oppression** model to further contextualize your
design problem. Consider where in the levels the problem was
created and how each level perpetuated it.

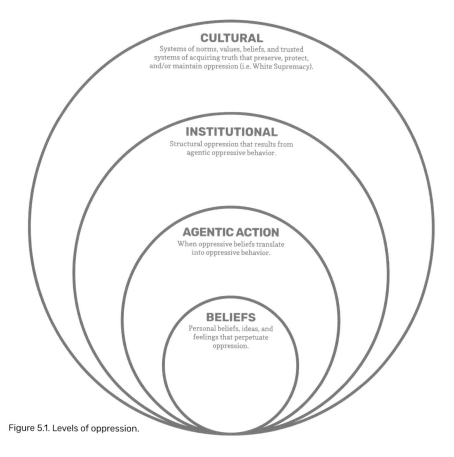

CULTURAL
Systems of norms, values, beliefs, and trusted
systems of acquiring truth that preserve, protect,
and/or maintain oppression (i.e. White Supremacy).

INSTITUTIONAL
Structural oppression that results from
agentic oppressive behavior.

AGENTIC ACTION
When oppressive beliefs translate
into oppressive behavior.

BELIEFS
Personal beliefs, ideas, and
feelings that perpetuate
oppression.

Figure 5.1. Levels of oppression.

oppressive behaviors. At this level, *cognitive dissonance*—the state of having
inconsistent or contradictory thoughts, beliefs, or attitudes, especially relating
to behavioral decisions—plays a huge role in the proclamation of values that
are not practiced by the individual. For instance, those in positions that benefit
from systems of oppression often proclaim that they were "taught not to see
color" or that "everyone is the same." While we hope everyone has these values,
merely proclaiming them does not make them true; rather, it just makes those
in power feel like good people. This is not to say that we should stop proclaiming
values associated with anti-oppression, but we must make clear that they are
goals we are still learning rather than absolute truths. This amount of specificity
is necessary in understanding the difference between being told a value and
learning the value itself. Learning requires a materialization or evidence of a
discernable set of skills—in this case, *anti-racism*. Pat Hutchings, Jillian Kinzie, and
George D. Kuh, in "Evidence of Student Learning," describe evidence as "essential

to improving student learning and responding to accountability expectations."[22] Yet we continue to lack evidence of an anti-racist ideology and claim that we hold those learned values. The sad fact is that what is actually learned is racialized and oppressive belief systems because these beliefs are what show up in the next level of oppression. It is our actions that act as evidence of our learned belief system, and it is only actions that we can measure and hold accountable to our expectations or the values that we claim to have.

The second level, which is situated outside of personal belief systems, is *agentic action*. This is the evidence that we were describing earlier, what we have formally defined as when oppressive beliefs translate into oppressive behavior. *Agentic* implies that an individual has the power to control or decide their actions. And those actions are inspired by the socialized, normalized, and learned ideologies they hold—essentially, our beliefs in action. Cognitive dissonance runs through each of these levels of oppression, but it shows up in agentic action as overt, covert, or a mixture of both. In the article "I Am Not a Racist But . . . ," Eduardo Bonilla-Silva and Tyrone A. Forman describe the cultural shift from overt to covert racism as a new racist ideology. The actions of those upholding white supremacy before the 1960s, during Jim Crow, was overt, while the racism that exists today after the civil rights movement is covert.[23] In regard to the covert forms of racism, Bonilla-Silva and Forman discuss the results of a survey that conflict with how United States citizens see themselves. "Why is it that a large proportion of Whites, who . . . agree with the principle of integration, do not mind their kids mixing with non-Whites, have no objection to interracial marriages, and do not mind people of color moving into their neighborhoods continue to live in all-White neighborhoods and send their kids to mostly White schools?" This further emphasizes how it is not enough to claim you do not hold prejudice; it is actions that continue to support racism. Regardless of how one may overtly or covertly choose to uphold white supremacist ideologies, the actionable ways racism may show up continue to uphold and support the systems of white supremacy, which are supported by the institution.

The third level in the levels of oppression is *institutional*. This level represents our policies, practices, laws, and other mandates that support oppression. Formally, we have defined this level as reinforced structural oppression that results from agentic oppressive behavior and is influenced by the culture. This level is situated outside of agentic action because it holds and supports both racialized and oppressive beliefs and actions. We would argue that the support goes both ways in that these institutional laws and practices influence actions and beliefs as well. These policies and other forms of institutional support are essentially oppressive actions set in stone and upheld by institutions that will enact punitive measures if those policies are not followed. Cognitive dissonance in the institution shows up often and is quite overt. In Racism Untaught workshops, a pervasive problem in organizations we work with is the lack of racial diversity in leadership. Many participants who see the lack of representation often point the finger at the department of human resources, the recruiters, or the executive-level leadership. While these can be true, participants also fail to see their own role in the normalization of whiteness in the culture of their workplace. For instance, we have witnessed non-executive-level, non-administrative-level employees point to colonial displays of knowledge and toxic cultures of expertise as the reasoning behind their support of one candidate over the other. Their rationale for choosing a more "qualified" candidate according to Eurocentric and Westernized ideologies and policies regarding education and displays of expertise happen without conversations about how racially privileged candidates may have had access to a doctoral degree or a particular certification. We often blame policy and standards that already exist when racialized bias shows up. However, we fail to understand our role in being able to question and dismantle these policies and standards that would keep the status quo. We blame institutional practices and tradition rather than using our agency to think and act critically to repair harm, provide opportunities, and open the door of access to the industry or academy. The institution and our personal actions perpetuate themselves in the broader cultural understanding of who deserves to be in what spaces.

The fourth and final level of oppression is *cultural*. Our culture is the norms, values, beliefs, and trusted systems of acquiring truth that preserve, protect, and maintain oppression—for example, the cultural norms of white supremacy, racial capitalism, and the patriarchy. We are socialized to look to these systems to govern our communities. We use these normalizations as a filter for what is right or wrong, who is assumed innocent or guilty, what safety means, who deserves to be in power, and why we uphold societal standards that exclude communities. And because the dominant culture (white, male, cisgender, straight, upper-class, Christian, etc.) decides the answers to these questions, we will continue to look at society with ideals decided for us by individuals who support (through belief and action) the systems of white supremacy, patriarchy, and capitalism. That is, unless we decide to take intentional collective action to find ways that we might create a community of interdependency built on concepts of transformative justice, liberation, love, and peace (further explored in chapter 6).

Just as our identities are multilayered and complex, so are forms of oppression. For us to encourage this critical and necessary analysis, we wanted to be sure that we developed a design intervention with intersections in mind. The levels of oppression model helps participants further contextualize instances or prompts of racialized design through a multi-layered lens. It is used as an intervention to prompt investigation of not only the artifact, system, or experience, but how that design could have even been created in the first place and sustained within our society through each level of oppression that exists. Ahead, we will break down a racialized artifact, system, and experience using the levels of oppression to further explore the use for the levels of oppression model as a design intervention.

Figure 5.2.
Confederate flag.

CONFEDERATE FLAG: AN ARTIFACT

The Confederate flag (see figure 5.2) was designed by Confederate congressman William Porcher Miles to further separate the visuals of the Union's battle flag and the Confederacy during the war—and "it's divisive even 160 years after it was designed."[24] It has been adopted globally by white supremacists and neo-Nazis as a tool of terrorism, intimidation, and a reminder that they sit on top of the racial order. In addition, it has now come to represent a nostalgic imagined narrative of a rebellious Southern pride. We break down the racialized artifact using the levels of oppression:

- *Beliefs:* Personal beliefs, ideas, and feelings that perpetuate oppression. *Rationale:* Users of the Confederate flag see it as a representation of Southern pride, having nothing to do with the hatred and intimidation of Black people.
- *Agentic action:* When oppressive beliefs translate into oppressive behavior. *Rationale:* The Confederate flag is used by white supremacists in protests and capital insurrections to show

disdain for policies or rulings that would provide equity to Black and brown communities.

- *Institutional:* Structural oppression that results from agentic oppressive behavior. *Rationale:* Southern monuments and government buildings include representations of the Confederate flag.
- *Cultural:* Systems of norms, values, beliefs, and trusted systems of acquiring truth that preserve, protect, and maintain oppression. *Rationale:* Pride in a falsified "American" identity enables a puritan and exclusive culture that holds on to cultural representations like the Confederate flag as symbols of a fabricated oppression.

Figure 5.3. Graduation cap.

ACADEMIA: A SYSTEM

The system of academia has racist ideologies embedded in the foundational traditions of the academy (see figure 5.3). From whose narrative is represented in the history books to who is teaching the history, the academy's devotion to the Eurocentric canon and the toxic culture of the expert continues to exclude racialized communities (further discussed in chapter 3). We break down the racialized system using the levels of oppression:

- *Beliefs:* Personal beliefs, ideas, and feelings that perpetuate oppression. *Rationale:* People of color are not smart enough and do not work hard enough to achieve a degree. If they do make it into the academy, it is because of a sports scholarship or affirmative action.
- *Agentic action:* When oppressive beliefs translate into oppressive behavior. *Rationale:* The academy continues to hire only tokenized representations of Black people, Indigenous people,

and people of color, while holding these same marginalized individuals to the same standard as their white counterparts.

- *Institutional:* Structural oppression that results from agentic oppressive behavior. *Rationale:* The system of academia underrepresents Black people, Indigenous people, and people of color in curricula, pedagogy, and among administration, faculty, staff, and students.
- *Cultural:* Systems of norms, values, beliefs, and trusted systems of acquiring truth that preserve, protect, and maintain oppression. *Rationale:* It is not common to see a nonwhite professor.

Figure 5.4. "Where are you *really* from?" and "What are you?" talking bubbles.

MICROAGGRESSION: AN EXPERIENCE

Black people, Indigenous people, and people of color are often asked, "What are you?" or "Where are you *really* from?" (see figure 5.4), regardless of where they are in the United States. These questions perpetuate the idea that nonwhite people do not belong in specific spaces. Because of this normality, people of color are often exoticized—objectified, othered, sexualized, and/or dehumanized. We break down the racialized experience using the levels of oppression:

- *Beliefs:* Personal beliefs, ideas, and feelings that perpetuate oppression. *Rationale:* White people believe that nonwhite people do not belong in predominantly white spaces.
- *Agentic action:* When oppressive beliefs translate into oppressive behavior. *Rationale:* When a white person encounters a Black person in their neighborhood, they call the police because they see their presence as a threat to their well-being.
- *Institutional:* Structural oppression that results from agentic oppressive behavior. *Rationale:* Corporations continue to hire

only people who "fit within the culture" and are similar to their white homogenous environment.

- *Cultural:* Systems of norms, values, beliefs, and trusted systems of acquiring truth that preserve, protect, and maintain oppression. *Rationale:* The culture of segregation still exists in hiring, real estate, and banking systems that do not allow Black people, Indigenous people, and people of color the opportunity for or access to economic advancement.

THE THESIS QUESTION

The second step of the Racism Untaught framework includes details on the specific ideas participants should consider to create an inclusive but oppressive-specific thesis question (see figure 5.5). This question is a pivotal intervention in the design research process because it allows participants to think through what they gleaned from the research and contextualization. To allow brainstorming to stay as open as possible, we have broken up the thesis question to allow for an easier discussion of what the group has decided on as the problem they want to address.

Because creating the thesis question is a challenge regarding ranking the symptoms of oppression and what is most important to solve, we use three sections for brainstorming. During this time, we suggest that participants be as specific as possible with concepts they would like to be addressed based on their racialized prompt. The three areas of the thesis brainstorming process correlate with the thesis question areas for input, which include actions, changes, and stakeholders. Once these three areas have been identified, participants can use them to complete their thesis question, "How might design be used to [action] in order to [create change] with [stakeholders]?"

During this portion of the thesis question process, it works best to have participants use those areas to individually consider (1) the action they want to pursue, (2) the change they want to make, and (3) with whom. We provide participants with individual stacks of sticky notes to write ideas down and place them in the category in which they belong. After a time period either set by the participants or within the timeframe of the workshop, participant groups then come back together to piece together the strongest ideas from each of the three areas. We emphasize that there is no good, bad, or best question and that racism will not be solved with this one question. We ask participants to remember that they are only approaching this one example of racialized design and not the whole system of racism. Consider the murder of George Floyd as the racialized experience. Creating a question specific to this incident will not solve all of racism, but it will address police brutality as a symptom of the racialized design of criminal justice. An example of what the thesis brainstorm session may look like is shown in table 5.1.

We are specific in our pursuit of creating a thesis question rather than a statement so that participants continue to question the current systems in place. Once they

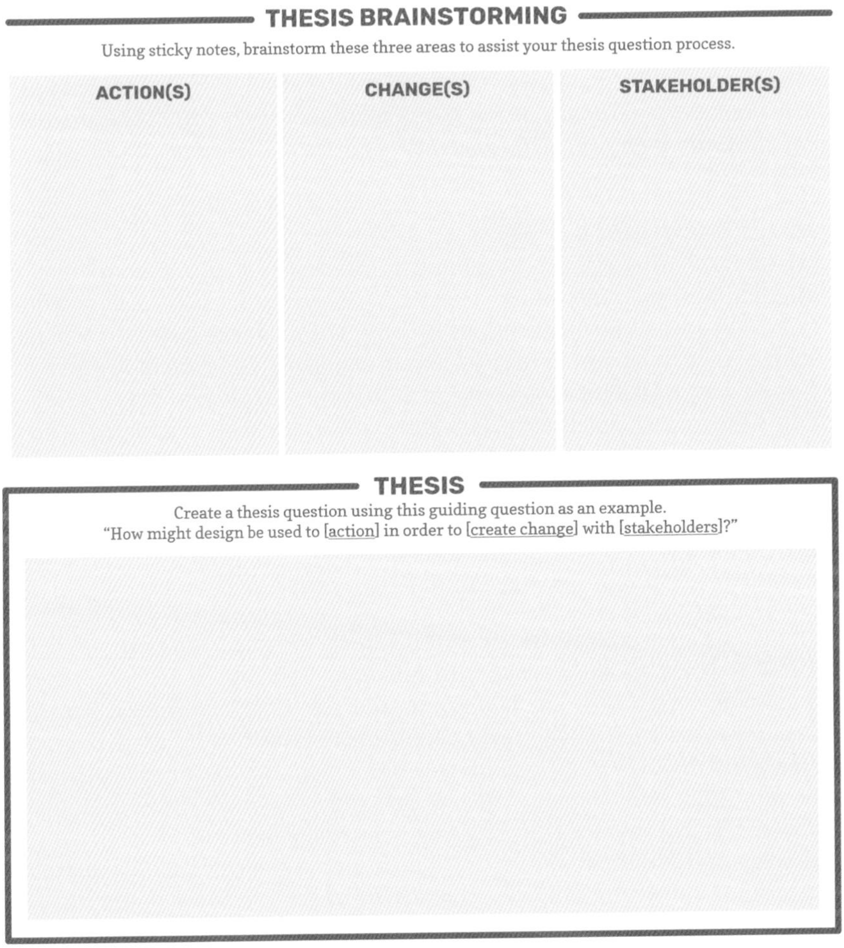

THESIS BRAINSTORMING

Using sticky notes, brainstorm these three areas to assist your thesis question process.

ACTION(S)	CHANGE(S)	STAKEHOLDER(S)

THESIS

Create a thesis question using this guiding question as an example.
"How might design be used to [action] in order to [create change] with [stakeholders]?"

Figure 5.5. Define step, thesis question.

Action(s)	Change(s)	Stakeholder(s)
Reformation laws	Police stop killing Black people	Black people
Abolition	New form of peacekeeping	Policy makers
Value Black life	Interdependent community policing	Local government officials

Table 5.1: Thesis question brainstorming

have a solid question, they write it on their workboard and refer to this question throughout the rest of the design research process. The final thesis question for the George Floyd example might look like this: "How might design *expose the fallacies and blatant racism of the systems of oppression that exist in policing* in order to *liberate and show the value of Black lives* with *United States citizens*?"

THE QUADRANT MAP

The third step in the Racism Untaught framework is meant to spark ideas for what could be. This step requires participants to brainstorm design avenues considering how certain artifacts, systems, and experiences might work together to answer their thesis question. After brainstorming and rapid iteration, the participants then take their ideas and map them on the quadrant map (see figure 5.6). This allows participants to gain a better understanding of their idea and first how far it will take their stakeholders from oppressive thought to anti-oppressive action, and then how far the idea moves culture norms from good intentions to positive impact. Participants do this part individually so they can fine-tune what they believe the goals of the group are before coming back together and explaining their idea and why they placed it where they did.

We often find that in critically assessing how their idea fits on the map, participants will begin to combine ideas, which will then move their ideas closer to the lower-right quadrant. The lower-right quadrant, denoted with a highlighted gold square, represents ideas that move stakeholders to the most anti-oppressive action and have the most positive impact. Often the most radical ideas end up in the lower-right quadrant. For example, considering the George Floyd example of a racialized design experience, an idea that may have good intentions but not move stakeholders to the most anti-oppressive action is police implicit bias training. While trainings about racism make those in power aware of the power they yield, often trainings leave attendees with nowhere to process and move their feelings of guilt or privileges into anti-oppressive actions. An idea that moves closer to anti-oppressive action but does not quite make it over to positive impact is defunding. What we mean by this is that defunding alone will not have the most impact. Here is where we might combine this idea with another to make this stronger, such as the redistribution of money into community programming that supports Black communities. This combined idea might then turn into abolishing the system of policing altogether and designing a community of interdependence with safety, protection, and the accommodation of physical, emotional, mental, social, and spiritual needs for all.

We have found that the quadrant map can be used not only in this phase of the framework, but in the steps that proceed it as participants consider their prototypes and final impact.

QUADRANT MAP

Use this **quadrant map** to help evaluate the value your ideas. On the
X-Axis, consider the intent of the idea in comparison to the impact?
On the Y-Axis, consider how far your idea shifts from the problem to
a positive design approach?

OPPRESSIVE THOUGHT

INTENT | IMPACT

ANTI-OPPRESSIVE ACTION

Figure 5.6. Ideate step,
quadrant map.

INDUSTRY CASE STUDY
Small Corporate Institution

RECRUITMENT PROCESS: INDUSTRY EXPERIENCE OF RECRUITMENT, HIRING, RETENTION, AND PROMOTION FOR EMPLOYEES OF COLOR

ORGANIZATION
Racism Untaught eight-hour workshop, two four-hour sessions for two consecutive days (see figure 5.7), online, spring 2022.

TEAM
Facilitators: Lisa Elzey Mercer and Terresa Moses.
Participants: Forty individuals, all from the same company, separated into six groups. The group focused on in this case study had seven participants and will be referred to as "the group." The racial makeup of the participants was two people of color and thirty-eight white people. The group focused on in this case study was composed of six white people.

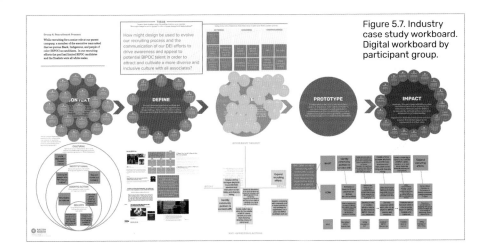

Figure 5.7. Industry case study workboard. Digital workboard by participant group.

◑ ONBOARDING ACTIVITIES: PRE-WORKSHOP

Participants were provided with an email inviting them to share space with us in the workshop. However, we asked them to complete a few onboarding activities approximately one week before the workshop began. We shared a document outlining all the activities participants were to complete. We entitled this shared informational document Racism Untaught + [insert partner name]. It included important links and pre-workshop activities, such as the pre-workshop survey, the community agreement online activity, the Socio-cultural Identities worksheet, the workshop facilitator's slide deck, the shared Social Identity Profile slide deck, the Racism Untaught worksheet (which includes a map of the design research process and levels of oppression), the workshop digital report-out slide deck, and the cards from the workboard document (which includes all the language from the workboard; see chapter 1 for more detailed descriptions).

◑ INTRODUCTION AND ONBOARDING: FIFTY-FIVE MINUTES

During the first session of the workshop, we read aloud a land acknowledgment, statement of unity, and community agreement. We acknowledged the additional agreements the participants had added to the pre-workshop activity. We provided participants with a link to an online collaborative document that included our names and phone numbers, and we let them know that they could contact us with any immediate group concerns to ensure anonymity.

◑ CONTEXT: ONE HOUR AND FIVE MINUTES

PROMPTS

In the pre-workshop activities, we asked participants if there were any instances of racism they had experienced or observed that they felt comfortable writing about. We asked them to tell their stories in the survey without using any personal identifiers to ensure that the stories did not identify anyone personally. Before the workshop, we anonymized the prompts even further to ensure that no persons could be directly associated with what was shared in the survey. The anonymized stories were used as prompts during the workshop. The workshops we have conducted often end with participants asking how their ideas that resulted from the workshop would be implemented in their workspace. This workshop had six different prompts for the six different groups, each of which depicted real racialized experiences from their environment. When the participants were broken into groups, they were also provided with links to the digital workboard that corresponded with the group number they worked with. One of the group prompts was as follows: "While recruiting for a senior role at our parent company, a member of the executive team asked that we pursue Black, Indigenous, and people of color as candidates. In our recruiting efforts the pool had limited Black, Indigenous, or person of color candidates, and the finalists were all white males."

CARDS

Once participants in the group read the prompt, they took turns reading a row from the elements of racism aloud to decide as a group if the term applied to the prompt. If it did, they moved the card up to the context circle; if not, the card remained where it was. A few of the cards they selected included the following:

- *Entitlement:* The ideology that an individual is inherently more deserving of privileges and or power that results in special treatment. *Rationale:* The belief that a person deserves a job only because they graduated from college or because of any other powers and privileges that they have been afforded due to their social identities.
- *Whiteness:* The embodied ideology that whiteness is the norm and this normative standard has the power to control the social, political, economic, and cultural behavior within society. *Rationale:* All the candidates were white men.
- *White social capital:* The networks of relationships among white people who live and work in a society, which enable the oppression of Black people, Indigenous people, and people of color. *Rationale:* That we tend to hire people that look like us due to our social circles.
- *Explicit bias:* Attitudes and beliefs about a person or group of people on a conscious level, usually expressed as a direct result of a perceived and/or socialized threat. *Rationale:* That our work environment needs to be more explicit about how normalized racism is reflected in our biases.

LEVELS OF OPPRESSION

In the second part of step one, the group worked together with the levels of oppression model to further contextualize the instances of oppression that showed up within the prompt they had been given (see figure 5.8). They were asked to consider how and where, at different levels, oppression was introduced, reinforced, and perpetuated:

- *Beliefs:* Personal beliefs, ideas, and feelings that perpetuate oppression. *Rationale:* An assumption that they may not fit in the culture of the company. They are not recruited because "they are not like us"; an assumption that candidates "are not white" based on something provided on the resume.
- *Agentic action:* When oppressive beliefs translate into oppressive behavior. *Rationale:* We rely heavily on referrals, and due to a name, previous education, location, or other element, a specific resume was not considered for the next step in the hiring process.
- *Institutional:* Structural oppression that results from agentic oppressive behavior. *Rationale:* Look for people who "fit" into our "culture" and how the company is marketed.
- *Cultural:* Systems of norms, values, beliefs, and trusted systems of acquiring truth that preserve, protect, and maintain oppression. *Rationale:* Social expectations that have shaped company culture.

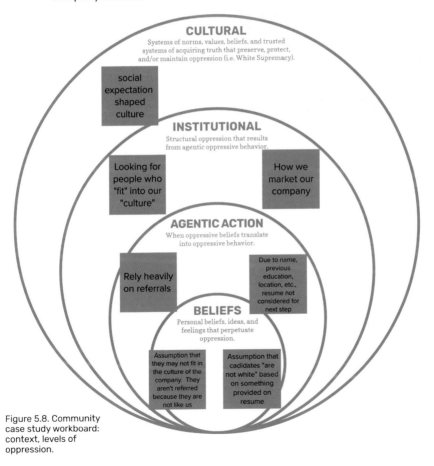

Figure 5.8. Community case study workboard: context, levels of oppression.

◀ DEFINE: ONE HOUR AND FIVE MINUTES

The groups were asked to begin by reviewing the cards in the define step. This provided participants with the opportunity to find value and understanding in the number of qualitative and quantitative research methods available for them to further contextualize and analyze the prompt. The group chose the following methods:

- *Needs assessment:* An essential tool to inform service planning, identifying the unmet needs of a population, and making changes to meet those unmet needs. This is a method.
- *Activity network:* A graphical method for showing dependencies between tasks or activities in a project. This is a method.
- *Expressive research:* A high value given to the views and perspectives of those who experience various phenomena and lived events. This is a theory.
- *Action research:* The act of research with the immediate follow up of evaluation, intervening in a continuous set of steps while making corrections. This is a method.

Figure 5.9. Community case study workboard: define. Participants selected research collected from the popular media search they conducted as a group.

Once this was completed, participants were asked to conduct a popular media search, a method for participants to search popular forms of media to gain further context on their prompt. Participants were encouraged to discuss the findings with each other, pull quotes from articles, and take screenshots of the articles or images used in them (see figure 5.9).

The question participants created from what they learned from secondary sources was: "How might design be used to evolve our recruiting process and the communication of our diversity, equity, and inclusion efforts to drive awareness and appeal to potential Black, Indigenous, or person of color talent in order to attract and cultivate a more diverse and inclusive culture with all associates?" When participants created their question, they began by using a breakdown we included to the right of the question, a space on the digital workboard separated into three different areas. This prompted them to consider: What *change* do they want to happen? What *actions* need to happen for that change to occur? *Who* needs to be involved for those changes to be sustainable? Each participant's voice was needed in this section to ensure that the question was created collaboratively (see figure 5.10). Some of the responses under each category included the following:

- *Action(s):* Outreach surveys for racially marginalized community members or organizations; think tank survey of current Black associates, Indigenous associates, or associates of color; more image-diverse recruiting materials; multi-touchpoint resume-vetting process; expanded recruiting efforts and locations (get out of our current comfort zone)
- *Change(s):* Attract, identify, and hire Black candidates, Indigenous candidates, or candidates of color; cultivate a more diverse and inclusive culture
- *Stakeholder(s):* Human resources; recruiters; hiring managers and department head(s); community leaders who hold racially marginalized identities

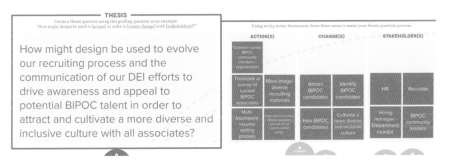

Figure 5.10. Community case study workboard: define. Participants' thesis question.

◀ IDEATE: THIRTY-FIVE MINUTES IN SESSION ONE, FIFTY MINUTES IN SESSION TWO

THE CARDS

The ideate step contained cards that were divided into the three identifiers in this research study: artifacts, systems, and experiences. Participants were prompted to review the cards in this step. They were asked to consider how they could combine these ideas to create a system that would help answer their thesis question. Some of the cards the participants chose in this group are as follows:

- *Interpersonal relationship:* Social associations, connections, or affiliations between two or more people. This fits within the experience section of design.
- *Large group relations:* The interactions within large groups of people. This fits within the experience section of design.
- *Campaign:* A connected series of operations designed to bring about a particular result. This fits within the experience section of design.

QUADRANT MAP

The quadrant map is an intervention meant to prompt conversation on ideation in collaborative spaces. Participants were asked between sessions to write down their ideas for answering the thesis question they had created based on everything they had completed in the workshop so far. Each participant wrote down an idea. Once the participants returned for the second session, their ideas were listed on a sticky note, and the groups were placed back into their breakout rooms to discuss where the sticky notes should be placed on the quadrant map (see figure 5.11). Some of their ideas included the following:

- Create a hiring manager playbook to provide best practices and instruction on fair hiring and diversity hiring.
- Update job descriptions to be more inclusive and ensure the language used does not appeal more to one group. Divide must-have skills from nice-to-have skills so that candidates can clearly see what is necessary.
- Identify community partners to connect with.
- Create content (e.g., videos for the websites of Black clients/vendors, Indigenous clients/vendors, or clients/vendors of color, or a case study featuring diversity among our client base).
- Invest in connecting with the community and/or expert partners to help develop the organization into a place that Black candidates, Indigenous candidates, or candidates of color seek out.

◀ PROTOTYPE: ONE HOUR AND TEN MINUTES

In this step of the framework, we introduced three different levels of prototypes: low, mid, and high fidelity. During an eight-hour workshop, the participants did not have time to complete the mid- and high-fidelity prototypes, so they were

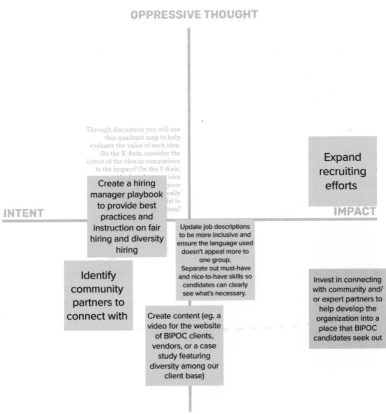

OPPRESSIVE THOUGHT

Through discussion you will use
this quadrant map to help
evaluate the value of each idea.
On the X-Axis, consider the
intent of the idea in comparison
to the impact? On the Y-Axis,
idea

INTENT

IMPACT

Create a hiring
manager playbook
to provide best
practices and
instruction on fair
hiring and diversity
hiring

Expand
recruiting
efforts

Update job descriptions
to be more inclusive and
ensure the language used
doesn't appeal more to
one group.
Separate out must-have
and nice-to-have skills so
candidates can clearly
see what's necessary.

Identify
community
partners to
connect with

Invest in connecting
with community and/
or expert partners to
help develop the
organization into a
place that BIPOC
candidates seek out

Create content (eg. a
video for the website
of BIPOC clients,
vendors, or a case
study featuring
diversity among our
client base)

ANTI-OPPRESSIVE ACTIONS

Figure 5.11. Community case
study workboard: ideate.

asked to focus on making a low-fidelity prototype. They were asked to review all
the prototype cards in this step.

The low-fidelity prototype is the initial, raw presentation of an idea. The
participants believed that the company was not reaching the right audience when
recruiting participants. They were concerned that the vetted resume process
was a potential source of bias and that a general awareness of inclusion and
diversity in their workplace may be lacking. They began to question what they
could do in their workspace to connect with the right candidates. They wanted to
begin looking at community partners and connections, consider the recruitment
materials they were using, the locations where these materials were distributed,
and the groups they had reached. They analyzed the content on their website
and wanted to add case studies that highlighted their work and projects that
were anti-racist.

They wanted to understand the investment into resources, partnerships, and content that would translate to Black people, Indigenous people, or people of color being interested in working at their company. Their idea was to develop new positions that were focused on expertise with Black and brown communities and businesses. They also considered hiring a new dedicated leader focused on diversity, equity, and inclusion. The hope was for this person to create a resource for Black and brown employees. They also hoped this person would create work initiatives that would ultimately build a task force and an expert team to be focused on the development and implementation of resources specifically for Black, Indigenous, or people of color employees (see figure 5.12).

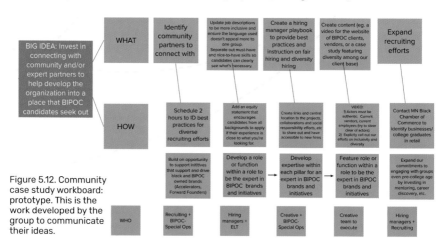

Figure 5.12. Community case study workboard: prototype. This is the work developed by the group to communicate their ideas.

◑ IMPACT: FORTY-FIVE MINUTES

The group was asked to select the impact cards they were most interested in implementing to further understand the impact of their ideas. In this step, we reminded all participants that the framework was iterative. When we further understand the impact of our work, we can do more research to help us ideate and prototype more ideas and ensure that we are working toward a positive impact. The team selected the following impact cards:

- *Implementation plan:* Addressing and creating the execution plan to realize solutions
- *Team formation plan:* Planning initiatives based on innovative solutions and forming teams around them—for example, task forces
- *Mission statement:* A short formal summary of the values of a company, organization, or individual

◑ FINAL PRESENTATION: FORTY-FIVE MINUTES

In the final presentations, the participants in the group presented the work they had completed together. We asked that only one or two individuals from each group present to ensure they met the time limit of five minutes. The groups were provided with a slide deck and were asked to fill in five slides per group, one slide per step of the framework. There was an introductory slide for each group that included the group's prompt.

CHALLENGES

Some of the challenges that participants brought up regarding the workshop included the design process, being vulnerable while talking about racism, trying to understand each of the elements of racism, and the length of the workshop being conducted over an online platform. Each of these is a challenge we have faced before and for which we continue to iterate solutions.

We do consider Zoom fatigue when we are conducting workshops. We provide participants with a worksheet that outlines the framework for them to take notes on for themselves outside of the digital workboard. In regard to understanding approximately seventy elements of racism, we tell participants that it is very difficult to learn all of them within the time frame of a workshop and encourage them to revisit the workboards or the list of elements we provide.

Comments from participants include the following:

> From the design piece to different ideas we came up with on how to solve for certain issues in our organization, I without a doubt see myself referencing and remembering what I learned over the last two days.[25]

> How we dissected the problem in digestible steps. It was so helpful to be able to pause and come back to each piece before moving forward. The guidance was truly phenomenal and I enjoyed that Terresa & Lisa would bop in and out of breakout rooms to help give us other thought starters or ask questions to facilitate deeper learnings.[26]

> I loved this course! Nice work, and thank you for helping us on our journey, such important work.[27]

> I liked this was not only for leadership but for all employees. Having leadership hear consistent messages of "we aren't doing enough" will hopefully help create a catalyst for change.[28]

WE NEED TO MOVE FROM COMPETITIVE IDEATION, TRYING TO PUSH OUR INDIVIDUAL IDEAS, TO COLLECTIVE IDEATION, COLLABORATIVE IDEATION. IT ISN'T ABOUT HAVING THE NUMBER ONE BEST IDEA, BUT HAVING IDEAS THAT COME FROM, AND WORK FOR, MORE PEOPLE.

—adrienne maree brown, *Emergent Strategies*[1]

A COLLECTIVE LIBERATORY FUTURE

Liberation cannot be created by one person. White colonial thinking continues to influence the ways in which we engage with one another in the fight against the very systems that oppress us all. We cannot allow individualism to narrow our ideas of what collective liberation looks like. We cannot put limits and rules on a future free of violence, or that future will not be free. This is one of the many reasons we encourage the use of the Racism Untaught framework as a group process. While there are individual learning experiences happening while engaging in the framework, those experiences run parallel to the collective vision. Our individual growth not only positively changes us, but positively supports the culture shifts necessary for our collective movement. Liberation will not come from a single person or idea; rather, a collective ideation process that considers a wide variety of experiences can craft an interdependent world meant for all of us to not only live but also thrive.

To get to what we envision as a collective liberatory future, we have outlined three areas of consideration or calls to action as one of many strategies for moving toward liberation: (1) understand the system (our client), (2) understand who we are (our audience) within and out of the system, and (3) understand and stay committed to the vision (our desired outcomes) (see figure 6.1).

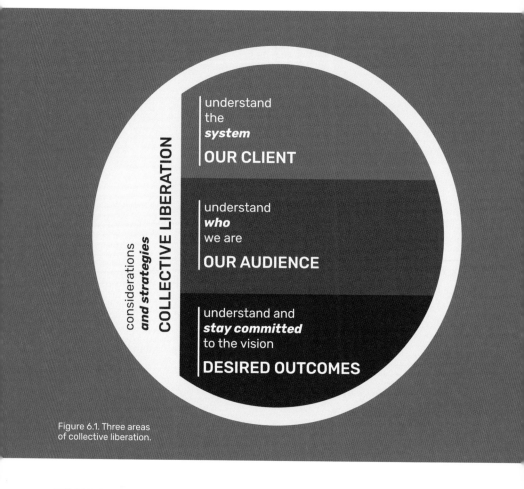

Figure 6.1. Three areas of collective liberation.

THE SYSTEM

In understanding the systems of oppression, we are calling you to action in understanding the reality of racialized danger and violence, the support you can find in intentional community, and collaboration and listening to learn.

REALITIES OF RACISM AND OPPRESSION

Author bell hooks described the system of oppression as a *white supremacist capitalist patriarchy*. The language she uses is inclusive of the intersectional systems of oppression at play that affect us all. This white supremacist capitalist patriarchy is continuous, pervasive, manipulative, and does not care about anyone.

While there are many symptoms of this system, one at the forefront in the wake of the George Floyd uprisings is police brutality. Since Floyd's murder, four other Black men have been murdered in the Minneapolis area by Minneapolis or Minneapolis-adjacent police departments. Violence against Black bodies is indicative of a system full of anti-Blackness that needs to be approached with an abolitionist design lens. The broader public knows that these are not isolated incidents, and yet we as a nation continue to allow this very real threat and racial trauma to permeate throughout communities. Police brutality is one of many symptoms of the systems that bell hooks describes as keeping in power those who are already in power and making it so that those who are oppressed to continue to lack the necessary resources to gain access to a life without a murderous expiration date.

With this continuous and institutionally supported threat of violence upon our communities, spaces must be created that support the study of the white supremacist capitalist patriarchy to craft anti-racist approaches. It is not enough to critically analyze racialized systems in classes and training modules with the title "diversity and inclusion." Racialized design is everywhere and affects everyone. For these reasons, we need to think more critically about how to bring, at a minimum, conversations about these realities into our workspaces, classrooms, and organizations. If we know that the white supremacist capitalist patriarchy affects us in all spaces, we have to make an intentional effort to understand how this system shows up in all of the spaces we inhabit.

For educators, and those with the power to educate within their institutions, this means that alongside your personal anti-racist growth, you are creating projects and opportunities to focus on these challenges in our society and to increase cultural awareness and create more anti-racist actions. As people who are consciously aware that racialized systems exist and are perpetually violent toward our communities, it is our responsibility to help those around us understand the role they must play in systemic racism and oppression as perpetrators of it or as those who dismantle it. This can be through direct teaching, modeling anti-racist behaviors, or showing up in the community. These conversations and projects will provide spaces to further explore and innovate in a collaborative and interdisciplinary environment.

FINDING COMMUNITY

Collaboration is not only important because we all bring unique skills to the proverbial table; in working together, we also build relationships. These relationships help us build empathy for experiences we do not share with others. In parallel to our own understanding of how we exist in systems of oppression, we begin to see the nuances of other's existence as well.

These relationships also build a community of trust, which is at the very foundation of a collective liberatory future. Trust can be built when we are radically willing to engage in individual and collective healing and foster nurturing environments for vulnerability.[2] Patrisse Cullors, one of the founders of the Black Lives Matter movement, writes in *An Abolitionist's Handbook*: "The concept of community building is really about whom we can trust, whom we can feel emotionally, spiritually and physically safe with, as well as reciprocal accountability. These are the key factors when building the community you want to be evolving inside of."[3] When we talk about transformative justice in our communities, this can only happen in communities built on trust and accountability.

Among many positive attributes in finding community, the last one we will mention is that community creates opportunities for accountability. Accountability recognizes a holistic process of acknowledgment, intervention, and restoration. It is in part a repertory act that can transform our communities—communities in which no one is canceled, and we can all find unique ways to contribute and support one another. These community concepts of collaboration, trust, and accountability can be applied to the design process. We can begin to critically analyze the ways in which we use design to create interdependent spaces, shifts, and changes.

WATCHING, LISTENING, AND LEARNING

As we explained in chapter 3, humility is necessary for our continued personal growth and anti-racist journeys. We can use this concept of humility to tackle the culture of expertise that often stifles progress due to the historically colonial pressure to know it all. As designers, it is our responsibility to understand the system we hope to change. This involves a critical analysis of what is happening around us that supports these systems. We cannot change what we do not understand, and we cannot understand without watching closely and listening intently.

Watch what your peers and leaders say versus what they do. What do they set into action? What is performative versus genuine? These questions could make the difference in understanding who you can work with to support collective liberation. And listen: Listen to those on the inside, living experiences drastically different from the dominant culture. Listen to Black people, Indigenous people, people of color, people with disabilities, women and nonbinary people, queer people, and trans people. Listening will only add to your process of learning.

We originally created the Racism Untaught toolkit to teach and educate about the very real threat of racialized design and ways in which people can engage in anti-racist design practices. Our framework is one of many frameworks, toolkits, training, modules, and workshops that provide opportunities to learn. Be a continuous learner; we have never fully arrived at the end of the knowledge that can be gained.

YOUR AGENCY

Your agency is your circle of influence within these systems of oppression. It is important that we all understand our positionality in those contexts, how we can create space for ourselves and others, our boundaries and ethical meters, and our abilities as designers.

EMPHASIS ON POSITIONALITY

Our society and culture continues to create racialized design even though we are not formally taught how to be racist. This system perpetuates itself, and without a critical look into how we play a role in changing said system, we are living contradictions, blaming others for racism and leaving ourselves out of justice-centered movements. It is imperative that we understand our identities (as discussed in chapter 3) and our roles in the movement toward collective liberation. This role brings about the nuance of being oppressed and having the capacity and positionality to oppress. Bring all these considerations to the table when you consider your role in socio-cultural change. Deepa Iyer emphasizes this point when she introduces her Social Change Ecosystem: "[We all] play different roles in pursuit of equity, liberation, inclusion, and justice."[4] And by choosing to do nothing—not to step into our roles toward liberation—we are perpetuating the very system that is oppressing us.

MAKE SPACE

In understanding the system and your agency, you are bound to make mistakes. Leave room and flexibility, for grace for yourself and grace for others. Do not let unspoken apologies, guilt, or embarrassment stop you from making and holding space with others. This is not in contradiction to accountability, and in fact adds to the definition. We must hold ourselves and others to the same standard of commitment to ensure we all make it to the future we are collectively envisioning. Making space for others when you have the power and or privilege to do so is imperative to creating collective power. So when you can, leave room for others at the table—or design a new table altogether, one where everyone's narrative, identity, and abilities are valued.

BOUNDARIES AND ETHICS

Sometimes we have said no to partners who want to work with us. It does not happen often, but it does happen. For us, these have been real in-time moments where we had to be clear on our goals and outcomes for specific projects. Life lessons in boundaries and ethics can take many forms, but we would encourage you to create your own code of ethics and stick to those boundaries. And over time, you will find that these boundaries shift with context and your ethics change due to new learnings. All these scenarios are completely validated as you continue your personal growth. Be clear about not only who you are, but what you stand for.

BE DESIGNERS

If our job as designers is to fix ugly things, why aren't we all talking about racism? Racism, capitalism, patriarchy, and other forms of systemic oppression have created an inaccessible society where it is impossible to thrive. We all have a hand in the design of these systems, so why are designers not thinking critically about using design strategies to create liberatory spaces? Thinking outside of the box is critical to outsmarting the system of violence that continues to oppress us. As a designer, you already have the tools to see problems and create solutions. Natalia Ilyin spoke to this sentiment in their chapter "What Design Activism Is and Is Not," stating that "designers can affect significant change. They can change societies. They can change who's in power. . . . Because they are trained in the tools of persuasion, they can tell the tale of the other side, of the 'underdog,' of the endangered species."[5] Shifting your lens and making this an intentional part of your practice can and should be learned. It should be an integral part of our growth as designers. We are not negating the fact that shifting your lens is a continual process and can be very difficult at times, but if you will not shift your design practices, who will, when will that happen, and can we wait that long? In her article "Black Designers: Still Missing in Action?" in *PRINT* magazine, Cheryl D. Holmes-Miller supports this point by stating to all designers everywhere, "It's time to be the solution; it's time to be seen, designing the solution now."[6]

We hope that Racism Untaught might be used as an additional tool for designers to positively impact our communities by developing new and inclusive designs at the local, state, and national levels. An effort must be placed on redesigning how individuals engage with and create artifacts, systems, and experiences to break down systemic racism. Because we, as creatives, designers, and artists, "are here to disturb the peace," as stated by James Baldwin in a 1961 conversation between him and Studs Terkel.[7] So let's start today, disturbing the peace of oppression and building solutions for our vision of a collective liberatory future.

THE VISION

The vision for collective liberation, in its entirety, will not be found in this book. Instead, we offer our ideas in the collective conversations centered on liberation, including decolonization and decentering whiteness, freedom, commitment, and liberatory futures.

DECOLONIZING AND DECENTERING

Buzzwords like *diversity*, *equity*, *inclusion*, and now *decolonization* tend to sugarcoat obvious issues caused by systemic racism to keep those who benefit from systems of oppression comfortable (discussed further in chapter 4). We cannot move past these issues unless we have the courage and bravery to call it what it is. For instance, it is common to hear "we need more diversity" rather than naming the reality that "harm and violence caused by white supremacy has stifled Black people's, Indigenous people's, and people of color's access to predominantly white spaces, and because of our willingness to uphold this standard, we have made it unsafe for people of color to want to engage in spaces with us." There are two completely different feelings of urgency in the language of both statements. Systems of oppression are very clear about who gains access and opportunity; it is time we are clear about destroying these systems of harm and violence. How can we see a vision for the future without a clear understanding of what affects our workplaces, campuses, and communities? When we use these terms without specific and intentional context, we enable our socio-cultural identity to be apathetic and compliant, ignoring the real issues of oppression.

Metaphors and analogies are helpful in the learning process; however, we cannot get stuck there because it promotes compliance and a recentering of the oppression we want to dismantle. Eve Tuck and K. Wayne Yang emphasize this point in their article "Decolonizing Is Not a Metaphor": "[Decolonization as a metaphor] recenters whiteness, it resettles theory, it extends innocence to the settler, it entertains a settler future."[8] This also implies that all of us, no matter our socio-cultural identity, have the ability and the power to decenter whiteness. Without context around what exactly is causing oppression and the future we hope to build, using language like *decolonization* does not help our causes because it still centers whiteness, rather than centering Black people, Indigenous people, and people of color in our just and collective liberatory futures. Lone metaphors and other soft language get in the way of focusing on meaningful and innovative ways to center our work on social impact or critical methodology. Many of these metaphors are treated as stopping points when we need to continue past their definitions toward collective liberation.

We see decolonization in our workplaces, educational institutions, and communities as an intentional deconstructing of colonial and white settler-imposed systems that oppress Black people, Indigenous people, and people of color. This is simply a recognition of and a gaining of awareness about these systems and their historical foundations. In education, Vanessa Lopez-Littleton and Brandi Blessett describe this as to "infuse co-curricular programming and services with components that create engaging cultural competence learning opportunities for students" and to create "new courses, curricula, and pedagogy . . . needed to respond to experiences of underrepresented and underserved students."[9] In the design industry, this may look like a restructuring of hierarchy in the responsibilities of workplace cultural ownership. Regardless of the spaces in which you are applying the concept of decolonization, we should be asking ourselves: How do I transform our spaces into a community of inquiry? How do I structure or sequence a series of readings, assignments, trainings, and intentional learning spaces that support a collective liberatory future? What types of activities need to be included in our spaces to support critical thinking and develop community trust and accountability? Who do I believe holds the knowledge and expertise in our space, and do I see socio-cultural experiential knowledge as valuable? And how does my positionality indicate or express my perception and understanding of a topic, project, or project outcome? These are just some of the questions we should be asking ourselves as we move toward a more specific concept of decentering.

After or in parallel with decolonizing, *decentering whiteness* is a concept that begins to value and validate the contributions of Black people, Indigenous people, and people of color within our industries, educational settings, and communities. Decentering offers a new way of considering expertise and even learning. It takes a more collective approach to understanding, placing the weight of our cultural workplace or educational standard on everyone in the space, not just those highest in the hierarchy. It is an inclusion of narratives and voices that often go underrepresented and undervalued. It is a normalization of all, not one. This collective and collaborative mindset moves us into liberation.

FREEDOM

Freedom is a nuanced concept that looks different to everyone, but there are just a few concepts that umbrella us all. First is the *gray area*. There is so much freedom in removing the colonial and puritan structure of good and bad. Removing the binary from our ways of doing, speaking, and just simply being adds a liberating complexity—an inclusionary existence. Multiple things can be true at once. And in knowing this, there is unfounded freedom in the gray area. When we let go of the black and white, we embrace our whole selves. And when we can embrace and love our whole selves, we can embrace and love others as well, gaining an empathy that only lived experience can teach. This gray area does not just apply to the personal aspects of our lives; in fact, we would progress much quicker if there was a radical acceptance of the gray. The understanding is that even as we strive for the creation and design of anti-racist artifacts, systems, and experiences, we must still live parallel to a system that perpetuates harm and violence. Understanding this helps us have more holistic conversations about the realities of oppression and its effects on our communities. For example, consider the nuances of environmental justice and its fight against fast fashion while we acknowledge that capitalism does not create opportunities for the majority to purchase sustainable clothing due to its cost. It is nuanced and wicked, which makes acknowledgment a path toward addressing foundational oppression and thus its wicked symptoms.

These nuanced parallels also apply to the freedom to make mistakes and the admission of regret or ignorance. The toxic binary we mentioned in chapter 3 remains true even in spaces dedicated to liberation and transformative justice. Just as we must intentionally create and engage the world in an anti-racist way, so too must we engage in our intentions to include nuance in our conversations and dreams about right and wrong. Because, as of now, *wrong* means *bad*, and that means being exiled from our society through punitive systems like prisons and social alienation. Angela Davis states in *Are Prisons Obsolete?*, "[Prison] relieves us of the responsibility of seriously engaging with the problems of our society, especially those produced by racism and, increasingly, global capitalism."[10] No one deserves punitive justice, so how can we imagine a world where police and prisons do not exist without recognition that one act does not define an individual? If we can accept the nuance in our identities, we must recognize it in the elements of racism we perpetuate. Without this acknowledgment, we cannot be specific about the nature of the harm we cause and thus we cannot move forward in dismantling what institutions supported that action in the first place. If we criminalize every person who has engaged in harmful actions birthed from systems of oppression, we will not be left with anyone in our collective liberatory future.

The last concept we will mention in the freedom that will exist in our vision of collective liberation is the freedom to just *be*. To just be, for us, means a freedom to feel and to create. The freedom to be oneself requires a space that allows for trust, vulnerability, and accountability. This means we must be conscious of how we are supporting one another in the vision, what we deem valuable, and whose humanity we are willing to see and have empathy for. This also means we can feel emotion, without judgment, from ourselves and others. We have to be able to admit when we are defensive about potential racialized harm we may have caused so that we can be held accountable and holistically heal with each other. This requires a level of trust that can only be gained in the building of community and authentic relationships. And if we say that we value this concept, then intentional time is needed to build these concepts. So if you have power to shift policies in your institution, set aside part of your workdays specifically for this. The fact is that working on the vision for collective liberation *is* work.

COMMITMENT

Working toward a collective liberatory future free from racial harm and violence takes commitment. Just as Karen Potts and Leslie Brown state in "Becoming an Anti-Oppressive Researcher," "Committing ourselves to anti-oppressive work means committing to social change and to taking an active role in that change."[11] This commitment comes from all of us, our organizations, and our communities. We should constantly question what collective liberation looks like, feels like, smells like, tastes like—and what, if anything, are we doing to get there. In a 1982 address entitled "Learning from the 60s," Audre Lorde delivered the following statement about commitment: "What we must do is commit ourselves to some future that can include each other and to work toward that future with the particular strengths of our individual identities. And in order to do this, we must allow each other our differences at the same time as we recognize our sameness."[12] This is a call to action. A commitment to disrupting the status quo, dismantling systems of oppression, and destroying colonial ways of thinking to allow space for nuance while we commit ourselves to a future that values all of us.

COLLECTIVE LIBERATION

We define *collective liberation* as transformational healing, protection, and creative freedom for all. A future that considers everyone in the decision-making process, understanding that when we design for those who sit in the margins of the margins, we are designing for everyone. In this liberatory lens, we would not define this consideration as some sort of reverse oppression; rather, we would understand how historically our society has been set up to exclude the marginalized and that liberation happens when those voices have the same access and opportunities as those who have benefited from systems of oppression for centuries. Collective liberation moves away from the individual and supports the collective good.

Although this is the final chapter, this is just the beginning of our journeys in the work of eradicating racialized and oppressive systems. This work does not end, and we cannot express how much you are needed in our vision of a collective liberatory future. We remain committed because of our hope that our work today will plant seeds for generations to come, who may eventually reap an equitable and anti-racist harvest of opportunities and access. We look toward a future where everyone has their physical, emotional, mental, social, and spiritual needs met. A collective future where we might create and heal together in communities based on love, grace, equity, transformative justice, and peace.

COMMUNITY CASE STUDY

Real Estate Agents

NOT IN MY BACKYARD: REAL ESTATE AGENTS IN MINNESOTA

ORGANIZATION
Racism Untaught workshop, one five-hour session (see figure 6.2), in-person, spring 2022

TEAM
Facilitators: Lisa Elzey Mercer, Terresa Moses, and Billie Conaway.
Participants: Thirty real estate agents, from different companies. All participants were guided through the first three steps of the framework in small groups of approximately six members. This case study will only feature one group's progress. The racial makeup of the group was all white.

Figure 6.2. Community case study workboard. This image shows all of the workboards at the end of the workshop.

❹ ONBOARDING ACTIVITIES: PRE-WORKSHOP

Participants were provided with an email that invited them to share space with us in the workshop. Within the email, we asked them to complete a few onboarding activities approximately one week before the workshop began. We shared an online document that we titled Racism Untaught + [insert partner name]. The document included important links and pre-workshop activities, such as the pre-workshop survey, the community agreement online activity, the Socio-cultural Identities worksheet, the workshop facilitator's slide deck, the shared Social Identity Profile slide deck, the Racism Untaught worksheet (which includes a map of the design research process and levels of oppression), the workshop digital report-out slide deck, and the cards from the workboard document (which includes all the language from the workboard; see chapter 1 for more detailed descriptions).

Most participants completed all of their pre-workshop activities; however, we always print out blank social identity cards for participants who do not come with that activity already completed.

❹ INTRODUCTION AND ONBOARDING: FIFTY-FIVE MINUTES

At the beginning of the workshop, we read aloud a land acknowledgment, statement of unity, and community agreement. We acknowledged the additional agreements and clarifications that the participants had added to the pre-workshop community agreement activity. We then give a brief overview of who we are and how and why we created the Racism Untaught framework. We discuss racialized design, the categories of artifacts, systems, and experiences, and positionality. After this introduction, in the next activity, we led by example by introducing ourselves again, along with a breakdown of our socio-cultural identities. Participants were then instructed to turn to their group members to introduce themselves and their identities in a similar fashion. We ended this segment with a few comments from the larger group and then with a five-minute break.

❹ CONTEXT: SIXTY-FIVE MINUTES
THE PROMPT: A RACIALIZED EXPERIENCE

In the pre-workshop activities, we asked participants to provide anonymized instances of racism they had experienced or observed and that they felt comfortable writing about. Before the workshop, we made sure that the prompts did not include recognizable identifiers to ensure that no particular persons could be directly associated with what was shared in the survey. These stories were used as prompts during the workshop. The workshops we have conducted often end with participants asking how their ideas that resulted from the workshop would be implemented in their workspace since they are solving for real instances of racism. This workshop had seven different prompts for the different groups. The prompt that will be the subject of this case study was as follows: "I have heard discussions among my white colleagues regarding Somali immigrants moving to an area causing a depreciation in property values."

THE CARDS

After reading through the prompt, we instructed the participants to decide which elements of racism applied to the prompt to help them further contextualize what happened in this racialized experience. Using the physical toolkit cards, they began to discuss the prompt in terms of which elements they agreed represented the experience (see figure 6.3). Some of the cards the participants pulled were as follows:

- *Anti-Black racism:* Elements of racism directed toward and experienced by Black people. *Rationale:* The participants named that there is a heightened racial bias against Black people in regard to conversations about property value.
- *Compliance culture:* Adhering to established norms that take the form of external laws, internal policies, and values meant to put an end to unwanted behaviors by associating those behaviors with negative, harmful, and violent stimulus. *Rationale:* The participants believed it was very likely that the person who heard the discussions said nothing to avoid discomfort.
- *Institutional racism:* Racial discrimination that derives from an individual's actions of a prejudiced institution or society. *Rationale:* Participants concluded that this discussion is indicative of a deeply embedded culture of racism within the institution of real estate.
- *Redlining:* The racially influenced and systematic denial of various residential services, including access to specific neighborhoods, through the selective raising of prices. *Rationale:* The participants discussed this racial bias as being the cause of systemic redlining within their communities.

LEVELS OF OPPRESSION

In the second part of step one, the group worked with the levels of oppression model to further contextualize the instances of oppression that showed up within the prompt they had been given (see figure 6.4). They were asked to consider how and where, at different levels, oppression was introduced, reinforced, and perpetuated. The following are examples of how the participants chose to break down the levels of oppression as related to their racialized prompts:

- *Beliefs:* Personal beliefs, ideas, and feelings that perpetuate oppression. *Rationale:* There is a stereotypical belief among real estate agents and clients that Blackness is equal to poverty, cheapness, and trashiness.
- *Agentic action:* When oppressive beliefs translate into oppressive behavior. *Rationale:* Personal beliefs translate into actions such as *blockbusting*, which is the convincing of white property owners to sell their houses at low prices by promoting fear that racial minorities will be moving into the neighborhood.

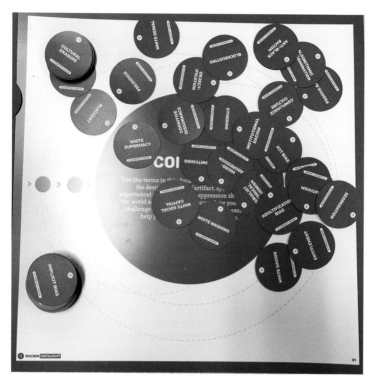

Figure 6.3.
Community case
study workboard:
context.

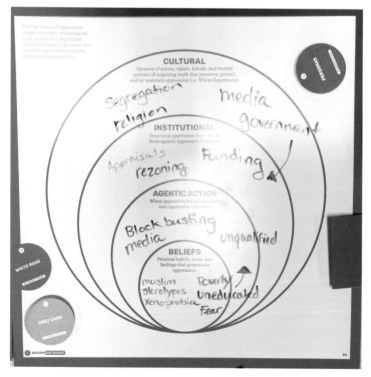

Figure 6.4.
Community case
study workboard:
context, levels of
oppression.

A Collective Liberatory Future

- *Institutional:* Structural oppression that results from agentic oppressive behavior. *Rationale:* Racialized beliefs and actions are perpetuated by a very biased appraisal process, lowering the value of homes just because the owners are Black.
- *Cultural:* Systems of norms, values, beliefs, and trusted systems of acquiring truth that preserve, protect, and maintain oppression. *Rationale:* There is still a widely accepted culture of segregation in the housing market.

◀ DEFINE: ONE HOUR AND FIVE MINUTES

The second step began with a review of the define step and how the team members would use the information they gathered to create their thesis questions. We instructed them to first review *theories*, which we described as a lens through which to look at racialized design, and then *methods*, which we described as ways of gathering data. This provided participants with the opportunity to understand the variety of qualitative and quantitative research methods available for them to further contextualize and analyze the prompt. The group chose the following methods and theories (see figure 6.5), although they only worked through the popular media search for the purposes of this training:

- *Culture of prejudice:* The theory that prejudice is embedded in our culture
- *Popular media search:* Searching popular forms of media to gain further context

Next, the participants engaged in the popular media search by pulling articles, reports, journals, books, videos, blogs, and imagery to help contextualize their prompt. In their search, they chose to explore topics such as refugees and resettlement, populations vulnerable to gentrification, communities that have higher racial diversity, how segregated and devalued neighborhoods affect children of color, the nationwide appraisal gap, and economic contributions to diverse neighborhoods.

The participants were then guided through the process of creating a thesis question, using this guiding question as an example: "How might design be used to [action] in order to [create change] with [stakeholders]?" We broke this down to them in three parts—actions, changes, and stakeholders—so they could more easily explore what they were interested in changing (see figure 6.6). In the actions category, they listed required training, education, and rewriting company policy. In the changes category, they listed proper valuation of homes owned by people of color and shifting office culture. And in the stakeholder category, they listed employees and company leadership. Through brainstorming and discussion, the participants crafted the following thesis question, which they used to guide them in creating an anti-racist approach for their racialized experience: "How might design be used to expose the inefficacy of the Realtor Code of Ethics in order to change industry and overall culture with colleagues, customers, clients, and community members?"

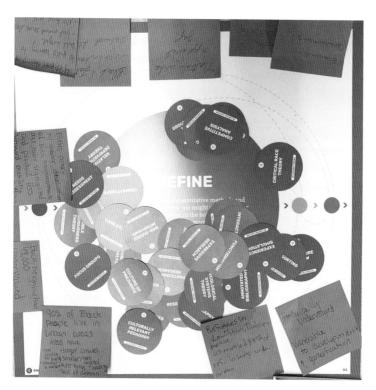

Figure 6.5.
Community
case study
workboard:
define.

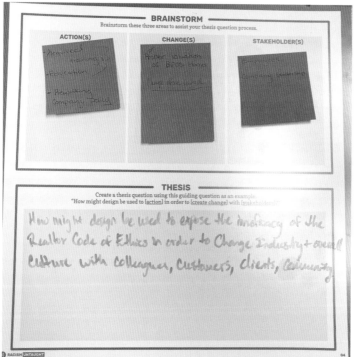

Figure 6.6.
Community
case study
workboard:
define, thesis
question.

◉ IDEATE: FORTY-FIVE MINUTES

THE CARDS

After crafting a thesis question together, the participants continued their work with their third and final step, ideate. Because this partner scheduled a five-hour workshop, we only had enough time to complete the framework up to step three. We explained to the participants that the ideate card set was meant to spark ideas and help them explore avenues through which they might answer the thesis question they created. Each card fell within one of the three categories of design explained in chapter 2. The participants were encouraged to use all three categories of design in the ideation process. We even encouraged the groupings of artifacts, systems, and experiences that might work together in a design approach. Some of the cards the group chose were as follows:

- *Campaign:* A connected series of operations designed to bring about a particular result. This is within the artifact section of design.
- *Labor and industry:* The system referring to workplaces and access to employment. This is within the system section of design.
- *Narrative:* A spoken or written account of connected events; a story. This is within the experience section of design.

THE QUADRANT MAP

The second part of the third step created opportunities for more specific ideas and for measuring the implementation of those ideas using the quadrant map (see figure 6.7). Each participant created a list of ideas based on the areas of design they pulled from the ideate deck of cards. Participants were encouraged to write down all their ideas, which they placed on individual sticky notes. Participants then placed their sticky notes on the quadrant map to gain a better understanding of first how far their idea would take their stakeholders from oppressive thought to anti-oppressive action, and then how far the idea moved cultural norms from good intentions to positive impact. In addition to their crafted thesis question, participants were encouraged to consider how they might be intentionally anti-racist in their new design approach.

The participants decided on a new, more rigorous licensure process, which they held in higher esteem than just a membership in a large organization for real estate agents. This new licensure process would require continual ethics and bias training to keep your real estate license. Participants discussed how they might move this idea into action in their organization, creating a campaign for a new code of ethics framed as a lived experience rather than a box to be checked.

◉ CHALLENGES

Some of the challenges participants faced was their proximity to other racially diverse experiences. Some ideas that were brought up in regard to housing throughout the workshop expressed a narrow lens of experience in regard to

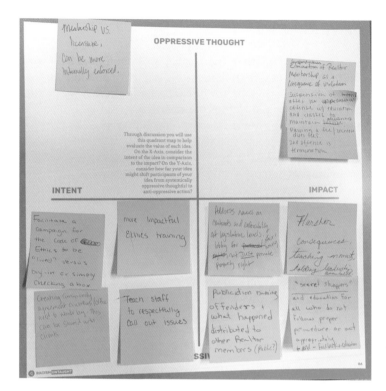

Figure 6.7. Community case study workboard: ideate, quadrant map.

race. This happens often in workshops with individuals whose organizations and workplaces reflect a white homogenous culture. Because of this challenge, we chose to draw upon our own experiences to help facilitate new ways of thinking and perhaps reveal a lens that they did not know existed. For instance, Terresa spoke to her experience as a Black woman in the academy who has certain powers that she has earned alongside her marginalized identities. Throughout the workshop, we repeated other nuanced stories and asked participants to question why certain elements exist in systems that they were critically exploring for the first time.

Five hours is not our ideal timeframe for a Racism Untaught workshop due to the lack of time for heavier discussion and analysis of systems of oppression. Many participants, though excited to have gone through the workshop, stated that they would have liked to complete all the steps of the framework to get to a solution. The following are direct quotes from the workshop participants:

The connection between small, everyday actions and broader systemic change. Specifically, how one can connect both "everyday" negative behavior to systemic racism and how pushing back against that can be part of changing systems as a whole.[13]

I felt like it helped me look at the challenges from a new perspective.[14]

THEY TRIED TO BURY US; THEY DID NOT KNOW WE WERE SEEDS.

—A Mexican battle cry for immigration and human rights

ACKNOWLEDGMENTS

We would like to thank our peers who are doing abolitionist and anti-racist work alongside us and to those who have reached back to pull us forward. We are thankful for the multitude of voices who have thought with us and continue to. This book would not have happened if it were not for the support of Antionette D. Carroll, president and CEO (founder) of Creative Reaction Lab, who supported the pilot workshop at the Design + Diversity conference. Our project advisors Heidi Bakk-Hansen, historian, researcher, and organizer; Dr. Gioconda Guerra Pérez, assistant vice chancellor for diversity, University of Illinois, Urbana-Champaign; Dr. Paula Pedersen, inclusive excellence, University of Minnesota, Duluth; Dr. Jeanine Weekes Schroer, philosopher and race theorist, University of Minnesota, Duluth; and Jennifer White-Johnson, art activist, designer, and educator.

We are thankful for participants who have engaged with the Racism Untaught framework and with us. To our students who have shared their stories and histories with us, who have spent their time thinking with us about how to discuss ethical, responsible, and various forms of racialized design. We are thankful for our academic, industry, and community partners who have helped us find, develop, and create new ways of working.

We are thankful to our peers and mentors who we have engaged with this work: the people we hold space with, who challenge us, help us grow and see new perspectives. Cheryl D. Miller, award-winning designer, author, and advocate; Anne H. Berry, assistant professor of graphic design in the Department of Art + Design at Cleveland State University; Lesley-Ann Noel, PhD, assistant professor of art and design at North Carolina State University; Omari Souza, assistant professor of graphic design at the University of North Texas; Gaby Hernandez, endowed associate professor of graphic design at the University of Arkansas; and Jacinda Walker, founder and creative director of designExplorr.

To Michael Gibson and Keith Owens, our professors, and graduate advisors at the University of North Texas. Your continued support and red pen of death over the last ten years have helped us in our navigation of the academy. We would like to thank our editor, Victoria Hindley, and the entire team at the MIT Press, who were willing to think with us about the direction of this book and its content. And to the readers of this work, thank you for engaging with us.

From Lisa: To my parents and those who came before them, my family, my partner, and our children. To my friends and mentors. It is through thoughtful conversations with each of you that I am where I am today. Thank you for your continued support, love, and encouragement.

From Terresa: To my ancestors, the historical abolitionists and freedom fighters, it is because of your dedication to our collective liberation that I am here today. To my mother, family, friends, fellow organizers, and mentors: thank you for your encouragement, critique, help, and the inspiration to keep going in the struggle.

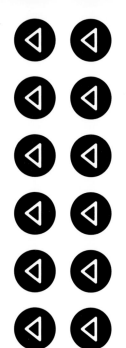

NOTES

FOREWORD

1. James Newton, "Slave Artisans and Craftsmen: The Roots of Afro-American Art," *Black Scholar* 9, no. 3 (1977): 35–42.
2. Jacquelyn Ogorchukwu Iyamah, "How Can Designers Build Interfaces That Avoid the 'White Default?,'" *Eye on Design*, March 14, 2022, https://eyeondesign.aiga.org/design-often-encourages -the-white-default-how-can-designers-create-more-inclusive-digital-interfaces/.

PREFACE

1. Qwo-Li Driskill (Cherokee), "Qwo-Li Driskill is Cherokee"? "Doubleweaving Two-Spirit Critiques: Building Alliances between Native and Queer Studies," *GLQ: A Journal of Lesbian and Gay Studies* 16, no. 1–2 (2010): 69–92.
2. "How George Floyd's Death Became a Catalyst for Change," National Museum of African American History and Culture, Smithsonian, May 25, 2021, https://nmaahc.si.edu/explore/stories/how -george-floyds-death-became-catalyst-change.

INTRODUCTION

1. bell hooks, *Teaching to Transgress: Education as the Practice of Freedom* (New York: Routledge, 1994), 12.
2. Patricia Hill Collins, *Black Feminist Thought: Knowledge, Consciousness, and the Politics of Empowerment*, 2nd ed. (New York: Routledge, 2009), 7.
3. Bethan Harries, "We Need to Talk About Race," *Sociology (Oxford)* 48, no. 6 (2014): 1107–1122, https://doi.org/10.1177/0038038514521714.
4. Kathy Glass, "Race-ing the Curriculum: Reflections on a Pedagogy of Social Change," in *Exploring Race in Predominantly White Classrooms: Scholars of Color Reflect*, ed. Maria del Guadalupe Davidson and George Yancy (New York: Routledge, 2014), 52.
5. Tiffany D. Joseph and Laura E. Hirshfield, "'Why Don't You Get Somebody New to Do It?' Race and Cultural Taxation in the Academy," *Ethnic and Racial Studies* 34, no. 1 (2011): 121–141, https://doi .org/10.1080/01419870.2010.496489.
6. Austin Channing Brown, *I'm Still Here* (New York: Crown, 2018), 170.
7. C. Kyle Rudick and Kathryn B. Golsan, "Civility and White Institutional Presence: An Exploration of White Students' Understanding of Race-Talk at a Traditionally White Institution," *Howard Journal of Communications* 29, no. 4 (2018): 335–352, https://doi.org/10.1080/10646175.2017.1392910.
8. "The Lens of Systemic Oppression," National Equity Project, accessed August 1, 2022, https://www.nationalequityproject.org/frameworks/lens-of-systemic-oppression.
9. hooks, *Teaching to Transgress*, 12.
10. As defined in the Racism Untaught toolkit: Cultural Taxation is a unique burden placed on Black, Indigenous, and people of color to carry out responsibility and service as the only represented minority within an organization.
11. Charlotte Huff, "Building a Better, More Diverse Faculty," *American Psychological Association* 52, no. 8 (2021): 25, https://www.apa.org/monitor/2021/11/news-diverse-faculty.
12. Barbara J. Fields and Karen Elise Fields, *Racecraft : The Soul of Inequity in American Life* (New York: Verso, 2012), 156.
13. Nicholas Daniel Hartlep, *Critical Race Theory: An Examination of Its Past, Present, and Future Implications* (ERIC Number ED506735, University of Wisconsin at Milwaukee, October 11, 2009), 6, https://eric.ed.gov/?id=ED506735.

There are five major components or tenets of CRT: (1) the notion that racism is ordinary and not aberrational, (2) the idea of an interest convergence, (3) the social construction of race, (4) the idea of storytelling and counterstorytelling, and (5) the notion that whites have actually been recipients of civil rights legislation.

14. Hartlep, *Critical Race Theory*, 6.

15. Daniel G. Solórzano and Tara J. Yosso, "Critical Race Methodology: Counter-Storytelling as an Analytical Framework for Education Research," *Qualitative Inquiry* 8, no. 1 (2002): 23–44.

16. Wendy Gunn, Ton Otto, and Rachel Charlotte Smith, *Design Anthropology* (New York: Bloomsbury, 2013), 2.

17. Terresa Moses, ART 3922 Course Syllabus (fall 2017).

18. Ellen Lupton, *Design Is Storytelling* (New York: Smithsonian Design Museum, 2017), 11.

19. Hemant Taneja, "The Era of 'Move Fast and Break Things' Is Over," *Harvard Business Review*, January 22, 2019, https://hbr.org/2019/01/the-era-of-move-fast-and-break-things-is-over.

20. Sarah Brown, "How Should Universities Respond to Racism?," *Chronicle of Higher Education*, December 3, 2021, https://www.chronicle.com/article/how-should-universities-respond -to-racism.

21. Arturo Escobar, *Designs for the Pluriverse: Radical Interdependence, Autonomy, and the Making of Worlds* (Durham, NC: Duke University Press, 2017), 67.

22. Tiffany Jewell, *This Book Is Anti-Racist: 20 Lessons on How to Wake Up, Take Action, and Do the Work* (London: Frances Lincoln Children's Books, 2020).

CHAPTER 1

1. Antionette Carroll, Twitter, June 24, 2020, 8:35 p.m., https://twitter.com/acarrolldesign /status/1275965708648583169?lang=en.

2. Donald A. Norman, *The Design of Everyday Things* (Philadelphia: Basic Books, 2013), 8.

3. "History," IDEO, accessed June 4, 2022, https://designthinking.ideo.com/history.

4. "History."

5. Charles Owen, "Design Thinking. What It Is. Why It Is Different. Where It Has New Value" (speech given at the International Conference on Design Research and Education for the Future, Gwangju City, Korea, October 21, 2005), https://www.id.iit.edu/wp-content/uploads/2015/03 /Design-thinking-what-it-is-owen_korea05.pdf.

6. Nigel Cross, "Designerly Ways of Knowing: Design Discipline versus Design Science," *Design Issues* 17, no. 3 (2001): 49–51, http://www.jstor.org/stable/1511801.

7. Horst W. J. Rittel and Melvin M. Webber, "Dilemmas in a General Theory of Planning," *Policy Sciences* 4, no. 2 (June 1973): 155–169, http://www.jstor.org/stable/4531523.

8. Rittel and Webber, "Dilemmas in a General Theory of Planning."

9. Richard Buchanan, "Wicked Problems in Design Thinking," *Design Issues* 8, no. 2 (Spring 1992): 5–21, http://www.jstor.org/stable/1511637.

10. Marie Davidová, "Multicentred Systemic Design Pedagogy through Real-Life Empathy Integral and Inclusive Practice-Based Education in the Research-by-Design Context," *Formakademisk* 13, no. 5 (2020): 1–7, https://doi.org/10.7577/formakademisk.3755.

11. Susan Gal, "John J. Gumperz's Discourse Strategies," *Journal of Linguistic Anthropology* 23, no. 3 (2013): 115–126, http://www.jstor.org/stable/43104337.

12. Gal, "John J. Gumperz's Discourse Strategies."

13. Janet K. Swim, Elizabeth D. Scott, Gretchen B. Sechrist, Bernadette Campbell, and Charles Stangor, "The Role of Intent and Harm in Judgments of Prejudice and Discrimination," *Journal of*

Personality and Social Psychology 84, no. 5 (2003): 944–959, https://doi.org/10.1037/0022
-3514.84.5.944.

14. Arlene Dávila, *Latinx Art* (Durham, NC: Duke University Press, 2020), 48.

15. Tarana Burke and Brene Brown, eds., *You Are Your Best Thing: Vulnerability, Shame, Resilience, and the Black Experience. An Anthology* (New York: Random House, 2021), 89.

16. "The Lens of Systemic Oppression," National Equity Project, accessed August 1, 2022, https://www.nationalequityproject.org/frameworks/lens-of-systemic-oppression.

17. Elizabeth B. Sanders and Pieter Jan Stappers, *Convivial Toolbox: Generative Research for the Front End of Design* (Amsterdam: Building Het Sieraad Publishers, 2012), 130.

18. Rikke Ørngreen and Karin Levinsen, "Workshops as a Research Methodology," *Electronic Journal of E-Learning* 15, no. 1 (2017): 70. ISSN 1479-4403.

19. Sanders and Stappers, *Convivial Toolbox*.

20. Katie Deney, "Situated Action," PB Works, November 19, 2009, http://510bds.pbworks.com/w/page/3872226/Situated%20Action.

21. Lucy A. Suchman, *Plans and Situated Actions: The Problem of Human-Machine Communication* (Cambridge: Cambridge University Press, 1987), 27–28.

22. Burke and Brown, *You Are Your Best Thing*, 60.

23. Arlene S. Hirsch, "An Inside Look at Workplace Racial Affinity Groups," Society for Human Resource Management, September 20, 2021, https://www.shrm.org/resourcesandtools/hr-topics/behavioral-competencies/global-and-cultural-effectiveness/pages/an-inside-look-at-workplace-racial-affinity-groups.aspx.

24. Participant, Racism Untaught industry workshop, 2021.

25. bell hooks, *Teaching to Transgress: Education as the Practice of Freedom* (New York: Routledge, 1994), 12.

26. "Native Land Digital," accessed May 2020, https://native-land.ca.

27. "Native Land Digital."

28. Sanders and Stappers, *Convivial Toolbox*, 45.

29. Miranda Fricker, *Epistemic Injustice: Power and the Ethics of Knowing* (Oxford: Oxford University Press, 2007), 145.

30. Nathan Shedroff, *Design Is the Problem: The Future of Design Must Be Sustainable* (Brooklyn: Rosenfeld Media, 2009), 77.

31. George Ella Lyon and Julie Landsman, "I Am From Project," accessed August 5, 2021, https://iamfromproject.com.

32. Paula J. Pedersen, "Where I'm REALLY From." Provided as a physical handout in the spring 2019 course referenced in this case study, and licensed under a Creative Commons Attribution-Noncommercial 4.0 International license.

33. Lyon and Landsman, "I Am From Project."

34. Marilyn Kern-Foxworth, *Aunt Jemima, Uncle Ben, and Rastus: Blacks in Advertising, Yesterday, Today, and Tomorrow* (Westport, CT: Greenwood Press, 1994).

35. Lawrence D. Reddick, "Educational Programs for the Improvement of Race Relations: Motion Pictures, Radio, the Press, and Libraries," *Journal of Negro Education* 13, no. 3 (1944): 367–389, https://doi.org/10.2307/2292454.

36. Student group, "Frank & Nancy" (unpublished student work, spring 2019), typescript.

37. Participant, Racism Untaught course, 2019.

38. Participant, Racism Untaught course, 2019.

39. Participant, Racism Untaught course, 2019.

40. Participant, Racism Untaught course, 2019.
41. Participant, Racism Untaught course, 2019.

CHAPTER 2

1. Lesley-Ann Noel and Renata M. Leitão, "Editorial: Not Just from the Centre," In *Proceedings of Design as a Catalyst for Change*, ed. C. Storni, K. Leahy, M. McMahon, P. Lloyd, and E. Bohemia (London: Design Research Society, 2018), 592–594, https://doi.org/10.21606/drs.2017.006.

2. Alison J. Clarke, *Design Anthropology: Object Cultures in Transition* (New York: Bloomsbury, 2017), 307.

3. Nicholas Daniel Hartlep, *Critical Race Theory: An Examination of Its Past, Present, and Future Implications* (ERIC Number ED506735, University of Wisconsin at Milwaukee, October 11, 2009), 6, https://eric.ed.gov/?id=ED506735.

4. Eduardo Bonilla-Silva, "Rethinking Racism: Toward a Structural Interpretation," *American Sociological Review* 62, no. 3 (1997): 465–480.

5. Eduardo Bonilla-Silva, "The Invisible Weight of Whiteness: The Racial Grammar of Everyday Life in America," Abstract, Duke University, https://scholars.duke.edu/display/pub866487.

6. Eduardo Bonilla-Silva, "The Invisible Weight of Whiteness: The Racial Grammar of Everyday Life in America," *Michigan Sociological Review* 26 (2012): 11.

7. Bonilla-Silva, "Invisible Weight of Whiteness," 1.

8. Bonilla-Silva, 11.

9. Zack Kucharski, "Gazette, KCRG-TV9 Photos Explained," *The Gazette*, April 3, 2015, https://www.thegazette.com/guest-columnists/gazette-kcrg-tv9-photos-explained/.

10. Bonilla-Silva, "Invisible Weight of Whiteness," 10.

11. "Elevating Voices: Visualizing Social Justice through Art," School of Social Work, University of Illinois, https://socialwork.illinois.edu/community-partnerships/community-engagment/elevating-voices-visualizing-social-justice-through-art.

12. "Elevating Voices."

13. Sue Hum, "Between the Eyes: The Racialized Gaze as Design," *College English* 77, no. 3 (2015): 191–215.

14. Hum, "Between the Eyes," 191.

15. Hum, 192.

16. Albert Bigelow Paine, *Th. Nast: His Period and His Pictures* (New York: Benjamin Blom, 1904), 592.

17. Hum, "Between the Eyes," 192.

18. Marc Leepson, "The North's Caustic Cartoonist," HistoryNet, April 10, 2018, https://www.historynet.com/norths-caustic-cartoonist.

19. JR, "Giants, Kikito, US-Mexico Border, 2017," https://www.jr-art.net/projects/giants-border-mexico.

20. Alexandra Schwartz, "The Artist JR Lifts a Mexican Child Over the Border Wall," *New Yorker*, September 11, 2017, https://www.newyorker.com/news/as-told-to/the-artist-jr-lifts-a-mexican-child-over-the-border-wall.

21. JR, "Giants, Kikito, US-Mexico Border."

22. Robert Miles, *Racism*, 2nd ed. (London: Routledge, 2003), 76.

23. Sylvia Ang, Elaine Lynn-Ee Ho, and Brenda S. A. Yeoh, "Migration and New Racism beyond Colour and the 'West': Co-ethnicity, Intersectionality and Postcoloniality," *Ethnic and Racial Studies* 45, no. 4 (2022): 585–594, https://doi.org/10.1080/01419870.2021.1925321.

24. Joyce Appleby, Lynn Hunt, and Margaret Jacob, *Telling the Truth about History* (New York: W. W. Norton, 1995), 18.

25. Appleby, Hunt, and Jacob, *Telling the Truth about History*, 18.

26. *Adiposity* refers to possessing unhealthy levels of body fat.

27. Margaret Hicken, Hedwig Lee, and Anna K. Hing, "The Weight of Racism: Vigilance and Racial Inequalities in Weight-Related Measures," *Social Science & Medicine* 199 (2018): 157–166, https://doi.org/10.1016/j.socscimed.2017.03.058.

28. Lennard J. Davis, ed., *The Disability Studies Reader: Constructing Normalcy* (London: Routledge, 2006), 3–15.

29. Davis, *Disability Studies Reader*, 3–15.

30. Davis, 3–15.

31. Ida B. Wells is an American investigative journalist, educator, and early civil rights leader and stated this quote as part of an address she gave to the Women's Era Club in 1893.

32. Lisa E. Mercer and Terresa Moses, "Identifying Racialized Design to Cultivate a Culture of Awareness in Design," *Design Journal* 22, no. S1 (2019): S1399–1407, https://doi.org/10.1080/14606925.2019.1594965.

33. *Merriam-Webster*, s.v. "artifact (*n.*)," accessed January 2, 2023, https://www.merriam-webster.com/dictionary/artifact.

34. Appleby, Hunt, and Jacob, *Telling the Truth about History*, 208.

35. Lisa Hix, "How America Bought and Sold Racism, and Why It Still Matters," Collectors Weekly, November 10, 2015, https://www.collectorsweekly.com/articles/how-america-bought-and-sold-racism.

36. Jillian Fellows, "Museum Curator: Racist Artifacts Can Help Teach against Intolerance," *Petoskey News-Review*, January 17, 2018, https://www.petoskeynews.com/story/news/local/2018/01/17/museum-curator-racist-artifacts-can-help-teach-against-intolerance/116503196/.

37. Logan Jaffe, "Confronting Racist Objects," *New York Times*, December 9, 2016, https://www.nytimes.com/interactive/2016/12/09/us/confronting-racist-objects.html.

38. David Pilgrim, "The Mammy Caricature," Jim Crow Museum, Ferris State University, October 2000, last edited 2012, https://ferris.edu/jimcrow/mammies/.

39. Jaffe, "Confronting Racist Objects."

40. Jaffe.

41. Langdon Winner, *The Whale and the Reactor*, 2nd ed. (Chicago: University of Chicago Press, 2020), 1.

42. "Thank you for caring enough to give us your feedback about the recent 'Re-civilized' NIVEA FOR MEN ad," Facebook, August 18, 2011, https://www.facebook.com/NIVEAusa/?brand_redir=351330671179.

43. "Ending the Era of Harmful 'Indian' Mascots," National Congress of American Indians, accessed March 5, 2019, http://www.ncai.org/proudtobe.

44. "Ending the Era of Harmful 'Indian' Mascots."

45. Jose A. Del Real, "An Icon or Insensitive Relic? Prospector Pete Is on Its Way Out," *New York Times*, October 3, 2018, https://www.nytimes.com/2018/10/03/us/cal-state-prospector-pete-statue.html.

46. "No 'R-word': US Groups Call to Drop NFL Team Name," Aljazeera, November 23, 2017, https://www.aljazeera.com/sports/2017/11/23/no-r-word-us-groups-call-to-drop-nfl-team-name.

47. John Keim, "Report: Investors Call on Nike, FedEx, PepsiCo to Cut Ties with Redskins over Name," ESPN, July 1, 2020, https://www.espn.com/nfl/story/_/id/29396653/report-investors-call-nike-fedex-pepsico-cut-ties-redskins-name.

48. John Keim, "Washington Selects Commanders as New NFL Team Name after Two-Season Process," ESPN, February 2, 2022, https://www.espn.com/nfl/story/_/id/33199548/washington-selects-commanders-new-team-name-two-season-search.

49. *Merriam-Webster*, s.v. "system (*n.*)," accessed January 2, 2023, https://www.merriam-webster.com/dictionary/system.

50. Donella H. Meadows, *Thinking in Systems* (White River Junction, VT: Chelsea Green, 2008), 3.
51. Wendy Gunn, Ton Otto, and Rachel Charlotte Smith, *Design Anthropology* (New York: Bloomsbury, 2013), 1.
52. Gunn, Otto, and Smith, *Design Anthropology*, 74.
53. Gunn, Otto, and Smith, 36.
54. Winner, *Whale and the Reactor*, 23.
55. Winner, 23.
56. Liz Sisley, "Shaker Barricades," Cleveland Historical, November 2017, https://clevelandhistorical.org/items/show/824.
57. Sisley, "Shaker Barricades."
58. Sisley.
59. "Criminal Justice Fact Sheet," National Association for the Advancement of Colored People, accessed December 15, 2021, https://naacp.org/resources/criminal-justice-fact-sheet.
60. *Merriam-Webster*, s.v. "experience (*n.*)," accessed January 2, 2023, https://www.merriam-webster.com/dictionary/experience.
61. Joe Neel, "Experiences of Discrimination in America," National Public Radio, October 24, 2017, https://www.npr.org/sections/thetwo-way/2017/10/24/559547557/webcast-experiences-of-discrimination-in-america.
62. Adrienne Green, "When Black Students Have to Balance Academia and Racism," *The Atlantic*, January 21, 2016, https://www.theatlantic.com/education/archive/2016/01/balancing-academia-racism/424887.
63. Ezio Manzini, *Design, When Everybody Designs : An Introduction to Design for Social Innovation* (Cambridge, MA: MIT Press, 2015), 3–4.
64. Samuel Sinyangwe, "Mapping Police Violence" Updated November 15, 2022. accessed 2017–2019, https://mappingpoliceviolence.org/.
65. Katie Nodjimbadem, "The Long, Painful History of Police Brutality in the US," *Smithsonian Magazine*, July 27, 2017, last updated May 29, 2020, https://www.smithsonianmag.com/smithsonian-institution/long-painful-history-police-brutality-in-the-us-180964098.
66. Daniel Victor, "Pepsi Pulls Ad Accused of Trivializing Black Lives Matter," *New York Times*, April 5, 2017.
67. Victor, "Pepsi Pulls Ad."
68. Emily Yahr, "Kendall Jenner Cries over Pepsi Ad Backlash in 'Keeping up with the Kardashians' Premiere," *Washington Post*, October 1, 2017.
69. Such as Mural or Miro.
70. "Clifton Strengths," Gallup Inc., accessed August 26, 2018, https://www.gallup.com/cliftonstrengths/en/252137/home.aspx.
71. "True Colors® International," accessed August 26, 2018, https://www.truecolorsintl.com/en-us/consulting-and-training-solutions.
72. "What Is DiSC®?," Discprofile.com, accessed August 26, 2018, https://www.discprofile.com/what-is-disc.
73. Deepa Iyer, Building Movement Project. SM, © 2020 Deepa Iyer. All rights reserved. All prior licenses revoked. https://buildingmovement.org/tools/social-change-ecosystem-map.
74. "Crystal," 2020, accessed August 26, 2018, https://www.crystalknows.com.
75. "This is a framework that can help individuals, networks, and organizations align and get in the right relationship with social change values, individual roles, and the broader ecosystem." Iyer, Building Movement Project.

CHAPTER 3

1. Kimberlé Crenshaw, "Mapping the Margins: Intersectionality, Identity Politics, and Violence against Women of Color," *Stanford Law Review* 43, no. 6 (1991): 241–299.
2. Participant, Racism Untaught industry workshop, fall 2021.
3. Christopher Tarman and David O. Sears, "The Conceptualization and Measurement of Symbolic Racism," *Journal of Politics* 67, no. 3 (2005): 731–761.
4. Margaret Hicken, Hedwig Lee, and Anna K. Hing, "The Weight of Racism: Vigilance and Racial Inequalities in Weight-Related Measures," *Social Science & Medicine* 199 (2018): 157–166, https://doi.org/10.1016/j.socscimed.2017.03.058.
5. Paulo Freire, *Pedagogy of the Oppressed* (New York: Bloomsbury Academic, 1970), 152.
6. Sightlines, "How Cheryl D. Miller Confronts White Supremacy in Graphic Design," *Sightlines*, November 13, 2021, https://sightlinesmag.org/how-cheryl-d-miller-confronts-white-supremacy-in-the-graphic-design-profession.
7. Ezio Manzini, *Design, When Everybody Designs : An Introduction to Design for Social Innovation* (Cambridge, MA: MIT Press, 2015), 2.
8. Crenshaw, "Mapping the Margins."
9. Kateryna Wowk et al., "Evolving Academic Culture to Meet Societal Needs," *Palgrave Communications* 3, no. 1 (2017), https://doi.org/10.1057/s41599-017-0040-1.
10. George Ella Lyon and Julie Landsman, "I Am From Project," accessed August 5, 2021, https://iamfromproject.com.
11. Crystal Raypole, "The Beginner's Guide to Trauma Responses," ed. Nathan Greene, *Healthline*, August 26, 2021, https://www.healthline.com/health/mental-health/fight-flight-freeze-fawn.
12. Crystal Raypole, "What It Really Means to Be Triggered," ed. Timothy J. Legg, *Healthline*, April 25, 2019, https://www.healthline.com/health/triggered.
13. Tarana Burke and Brené Brown, eds., *You Are Your Best Thing: Vulnerability, Shame, Resilience, and the Black Experience. An Anthology* (New York: Random House, 2021), 187.
14. M. E. Esquilin and M. Funk, "Campus Bias Incidents: What Could Faculty Do? Navigating Discussions in the Classroom," resource presented at Bryant University, Smithfield, RI, November 2019.
15. Graham D. Bodie et al., "The Role of 'Active Listening' in Informal Helping Conversations: Impact on Perceptions of Listener Helpfulness, Sensitivity, and Supportiveness and Disclosure Emotional Improvement," *Western Journal of Communication* 79, no. 2 (2015): 151–173, https://doi.org/10.1080/10570314.2014.943429.
16. Miliann Kang et al., *Introduction to Women, Gender, Sexuality Studies* (Amherst: University of Massachusetts Amherst Libraries, 2017), 48.
17. Anne Bonds and Joshua Inwood, "Beyond White Privilege: Geographies of White Supremacy and Settler Colonialism," *Progress in Human Geography* 6, no. 40, (2016): 715–733.
18. bell hooks, *Teaching to Transgress: Education as the Practice of Freedom* (New York: Routledge, 1994), 12.
19. Chimamanda Ngozi Adichie, "The Danger of a Single Story," filmed July 29, 2009 at TEDGlobal 2009, TED.com video, 18:33, https://www.ted.com/talks/chimamanda_ngozi_adichie_the_danger_of_a_single_story/transcript?language=en.
20. Keith Jenkins, *Rethinking History* (New York: Routledge, 2003), 7–32.
21. *Individual oppression* is fueled by personal beliefs, ideas, and feelings that perpetuate oppression. *Agentic action* occurs when oppressive beliefs translate into oppressive behavior. *Institutional oppression* occurs when structural oppression results from agentic, oppressive behavior. *Cultural oppression* is fueled by well-entrenched systems of norms, values, beliefs, and trusted systems of acquiring truth that preserve, protect, or maintain oppression.

22. Freire, *Pedagogy of the Oppressed*, 129.

23. Brenda Campbell Jones, Shannon Keeny, and Franklin Campbell Jones, *Culture, Class, and Race* (Alexandria, VA: ASCD, 2020), 489.

24. Campbell Jones, Keeny, and Campbell Jones, *Culture, Class, and Race*, 791.

25. Jan E. Stets and Peter J. Burke, "Identity Theory and Social Identity Theory," *Social Psychology Quarterly* 63, no. 3 (2000): 225.

26. Stets and Burke, "Identity Theory and Social Identity Theory," 230.

27. Finlo Rohrer, "Can the Art of a Pedophile be Celebrated?," *BBC News Magazine*, September 5, 2007, http://news.bbc.co.uk/2/hi/uk_news/magazine/6979731.stm.

28. "Eric Gill: Our Response," Ditchling Museum of Art + Craft, reviewed June 2022, https://www.ditchlingmuseumartcraft.org.uk/eric-gill-our-response/.

29. Rohrer, "Art of a Pedophile."

30. Sue Hum, "Between the Eyes: The Racialized Gaze as Design," *College English* 77, no. 3 (2015) 191–215, http://www.jstor.org/stable/24238161.

31. Antionette Carroll, "Can Design Dismantle Racism?," filmed October 2017 in St. Louis, MO, at TEDxGatewayArch, YouTube video, 12:47, TEDx Talks, posted January 11, 2018.

32. Tony Fry, "Design for/by 'The Global South,'" *Design Philosophy Papers* 15, no. 1 (2017): 28.

33. Freire, *Pedagogy of the Oppressed*, 9.

34. Ruth Morris, *Stories of Transformative Justice* (Toronto: Canadian Scholars/Women's Press, 2000).

35. Resmaa Menakem, *My Grandmother's Hands: Racialized Trauma and the Pathway to Mending Our Hearts and Bodies* (Las Vegas: Central Recovery Press, 2017).

36. hooks, *Teaching Community*, 102.

37. Participant, Racism Untaught industry workshop, 2022.

38. Kathy Obear, "Diversity and Inclusion Bingo," Training of Facilitators, Deepening Capacity of Lead Equity and Inclusion sessions, handout received May 16, 2017.

39. Lyon and Landsman, "I Am From Project."

40. Paula J. Pedersen, "Where I'm REALLY From." Provided as a physical handout in the spring 2019 course referenced in this case study, and licensed under a Creative Commons Attribution-Noncommercial 4.0 International license.

41. Adrienne maree brown, *Emergent Strategy* (Chico, CA: AK Press, 2017), 158.

42. Audre Lorde, *Sister Outsider* (New York: Random House, 2007), 104.

43. John Thackara, *In the Bubble: Designing in a Complex World* (Cambridge, MA: MIT Press, 2005), 248–249.

44. Linda Tuhiwai Smith, *Decolonizing Methodologies* (London: Bloomsbury, 1999), 1.

45. Smith, *Decolonizing Methodologies*, 146.

46. Smith, 214.

47. Participant, Racism Untaught community workshop, 2021.

48. Participant, Racism Untaught industry workshop, 2021.

49. Participant, Racism Untaught industry workshop, 2021.

50. Participant, Racism Untaught industry workshop, 2021.

CHAPTER 4

1. Joy DeGruy, "Racism does not always look the same. In our definition of racism we need to include prejudice, discrimination, bias, and bigotry. These are all manifestations of the same root problem—racism." Twitter, October 25, 2021, 3:20 p.m. https://twitter.com/drjoydegruy/status /1452731733997088769?lang=en.

2. Julia Morris, *A Degree in a Book: Anthropology* (London: Arcturus, 2021), 69.

3. James Baldwin, *The Fire Next Time* (New York: Dial Press, 1963), 69.

4. Maria Popova, "Audre Lorde on the Vulnerability of Visibility and Our Responsibility, to Ourselves and Others, to Break Our Silences," *The Marginalian* (blog), May 20, 2016, https://www.themarginalian.org/2016/05/20/audre-lorde-silence-visibility/.

5. Brené Brown, *Atlas of the Heart: Mapping Meaningful Connection and the Language of Human Experience* (New York: Random House, 2021), xxi.

6. Brown, *Atlas of the Heart*, xxi.

7. Barbara J. Fields and Karen Elise Fields, *Racecraft: The Soul of Inequality in American Life* (New York: Verso, 2012), 11.

8. Fields and Fields, *Racecraft*, 11.

9. Abigail C. Saguy, *What Is Sexual Harassment? From Capitol Hill to the Sorbonne* (Oakland: University of California Press, 2003), 1–18.

10. Miranda Fricker, *Epistemic Injustice: Power and the Ethics of Knowing* (Oxford: Oxford University Press, 2007), 150.

11. Fricker, *Epistemic Injustice*, 155.

12. Brown, *Atlas of the Heart*, xx.

13. Participant, Racism Untaught conference workshop, 2019.

14. Brown, *Atlas of the Heart*, 236.

15. Tarana Burke and Brené Brown, eds., *You Are Your Best Thing: Vulnerability, Shame, Resilience, and the Black Experience. An Anthology* (New York: Random House, 2021), 184.

16. Burke and Brown, *You Are Your Best Thing*, 24.

17. Brene Brown, host, "The Language of Emotion and Human Experience," *Atlas of the Heart*, season 1, episode 1, HBO, 2022, 47 min.

18. Brown, "Language of Emotion and Human Experience."

19. Lorde, *Sister Outsider*, 30.

20. Lorde, 31.

21. Ezio Manzini, *Design, When Everybody Designs : An Introduction to Design for Social Innovation* (Cambridge, MA: MIT Press, 2015), 34.

22. D. A. Schön, *The Reflective Practitioner* (New York: Basic Books, 1983), 274.

23. Anika Fiebich, "Perceiving Affordances and Social Cognition," in *Perspectives on Social Ontology and Social Cognition*, Studies in the Philosophy of Sociality, vol. 4, ed. M. Gallotti and J. Michael (Dordrecht: Springer, 2014), 144–196, https://doi.org/10.1007/978-94-017-9147-2_11.

24. Lisa E. Mercer and Terresa Moses, "Identifying Racialized Design to Cultivate a Culture of Awareness in Design," *Design Journal* 22, no. S1 (2019): S1399–1407, https://doi.org/10.1080/14606925.2019.1594965.

25. Schön, *Reflective Practitioner*.

26. Manzini, *Design, When Everybody Designs*, 35.

27. Manzini, 63.

28. Manzini, 105.

29. Participant, Racism Untaught industry workshop, 2021.

30. Kimberlé Crenshaw, "Intersectionality, More than Two Decades Later," Columbia Law School, June 8, 2017, https://www.law.columbia.edu/news/archive/kimberle-crenshaw-intersectionality-more-two-decades-later.

31. Heineken, "Heineken 2018 Lighter Is Better, Advert. Racist?," YouTube video, 30 seconds, March 26, 2018. https://www.youtube.com/watch?v=g_u_-OD1_z0&t=4s.

32. Amy Barto, "Disproportionate Identification of Students of Color in Special Education," Learning Disabilities Association of America, accessed May 30, 2022, https://ldaamerica.org/lda_today /disproportionate-identification-of-students-of-color-in-special-education/.

33. Langdon Winner, *The Whale and the Reactor*, 2nd ed. (Chicago: University of Chicago Press, 2020), 22.

34. History.com editors, "Segregation in the United States," History.com, November 28, 2018, last updated January 18, 2022, https://www.history.com/topics/black-history/segregation-united-states.

35. Student, "Life's A Bridge" (unpublished student work, fall 2019), typescript.

36. Student, "Life's a Bridge."

37. Participant, Racism Untaught course, 2021.

38. Participant, Racism Untaught course, 2021.

39. Participant, Racism Untaught course, 2021.

40. Participant, Racism Untaught course, 2021.

41. Participant, Racism Untaught course, 2021.

CHAPTER 5

1. Jeanine Weekes Schroer, "The Practice of Personhood: Understanding Individual Responsibility for Oppression" (PhD diss., University of Illinois at Chicago, 2005), 25.

2. Paulo Freire, *Pedagogy of the Oppressed* (New York: Bloomsbury Academic, 1970), 29.

3. Terresa Moses, "Who Holds Knowledge? The Effects of Television on the Assumed Knowledge of Women of Color in Higher Education," *International Journal of Diversity in Education* 22, no. 2 (2022): 25–39, https://doi.org/10.18848/2327-0020/CGP/v22i02/25-39.

4. Dr. Kristi Siegel, "Introduction to Modern Literacy Theory," accessed June 5, 2022, http://mseffie .com/Heart_of_Darkness_WebQuest/Resources/Entries/2011/1/1_Postcolonial_Criticism.html.

5. Nikole Hannah-Jones, Caitlin Roper, Ilena Silverman, and Jake Silverstein, eds., *A New Origin Story: The 1619 Project* (New York: One World, 2021).

6. Hannah-Jones et al., *A New Origin Story*.

7. Dark Matter University, "About," accessed August 28, 2021, https://darkmatteruniversity.org/About.

8. Dark Matter University, "About."

9. Dark Matter University, "About."

10. Sasha Costanza-Chock, *Design Justice* (Cambridge, MA: MIT Press, 2020), xvii.

11. Costanza-Chock, *Design Justice*, 6.

12. Lesley-Ann Noel, "Envisioning a Pluriversal Design Education," in *Proceedings of Pivot 2020: Designing a World of Many Centers*, ed. Renata Marques Leitão, Lesley-Ann Noel, and Laura Murphy (London: Design Research Society, 2020), 69–78.

13. Noel, "Envisioning a Pluriversal Design Education," 70.

14. DesignExplorr, "About," accessed June 6, 2022, https://designexplorr.com/about.

15. DesignExplorr, "About."

16. Creative Reaction Lab, "About Us," accessed June 6, 2022, https://www.creativereactionlab.com /about-us.

17. Creative Reaction Lab, "About Us."

18. "Interconnectedness," in *Inclusive Design Guide* (Inclusive Design Research Centre at OCAD University), accessed June 5, 2022, https://guide.inclusivedesign.ca/insights/interconnectedness.

19. Karen Potts and Leslie Brown, "Becoming an Anti-oppressive Researcher," in *Research as Resistance: Critical, Indigenous and Anti-oppressive Approaches*, ed. Leslie Brown and Susan Strega (Toronto: Canadian Scholars/Women's Press, 2005), 255–286.

20. John Mathers, "Design Interventions," *Royal Society for the Encouragement of Arts, Manufactures and Commerce Journal* 161, no. 5561 (2015): 28.

21. Linda Tuhiwai Smith, *Decolonizing Methodologies* (London: Bloomsbury, 1999), 168.

22. Pat Hutchings, Jillian Kinzie, and George D. Kuh, "Evidence of Student Learning: What Counts and What Matters for Improvement," in *Using Evidence of Student Learning to Improve Higher Education*, ed. George D. Kuh (San Francisco: Jossey-Bass, 2015), 83.

23. Eduardo Bonilla-Silva and Tyrone A. Forman, "'I Am Not a Racist But . . .': Mapping White College Students' Racial Ideology in the USA," *Discourse & Society* 11, no. 1 (2000): 50–85, https://doi.org/10.1177/0957926500011001003.

24. Erin Blakemore, "How the Confederate Battle Flag Became an Enduring Symbol of Racism," *National Geographic*, January 12, 2021, https://www.nationalgeographic.com/history/article/how-confederate-battle-flag-became-symbol-racism#:~:text=Known%20as%20the%20%E2%80%9CStars%20and,to%20tell%20the%20two%20apart.

25. Participant, Racism Untaught industry workshop, 2022.

26. Participant, Racism Untaught industry workshop, 2022.

27. Participant, Racism Untaught industry workshop, 2022.

28. Participant, Racism Untaught industry workshop, 2022.

CHAPTER 6

1. adrienne maree brown, *Emergent Strategy* (Chico, CA: AK Press, 2017), 59.

2. "Black Liberation Lab," https://blackliberationlab.org.

3. Patrisse Cullors, *An Abolitionist's Handbook* (New York: St. Martin's Press, 2021), 217.

4. Deepa Iyer, Building Movement Project. SM, © 2020 Deepa Iyer. All rights reserved. All prior licenses revoked. https://buildingmovement.org/tools/social-change-ecosystem-map.

5. Natalia Ilyin, "What Design Activism Is and Is Not: A Primer for Students," in *Developing Citizen Designers*, ed. Elizabeth Resnick (London: Bloomsbury Visual Arts, 2016), 64.

6. Cheryl D. Holmes-Miller, "Black Designers: Still Missing in Action?," *PRINT* 70, no. 2 (Summer 2016): 89.

7. James Baldwin, interview by Studs Terkel, *Studs Terkel Radio Archive*, Chicago History Museum, July 15, 1961, https://studsterkel.wfmt.com/programs/james-baldwin-discusses-his-book-nobody-knows-my-name-more-notes-native-son.

8. Eve Tuck and K. Wayne Yang, "Decolonizing Is Not a Metaphor," *Decolonization: Indigeneity, Education & Society* 1, no. 1 (2012): 3.

9. Vanessa Lopez-Littleton and Brandi Blessett, "A Framework for Integrating Cultural Competency into the Curriculum of Public Administration Programs," *Journal of Public Affairs Education* 21, no. 4 (2015): 557–574, https://doi.org/10.1080/15236803.2015.12002220.

10. Angela Davis, *Are Prisons Obsolete?* (New York: Seven Stories Press, 2003), 16.

11. Karen Potts and Leslie Brown, "Becoming an Anti-oppressive Researcher," in *Research as Resistance: Critical, Indigenous and Anti-oppressive Approaches*, ed. Leslie Brown and Susan Strega (Toronto: Canadian Scholars/Women's Press, 2005), 255.

12. "(1982) Audre Lorde, 'Learning from the 60s,'" BlackPast, August 12, 2012, https://www.blackpast.org/african-american-history/1982-audre-lorde-learning-60s.

13. Participant, Racism Untaught community workshop, 2022.

14. Participant, Racism Untaught community workshop, 2022.

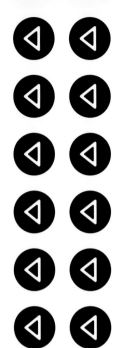

BIBLIOGRAPHY

"(1982) Audre Lorde, 'Learning from the 60s.'" BlackPast, August 12, 2012. https://www.blackpast.org /african-american-history/1982-audre-lorde-learning-60s .

"About." Dark Matter University. Accessed August 28, 2021, https://darkmatteruniversity.org/About.

"About." designExplorr. Accessed June 6, 2022. https://designexplorr.com/about.

"About Us." Creative Reaction Lab. Accessed June 6, 2022. https://www.creativereactionlab.com /about-us.

Adichie, Chimamanda Ngozi. "The Danger of a Single Story." Filmed July 2009 at TEDGlobal 2009. TED. com video, 18:33. https://www.ted.com/talks/chimamanda_ngozi_adichie_the_danger_of_a _single_story/transcript?language=en.

Ang, Sylvia, Elaine Lynn-Ee Ho, and Brenda S. A. Yeoh. "Migration and New Racism beyond Colour and the 'West': Co-ethnicity, Intersectionality and Postcoloniality." *Ethnic and Racial Studies* 45, no. 4 (2022): 585–594. https://doi.org/10.1080/01419870.2021.1925321.

Appleby, Joyce, Lynn Hunt, and Margaret Jacob. *Telling the Truth about History*. New York: W. W. Norton, 1995.

Baldwin, James. *The Fire Next Time*. New York: Dial Press, 1963.

Baldwin, James. Interview by Studs Terkel. *Studs Terkel Radio Archive*, Chicago History Museum, July 15, 1961. https://studsterkel.wfmt.com/programs/james-baldwin-discusses-his-book-nobody -knows-my-name-more-notes-native-son.

Barto, Amy. "Disproportionate Identification of Students of Color in Special Education." Learning Disabilities Association of America. Accessed May 30, 2022. https://ldaamerica.org/lda_today /disproportionate-identification-of-students-of-color-in-special-education.

Blakemore, Erin. "How the Confederate Battle Flag Became an Enduring Symbol of Racism." *National Geographic*. January 12, 2021. https://www.nationalgeographic.com/history/article/how -confederate-battle-flag-became-symbol-racism.

Bodie, Graham D., Andrea J. Vickery, Kaitlin Cannava, and Susanne M. Jones. "The Role of 'Active Listening' in Informal Helping Conversations: Impact on Perceptions of Listener Helpfulness, Sensitivity, and Supportiveness and Discloser Emotional Improvement." *Western Journal of Communication* 79, no. 2 (2015): 151–173. https://doi.org/10.1080/10570314.2014.943429.

Bonds, Anne, and Joshua Inwood. "Beyond White Privilege: Geographies of White Supremacy and Settler Colonialism." *Progress in Human Geography* 6, no. 40 (2016): 715–733.

Bonilla-Silva, Eduardo. "The Invisible Weight of Whiteness: The Racial Grammar of Everyday Life in America." *Michigan Sociological Review* 26 (2012): 1–15.

Bonilla-Silva, Eduardo. "Rethinking Racism: Toward a Structural Interpretation." *American Sociological Review* 62, no. 3 (1997): 465–480.

Bonilla-Silva, Eduardo, and Tyrone A. Forman. "'I Am Not Racist But . . .': Mapping White College Students' Racial Ideology in the USA." *Discourse & Society* 11, no. 1 (2000): 50–85. https://doi.org/10.1177/0957926500011001003.

brown, adrienne maree. *Emergent Strategy*. Chico, CA: AK Press, 2017.

Brown, Austin Channing. *I'm Still Here*. New York: Crown, 2018.

Brown, Brené. *Atlas of the Heart: Mapping Meaningful Connection and the Language of Human Experience*. New York: Random House, 2021.

Brown, Brené, host. "The Language of Emotion and Human Experience." *Atlas of the Heart*, season 1, episode 1. HBO, 2022. 47 min.

Brown, Sarah. "How Should Universities Respond to Racism?" *Chronicle of Higher Education*, December 3, 2021. https://www.chronicle.com/article/how-should-universities-respond-to-racism.

Buchanan, Richard. "Wicked Problems in Design Thinking." *Design Issues* 8, no. 2 (Spring 1992): 5–21. http://www.jstor.org/stable/1511637.

Burke, Tarana, and Brené Brown, eds. *You Are Your Best Thing: Vulnerability, Shame, Resilience, and the Black Experience: An Anthology*. New York: Random House, 2021.

Campbell Jones, Brenda, Shannon Keeny, and Franklin Campbell Jones. *Culture, Class, and Race: Constructive Conversations that Unite and Energize Your School and Community*. Alexandria, VA: Association for Supervision and Curriculum Development, 2020.

Carroll, Antionette. "Can Design Dismantle Racism?" Filmed October 2017, in St. Louis, MO, at TEDxGatewayArch. YouTube video, 12:47. TEDx Talks, posted January 11, 2018. https://www.youtube.com/watch?v=cNIsMqiBmSA.

Carroll, Antionette. "Designing for Justice." Filmed May 2017 at TEDxHerndon. TED.com video, 12:47. https://www.ted.com/talks/antionette_carroll_designing_for_justice.

Carroll, Antionette. "Like all systems, systems of oppression, inequality, and inequity are by design. Therefore, they can be redesigned. In order for us to redesign these systems, we need a new type of leader." Twitter, June 24, 2020, 8:35 p.m. https://twitter.com/acarrolldesign /status/1275965708648583169?lang=en.

Clarke, Alison J. *Design Anthropology: Object Cultures in Transition*. New York: Bloomsbury, 2017.

Collins, Patricia Hill. *Black Feminist Thought: Knowledge, Consciousness, and the Politics of Empowerment*. 2nd ed. New York: Routledge, 2022.

Costanza-Chock, Sasha. *Design Justice: Community-Led Practices to Build the Worlds We Need*. Cambridge, MA: MIT Press, 2020.

Crenshaw, Kimberlé. "Intersectionality, More than Two Decades Later." Columbia Law School, June 8, 2017. https://www.law.columbia.edu/news/archive/kimberle-crenshaw-intersectionality-more -two-decades-later.

Crenshaw, Kimberle. "Mapping the Margins: Intersectionality, Identity Politics, and Violence against Women of Color." *Stanford Law Review* 43, no. 6 (1991): 241–299. https://doi.org/10.2307/1229039.

"Criminal Justice Fact Sheet." National Association for the Advancement of Colored People. Accessed December 15, 2021. https://naacp.org/resources/criminal-justice-fact-sheet.

Cross, Nigel. "Designerly Ways of Knowing: Design Discipline versus Design Science." *Design Issues* 17, no. 3 (2001): 49–55. http://www.jstor.org/stable/151180.

Cullors, Patrisse. *An Abolitionist's Handbook*. New York: St. Martin's Press, 2021.

Davidová, Marie. "Multicentred Systemic Design Pedagogy through Real-Life Empathy: Integral and Inclusive Practice-Based Education in the Research-by-Design Context." *Formakademisk* 13, no. 5 (2020): 1–7. https://doi.org/10.7577/formakademisk.3755.

Dávila, Arlene. *Latinx Art*. Durham, NC: Duke University Press, 2020.

Davis, Angela. *Are Prisons Obsolete?* New York: Seven Stories Press, 2003.

Davis, Lennard J., ed. *The Disability Studies Reader: Constructing Normalcy*. London: Routledge, 2006.

DeGruy, Joy. "Racism does not always look the same. In our definition of racism we need to include prejudice, discrimination, bias, and bigotry. These are all manifestations of the same root problem— racism." Twitter, October 25, 2021, 3:20 p.m. https://twitter.com/drjoydegruy /status/1452731733997088769?lang=en.

Del Real, Jose A. "An Icon or Insensitive Relic? Prospector Pete Is on Its Way Out." *New York Times*, October 3, 2018. https://www.nytimes.com/2018/10/03/us/cal-state-prospector-pete-statue.html.

Deney, Katie. "Situated Action." PB Works, November 19, 2009. http://510bds.pbworks.com/w/page/3872226/Situated%20Action.

Driskill, Qwo-Li. "Doubleweaving Two-Spirit Critiques: Building Alliances between Native and Queer Studies." *GLQ: A Journal of Lesbian and Gay Studies* 16, no. 1–2 (2010): 69–92.

"Elevating Voices: Visualizing Social Justice through Art." School of Social Work, University of Illinois. Accessed May 20, 2022. https://socialwork.illinois.edu/community-partnerships/community-engagment/elevating-voices-visualizing-social-justice-through-art/.

"Eric Gill: Our Response." Ditchling Museum of Art + Craft. Reviewed June 2022. Escobar, Arturo. *Designs for the Pluriverse: Radical Interdependence, Autonomy, and the Making of Worlds.* Durham, NC: Duke University Press, 2017.

Esquilin, M. E., and M. Funk. "Campus Bias Incidents: What Could Faculty Do? Navigating Discussions in the Classroom." Resource presented at Bryant University, Smithfield, RI, November 2019. https://cte.bryant.edu/wp-content/uploads/2018/10/Bryant-handouts-Nov-2019-PDF.pdf [discontinued].

Fellows, Jillian. "Museum Curator: Racist Artifacts Can Help Teach against Intolerance." *Petoskey News-Review*, January 17, 2018. https://www.petoskeynews.com/story/news/local/2018/01/17/museum-curator-racist-artifacts-can-help-teach-against-intolerance/116503196/.

Fiebich, Anika. "Perceiving Affordances and Social Cognition." In *Perspectives on Social Ontology and Social Cognition*, Studies in the Philosophy of Sociality, vol. 4, edited by M. Gallotti and J. Michael, 149–166. Dordrecht: Springer, 2014. https://doi.org/10.1007/978-94-017-9147-2_11.

Fields, Barbara J., and Karen Elise Fields. *Racecraft: The Soul of Inequality in American Life.* New York: Verso, 2012.

Freire, Paulo. *Pedagogy of the Oppressed.* New York: Bloomsbury Academic, 1970.

Fricker, Miranda. *Epistemic Injustice: Power and the Ethics of Knowing.* Oxford: Oxford University Press, 2009.

Fry, Tony. "Design for/by 'The Global South.'" *Design Philosophy Papers* 15, no. 1 (2017): 3–37. https://doi.org/10.1080/14487136.2017.1303242.

Gal, Susan. "John J. Gumperz's Discourse Strategies." *Journal of Linguistic Anthropology* 23, no. 3 (2013): 115–126. http://www.jstor.org/stable/43104337.

Gallup Inc. "Clifton Strengths." Accessed August 26, 2018. https://www.gallup.com/cliftonstrengths/en/252137/home.aspx.

Glass, Kathy. "Race-ing the Curriculum: Reflections on a Pedagogy of Social Change." In *Exploring Race in Predominantly White Classrooms: Scholars of Color Reflect*, edited by Maria del Guadalupe Davidson and George Yancy, 50–61. New York: Routledge, 2014. https://doi.org/10.4324/9780203416716.

Green, Adrienne. "When Black Students Have to Balance Academia and Racism." *The Atlantic*, January 21, 2016. https://www.theatlantic.com/education/archive/2016/01/balancing-academia-racism/424887.

Gunn, Wendy, Ton Otto, and Rachel Charlotte Smith. *Design Anthropology*. New York: Bloomsbury, 2013.

Hannah-Jones, Nikole, Caitlin Roper, Ilena Silverman, and Jake Silverstein, eds. *A New Origin Story: The 1619 Project.* New York: One World, 2021.

Harries, Bethan. "We Need to Talk About Race." *Sociology (Oxford)* 48, no. 6 (2014): 1107–1122. https://doi.org/10.1177/0038038514521714.

Hartlep, Nicholas Daniel. "Critical Race Theory: An Examination of Its Past, Present, and Future Implications." ERIC Number ED506735. University of Wisconsin at Milwaukee, October 11, 2009. https://eric.ed.gov/?id=ED506735.

Heineken. "Heineken 2018, Lighter Is Better, Advert. Racist?" YouTube video, 30 seconds. March 26, 2018. https://www.youtube.com/watch?v=g_u_-OD1_z0&t=4s.

Hicken, Margaret T., Hedwig Lee, and Anna K. Hing. "The Weight of Racism: Vigilance and Racial Inequalities in Weight-Related Measures." *Social Science & Medicine* 199 (2018): 157–166. https://doi.org/10.1016/j.socscimed.2017.03.058.

Hirsch, Arlene S. "An Inside Look at Workplace Racial Affinity Groups." Society for Human Resource Management, September 20, 2021. https://www.shrm.org/resourcesandtools/hr-topics/behavioral-competencies/global-and-cultural-effectiveness/pages/an-inside-look-at-workplace-racial-affinity-groups.aspx.

History.com editors. "Segregation in the United States." History.com, November 28, 2018, last updated January 18, 2022. https://www.history.com/topics/black-history/segregation-united-states.

Hix, Lisa. "How America Bought and Sold Racism, and Why It Still Matters." Collectors Weekly, November 10, 2015. https://www.collectorsweekly.com/articles/how-america-bought-and-sold-racism/.

Holmes-Miller, Cheryl D. "Black Designers: Still Missing in Action?" *PRINT* 70, no. 2 (Summer 2016): 82–89.

hooks, bell. *Teaching Community*. New York: Taylor and Francis, 2003.

hooks, bell. *Teaching to Transgress: Education as the Practice of Freedom*. New York: Routledge, 1994.

"How George Floyd's Death Became a Catalyst for Change." National Museum of African American History and Culture, Smithsonian. June 15, 2021. https://nmaahc.si.edu/explore/stories/how-george-floyds-death-became-catalyst-change.

Huff, Charlotte. "Building a Better, More Diverse Faculty." *American Psychological Association* 52, no. 8 (2021). https://www.apa.org/monitor/2021/11/news-diverse-faculty.

Hum, Sue. "Between the Eyes: The Racialized Gaze as Design." *College English* 77, no. 3 (2015): 191–215. http://www.jstor.org/stable/24238161.

Hutchings, Pat, Jillian Kinzie, and George D. Kuh. "Evidence of Student Learning: What Counts and What Matters for Improvement." In *Using Evidence of Student Learning to Improve Higher Education*, edited by George D. Kuh, 27–50. San Francisco: Jossey-Bass, 2015.

IDEO. "History." Accessed June 4, 2022. https://designthinking.ideo.com/history.

Ilyin, Natalia. "What Design Activism Is and Is Not: A Primer for Students." In *Developing Citizen Designers*, edited by Elizabeth Resnick, 64–65. London: Bloomsbury Visual Arts, 2016.

"Interconnectedness." In *Inclusive Design Guide*. Inclusive Design Research Center at OCAD University. Accessed June 5, 2022. https://guide.inclusivedesign.ca/insights/interconnectedness.

Iyamah, Jacquelyn Ogorchukwu. "How Can Designers Build Interfaces That Avoid the 'White Defaullt?'" *Eye on Design*, March 14, 2022. https://eyeondesign.aiga.org/design-often-encourages-the-white-default-how-can-designers-create-more-inclusive-digital-interfaces.

Iyer, Deepa. Building Movement Project. SM, © 2020 Deepa Iyer. All rights reserved. All prior licenses revoked. https://buildingmovement.org/tools/social-change-ecosystem-map.

Jaffe, Logan. "Confronting Racist Objects." *New York Times*, December 9, 2016. https://www.nytimes.com/interactive/2016/12/09/us/confronting-racist-objects.html.

Jenkins, Keith. *Rethinking History*. New York: Routledge, 2003.

Jewell, Tiffany. *This Book Is Anti-Racist: 20 Lessons on How to Wake Up, Take Action, and Do the Work*. London: Frances Lincoln Children's Books, 2020.

Joseph, Tiffany D., and Laura E. Hirshfield. "'Why Don't You Get Somebody New to Do It?' Race and Cultural Taxation in the Academy." *Ethnic and Racial Studies* 34, no. 1 (2011): 121–141. https://doi.org/10.1080/01419870.2010.496489.

JR. "Giants, Kikito, US-Mexico Border, 2017." Accessed June 25, 2022. https://www.jr-art.net/projects

/giants-border-mexico.

Kang, Miliann, Donovan Lessard, Laura Heston, and Sonny Nordmarken. *Introduction to Women, Gender, Sexuality Studies*. Amherst, MA: University of Massachusetts Amherst Libraries, 2017.

Keim, John. "Report: Investors Call on Nike, FedEx, PepsiCo to Cut Ties with Redskins over Name." ESPN, July 1, 2020. https://www.espn.com/nfl/story/_/id/29396653/report-investors-call-nike -fedex-pepsico-cut-ties-redskins-name.

Keim, John. "Washington Selects Commanders as New NFL Team Name after Two-Season Process." ESPN, February 2, 2022. https://www.espn.com/nfl/story/_/id/33199548/washington-selects -commanders-new-team-name-two-season-search.

Kern-Foxworth, Marilyn. *Aunt Jemima, Uncle Ben, and Rastus: Blacks in Advertising, Yesterday, Today, and Tomorrow*. Westport, CT: Greenwood Press, 1994.

Kucharski, Zack. "Gazette, KCRG-TV9 Photos Explained." *The Gazette*, April 3, 2015. https://www.thegazette.com/guest-columnists/gazette-kcrg-tv9-photos-explained.

Leepson, Marc. "The North's Caustic Cartoonist." HistoryNet, April 10, 2018. https://www.historynet.com/norths-caustic-cartoonist/.

Lopez-Littleton, Vanessa, and Brandi Blessett. "A Framework for Integrating Cultural Competency into the Curriculum of Public Administration Programs." *Journal of Public Affairs Education* 21, no. 4 (2015): 557–574. https://doi.org/10.1080/15236803.2015.12002220.

Lorde, Audre. *Sister Outsider*. New York: Random House, 2007.

Lupton, Ellen. *Design Is Storytelling*. New York: Smithsonian Design Museum, 2017.

Manzini, Ezio. *Design, When Everybody Designs: An Introduction to Design for Social Innovation*. Cambridge, MA: MIT Press, 2015.

Mathers, John. "Design Interventions." *Royal Society for the Encouragement of Arts, Manufactures and Commerce Journal* 161, no. 5561 (2015): 24–29.

Meadows, Donella H. *Thinking in Systems*. White River Junction, VT: Chelsea Green, 2008.

Mercer, Lisa E., and Terresa Moses. "Identifying Racialized Design to Cultivate a Culture of Awareness in Design." *Design Journal* 22, no. S1 (2019): S1399–1407.*My Grandmother's Hands: Racialized Trauma and the Pathway to Mending Our Hearts and Bodies*. Las Vegas: Central Recovery Press, 2017.

Miles, Robert. *Racism*. 2nd ed. London: Routledge, 2003.

Miller, Cheryl D. "Black Designers Missing in Action." *PRINT* 41, no. 5 (September/October 1987): 58–65, 136–138.

Miller, Cheryl D. "Transcending the Problems of the Black Graphic Designer to Success in the Marketplace." Master's thesis, Pratt Institute, New York, 1985. Stanford Digital Repository.

Morris, Ruth. *Stories of Transformative Justice*. Toronto: Canadian Scholars/Women's Press, 2000.

Morris, Julia. *A Degree in a Book: Anthropology*. London: Arcturus, 2021.

Moses, Terresa. "Who Holds Knowledge? The Effects of Television on the Assumed Knowledge of Women of Color in Higher Education." *International Journal of Diversity in Education* 22, no. 2 (2022): 25–39. https://doi.org/10.18848/2327-0020/CGP/v22i02/25-39.

National Congress of American Indians. "Ending the Era of Harmful 'Indian' Mascots." Accessed March 5, 2019. http://www.ncai.org/proudtobe.

National Equity Project. "The Lens of Systemic Oppression." Accessed August 1, 2022. https://www.nationalequityproject.org/frameworks/lens-of-systemic-oppression.

Neel, Joe. "Experiences of Discrimination in America." National Public Radio, October 24, 2017. https://www.npr.org/sections/thetwo-way/2017/10/24/559547557/webcast-experiences-of -discrimination-in-ameri.

Newton, James E. "Slave Artisans and Craftsmen: The Roots of Afro-American Art." *Black Scholar* 9, no. 3 (1977): 35–42.

Nodjimbadem, Katie. "The Long, Painful History of Police Brutality in the US." *Smithsonian Magazine*, July 27, 2017. Last updated May 29, 2020. https://www.smithsonianmag.com/smithsonian -institution/long-painful-history-police-brutality-in-the-us-180964098.

Noel, Lesley-Ann. "Envisioning a Pluriversal Design Education." In *Proceedings of Pivot 2020: Designing a World of Many Centers*, edited by Renata Marques Leitão, Lesley-Ann Noel, and Laura Murphy, 69–78. London: Design Research Society, 2020.

Noel, Lesley-Ann, and Renata M. Leitão. "Editorial: Not Just from the Centre." In *Proceedings of Design as a Catalyst for Change*, edited by C. Storni, K. Leahy, M. McMahon, P. Lloyd, and E. Bohemia, 592–594. London: Design Research Society, 2018. https://doi.org/10.21606/drs.2017.006.

Norman, Donald A. *The Design of Everyday Things*. Philadelphia: Basic Books, 2013.

"No 'R-word': US Groups Call to Drop NFL Team Name." Aljazeera, November 23, 2017. https://www.aljazeera.com/sports/2017/11/23/no-r-word-us-groups-call-to-drop-nfl-team-name.

Ørngreen, Rikke, and Karin Levinsen. "Workshops as a Research Methodology." *Electronic Journal of e-Learning* 15, no. 1 (2017): 70–81.

Owen, Charles. "Design Thinking. What It Is. Why It Is Different. Where It Has New Value." Speech given at the International Conference on Design Research and Education for the Future, Gwangju City, Korea, October 21, 2005. https://www.id.iit.edu/wp-content/uploads/2015/03/Design-thinking -what-it-is-owen_korea05.pdf.

Paine, Albert Bigelow. *Th. Nast: His Period and His Pictures*. New York: Benjamin Blom, 1904.

Pilgrim, David. "The Mammy Caricature." Jim Crow Museum, Ferris State University, October 2000, last edited 2012. https://ferris.edu/jimcrow/mammies/.

Popova, Maria. "Audre Lorde on the Vulnerability of Visibility and Our Responsibility, to Ourselves and Others, to Break Our Silences." *The Marginalian* (blog), May 20, 2016. https://www.themarginalian .org/2016/05/20/audre-lorde-silence-visibility.

Potts, Karen, and Leslie Brown. "Becoming an Anti-Oppressive Researcher." In *Research as Resistance: Critical, Indigenous and Anti-oppressive Approaches*, edited by Leslie Brown and Susan Strega, 255–286. Toronto: Canadian Scholars/Women's Press, 2005.

Raypole, Crystal. "The Beginner's Guide to Trauma Responses." Edited by Nathan Greene. *Healthline*, August 26, 2021. https://www.healthline.com/health/mental-health/fight-flight-freeze-fawn.

Raypole, Crystal. "What It Really Means to be Triggered." Edited by Timothy J. Legg. *Healthline*, April 25, 2019. https://www.healthline.com/health/triggered.

Reddick, Lawrence D. "Educational Programs for the Improvement of Race Relations: Motion Pictures, Radio, the Press, and Libraries." *Journal of Negro Education* 13, no. 3 (1944): 367–389. https://doi.org/10.2307/2292454.

Rittel, Horst W. J., and Melvin M. Webber. "Dilemmas in a General Theory of Planning." *Policy Sciences* 4, no. 2 (June 1973): 155–169. http://www.jstor.org/stable/4531523.

Rohrer, Finlo. "Can the Art of a Pedophile be Celebrated?" *BBC News Magazine*, September 5, 2007. Accessed August 5, 2021. http://news.bbc.co.uk/2/hi/uk_news/magazine/6979731.stm.

Rudick, C. Kyle, and Kathryn B. Golsan. "Civility and White Institutional Presence: An Exploration of White Students' Understanding of Race-Talk at a Traditionally White Institution." *Howard Journal of Communications* 29, no. 4 (2018): 335–352. https://doi.org/10.1080/10646175.2017.1392910.

Saguy, Abigail C. *What Is Sexual Harassment? From Capitol Hill to the Sorbonne*. Oakland: University of California Press, 2003.

Sanders, Elizabeth B., and Pieter Jan Stappers. *Convivial Toolbox: Generative Research for the Front*

End of Design. Amsterdam: Building Het Sieraad Publishers, 2012.

Schön, D. A. *The Reflective Practitioner*. New York: Basic Books, 1983.

Schroer, Jeanine Weekes. "The Practice of Personhood: Understanding Individual Responsibility for Oppression." PhD diss., University of Illinois at Chicago, 2005.

Shedroff, Nathan. *Design Is the Problem: The Future of Design Must Be Sustainable*. Brooklyn: Rosenfeld Media, 2009.

Siegel, Kristi. "Introduction to Modern Literacy Theory." Accessed June 5, 2022. http://mseffie.com /Heart_of_Darkness_WebQuest/Resources/Entries/2011/1/1_Postcolonial_Criticism.html.

Sightlines. "How Cheryl D. Miller Confronts White Supremacy in Graphic Design." *Sightlines*, November 13, 2021. https://sightlinesmag.org/how-cheryl-d-miller-confronts-white-supremacy-in-the -graphic-design-profession.

Sinyangwe, Samuel. "Mapping Police Violence." Updated November 15, 2022. Accessed 2017–2019. https://mappingpoliceviolence.org/.

Schwartz, Alexandra. "The Artist JR Lifts a Mexican Child over the Border Wall." *New Yorker*, September 11, 2017. https://www.newyorker.com/news/as-told-to/the-artist-jr-lifts-a-mexican-child-over -the-border-wall.

Sisley, Liz. "Shaker Barricades." Cleveland Historical, November 2017. https://clevelandhistorical.org /items/show/824.

Smith, Linda Tuhiwai. *Decolonizing Methodologies*. London: Bloomsbury, 1999.

Solórzano, Daniel G., and Tara J. Yosso. "Critical Race Methodology: Counter-Storytelling as an Analytical Framework for Education Research." *Qualitative Inquiry* 8, no. 1 (2002): 23–44. https://doi.org/10.1177/107780040200800103.

Stets, Jan E., and Peter J. Burke. "Identity Theory and Social Identity Theory." *Social Psychology Quarterly* 63, no. 3 (2000): 224–237. https://doi.org/10.2307/2695870.

Suchman, Lucy A. *Plans and Situated Action: The Problem of Human-Machine Communication*. Cambridge: Cambridge University Press, 1987.

Swim, Janet K., Elizabeth D. Scott, Gretchen B. Sechrist, Bernadette Campbell, and Charles Stangor. "The Role of Intent and Harm in Judgments of Prejudice and Discrimination." *Journal of Personality and Social Psychology* 84, no. 5 (2003): 944–959. https://doi.org/10.1037/0022-3514.84.5.944.

Taneja, Hemant. "The Era of 'Move Fast and Break Things' Is Over." *Harvard Business Review*, January 22, 2019. https://hbr.org/2019/01/the-era-of-move-fast-and-break-things-is-over.

Tarman, Christopher, and David O. Sears. "The Conceptualization and Measurement of Symbolic Racism." *Journal of Politics* 67, no. 3 (2005): 731–761. https://doi.org/10.1111/j.1468 -2508.2005.00337.x.

Thackara, John. *In the Bubble: Designing in a Complex World*. Cambridge, MA: MIT Press, 2005.

Tuck, Eve, and K. Wayne Yang. "Decolonizing Is Not a Metaphor." *Decolonization: Indigeneity, Education & Society* 1, no. 1 (2012): 1–40.

Victor, Daniel. "Pepsi Pulls Ad Accused of Trivializing Black Lives Matter." *New York Times*, April 5, 2017.

"What Is DiSC?" Discprofile. Accessed August 26, 2018. https://www.discprofile.com/what-is-disc.

Winner, Langdon. *The Whale and the Reactor: A Search for Limits in an Age of High Technology*. 2nd ed. Chicago: University of Chicago Press, 2020.

Wowk, Kateryna, Larry McKinney, Frank Muller-Karger, Russell Moll, Susan Avery, Elva Escobar-Briones, David Yoskowitz, and Richard McLaughlin. "Evolving Academic Culture to Meet Societal Needs." *Palgrave Communications* 3, no. 1 (2017): 1–7.

Yahr, Emily. "Kendall Jenner Cries over Pepsi Ad Backlash in 'Keeping up with the Kardashians' Premiere." *Washington Post*, October 1, 2017.

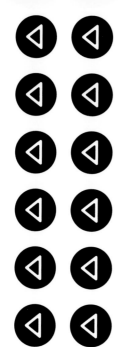

INDEX

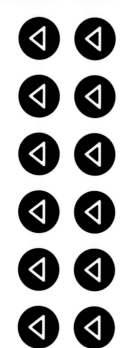